THE DYNAMICS OF PUBLIC SERVICE CONTRACTING

Other titles available from The Policy Press include:

Trust and contracts: Relationships in local government, health and public services
Edited by Andrew Coulson
Paperback ISBN 1 86134 086 9 £16.99
Hardback   ISBN 1 86134 107 5 £40.00

A revolution in social policy: Quasi-market reforms in the 1990s
Edited by Will Bartlett, Jennifer A. Roberts and Julian Le Grand
Paperback ISBN 1 86134 060 5 £16.95
Hardback   ISBN 1 86134 111 3 £40.00

Partnership against poverty and social exclusion? Local regeneration strategies and exlcuded communities in the UK
Mike Geddes
Paperback ISBN 1 86134 071 0 £12.95

Making partnerships work in community care: A guide for practitioners in housing, health and social services
Robin Means, Maria Brenton, Lyn Harrison and Frances Heywood
Paperback ISBN 1 86134 058 3 £14.95

Forthcoming February 1999

Implementing holistic government: Joined-up action on the ground
David Wilkinson and Elaine Applebee
Paperback ISBN 1 86134 143 1 £14.99

All the above titles are available from
Biblios Publishers' Distribution Services Ltd, Star Road,
Partridge Green, West Sussex RH13 8LD, UK
Telephone +44 (0)1403 710851, Fax +44 (0)1403 711143

THE DYNAMICS OF PUBLIC SERVICE CONTRACTING

The British experience

Young-Chool Choi

The POLICY PRESS

First published in Great Britain in 1999 by

The Policy Press
University of Bristol
Rodney Lodge
Grange Road
Bristol BS8 4EA
UK

Tel   +44 (0)117 973 8797
Fax   +44 (0) 117 973 7308
e-mail   tpp@bristol.ac.uk
http://www.bristol.ac.uk/Publications/TPP

© The Policy Press, 1999
British Library Cataloguing in Publication Data
A catalogue record for this book is available from the British Library

ISBN 1 86134 139 3

Young-Chool Choi is Assistant Professor at the Department of Public Administration, Chungbuk National University, South Korea, and Visiting Fellow at the Department of Social Policy, University of Newcastle upon Tyne.

Cover design: Qube Design Associates, Bristol.

Photographs supplied by kind permission of John Birdsall Photography, Nottingham.

Printed and bound in Great Britain by Hobbs the Printers Ltd, Southampton.

Contents

List of tables and figures

Tables

Figures

Preface

The study described in this book investigates the factors influencing compulsory competitive tendering (CCT). It also attempts to show the importance of the politics of transaction costs in relation to the implementation of CCT policy.

In Britain during the last decade there has been sustained 'top-down' pressure to privatise local government services. Empirical policy output studies associated with competitive tendering decisions at the local level, and research on the political dynamics underlying CCT policy implementation and policy output, have been largely unexplored in research literature. This is due to the inordinate emphasis on an economic approach derived from public choice theory and on the theoretical pros and cons of CCT policy, which represent partisan views. Spatial variations in CCT output or the effects of privatisation have largely been neglected and the dynamic relationships between policy implementation and policy output have received less attention than they should. This work seeks to remedy the neglect of these topics by examining the determinants of CCT policy output and investigating how the output has been made.

The theoretical questions addressed in this study focus on specific aspects of privatisation. The questions are: 'What determines the local variation in CCT output?' and, 'How do the determinants affect it?'

In examining the determinants of CCT output, the investigation will centre on the 296 non-metropolitan districts in England, employing path analysis. The contributions of a transaction cost approach to an analysis of the continuous trade-off between the parties involved are now widely recognised. However, one dimension of the transaction cost approach, the politics, is much less developed. For this reason, four local authorities will be case studied in an attempt to explain better the political dynamic underlying CCT policy implementation and policy output. This will be carried out by applying the politics of transaction cost perspective, drawn from transaction cost economics, to the four selected districts.

This research found that in the path analysis for 1991 the political variable, *party control*, was the strongest determinant influencing the CCT output, whereas in the analysis for 1994 the strategic variable, *geographical location*, was the strongest. This implies that as time went on private contractors also influenced significantly the decisions about who won the contract, resulting in a notable geographical variation in CCT output. In view of that we need more in-depth case study analysis to further our understanding of how CCT output has been generated.

Following case study analysis of the four local authorities, the CCT output is shown to be the output of interactions between contexts, motivations and strategies associated with transaction costs on the part of the three main interested parties: central government, the local authority, and private companies.

The politics of the transaction costs incurred by the three main interested parties can facilitate or impede privatisation. The consequence of this is considerable local variation in CCT output, leading to a greater likelihood of privatisation in certain local contexts. At the same time, the way in which CCT output has been generated is explained by the politics of the transaction costs used, manipulated or transferred by the main parties involved in the contested tendering process. Unless there are fair competition rules and a level playing field for the interested parties in the tendering process, it is likely to become a cat-and-mouse game, resulting in endless efforts on the part of the parties concerned to use, shift or manipulate transaction costs to their own advantage. Finally, the book suggests how transaction costs can be minimised to implement CCT policy successfully.

Following the coming to power of the Labour Government in 1997, the nature of CCT policy has changed considerably. The Government's White Paper on modernising local government, *Modern local government – in touch with the people*, which was issued in July 1998, made it clear that CCT will be replaced by a 'Best Value' system. Even so, competition will continue to play an important role, and contracting will also play a key part in the Government's strategy in relation to the 'Best Value' framework in local government. UK interest in the issues addressed in this book is set to increase as efforts to understand the dynamics of contracting, and the search for best practice and new models of contracting, continue. Other countries wishing to restructure their public sectors will also be keen to learn lessons and draw implications from the experience of the UK, which has been one of the pioneers in local government contracting. This book also aims to contribute to the successful restructuring of the public sector management in transitional countries at the central and local level.

Foreword

Studies of policy processes these days always have to contend with the pace of policy change. As the number of studies of the purchaser–provider system in the health service or the new arrangements for community care begin to increase so new innovations emerge which may make the findings of those studies irrelevant. In the same vein this is a study of local government innovation – compulsory competitive tendering (CCT) – emerging at a time when new approaches to external commissioning of services based on the notion of the search for 'Best Value' is preoccupying practical policy makers. It may be regarded as unfortunate that our policy makers do not stop to evaluate the old before they rush into the new, but this is inevitable, particularly when the old comprises something as politically contentious as CCT. The hope is that systematic studies of abandoned policies will provide insights into new policies. That is what this book does.

Several special features of the research study allows the book to achieve this. First, the study uses a research method that – while it has been elaborated extensively all over the world – has been given comparatively little attention in recent British policy studies: the statistical analysis of the relationships between policy inputs and outputs. In doing so it addresses, appropriately in relation to so politicised a topic as CCT, that fundamental question for political science: does politics matter? It shows that despite strenuous efforts by central government to prevent local authorities evading the political thrust of the CCT initiative, the political 'colour' of local authorities influenced the extent to which they privatised services. However, through its examination of CCT at two points in time it also shows how that political influence on outputs weakened over time, suggesting that factors influencing the behaviour of private organisations as bidders for local government services began to have a greater influence.

Second, to offer an approach to exploring why outcomes were subject to local influences, despite the efforts of central government to influence the slope of the CCT 'playing field', the study builds on the pioneering work of the late Keiron Walsh in using transaction cost theory to explain policy processes. It sets out to overcome the considerable difficulties with the pragmatic application of transaction cost theory to use it to evaluate the 'gaming' that goes on in relation to the negotiation and regulation of tendering processes.

Third, it uses qualitative case studies of the tendering process in four local authorities to explore that gaming process and to deepen understanding of the factors which influence or inhibit the statistical associations demonstrated.

Fourth, a remarkable feature of this book is that it offers the insights of a foreign scholar on a field of study – British local government – which is rarely examined from the outside. Dr Choi offers detached insights on some domestic preoccupations, and an analysis which will inform efforts in other countries to learn from the CCT experience in Britain. On the latter he offers evidence that policy copying can be problematical if the peculiar political circumstances in which ideas are developed and implemented are not taken into account.

It is these features of this book which make it relevant despite the demise of CCT. It is to be hoped that other scholars will take up the challenge offered by this study to apply its methods and theories to 'Best Value' and to other emergent influences on central–local government relations in Britain. The end of a period in which those relations have been conflict-ridden and heavily influenced by dogma is precisely one in which new attention needs to be given to the way in which the complex transactions between central and local government actually work.

Michael Hill
Visting Professor, Department of Social Policy and Politics
Goldsmiths College, University of London

Acknowledgements

This book is based on a PhD thesis submitted to the University of Newcastle upon Tyne, England in 1998. The primary debt I should like to record is to my academic supervisor, Professor Michael Hill, who provided me throughout with considerable assistance and support in the sometimes difficult circumstances occasioned by geographical distance. To him my warmest thanks.

Next, my sincere thanks are due to Dr Howard Davis, University of Warwick, who as my external examiner shared with me his expert knowledge of compulsory competitive tendering (CCT) in Britain and provided me with valuable feedback on my work. I would like also to thank everyone in the Department of Social Policy, Newcastle University, for providing me with such a warm and encouraging environment for study. In particular I wish to thank Dr Robin Humphrey for his unfailing support, and Dr Peter Selman, who as Head of Department offered me useful teaching opportunities which helped me to test and refine my ideas.

I wish to express my sincere thanks to the academic staff in the Department of Public Administration, Chungbuk National University, Korea for the understanding they have shown concerning my period of study abroad and for being prepared to take on the extra workload caused by my absence.

I owe a deep debt of gratitude to my parents and parents-in-law for their understanding and support, without which I could not have completed this project. I would like also to express my gratitude to my elder brother, Professor Oe-Chool Choi, and his wife, Professor In-Jeon Park, for their constant encouragement of a fellow academic. I must also thank my wife, Ji-Hyun, for the unwavering support she gave me both as a friend and as an advisor.

In conclusion I would like to mention my two sons, Min-Je and Min-Hyuk, who adjusted so speedily and so well to life in another country. I hope that reading this book in the future they may understand the reasons for my preoccupation and be spurred to respond to their own challenges.

List of acronyms

AMA	Association of Metropolitan Authorities
ANOVA	analysis of variance
BART	Bay Area Rapid Transit
CIPFA	Chartered Institute of Public Finance and Accounting
CCT	compulsory competitive tendering
DoE	Department of the Environment
DLO	direct labour organisation
DSO	direct service organisation
EC	European Community
ECU	European currency unit
EEC	European Economic Community
EU	European Union
GMBATU	General Municipal, Boilermakers and Allied Trade Union
GMWU	General Municipal Workers' Union
ICMA	International City Management Association
NALGO	National and Local Government Officers' Association
NHS	National Health Service
NUPE	National Union of Public Employees
OLS	ordinary least squares
OLJEC	Official Journal of the European Communities
PFI	Private Finance Initiative
PSBR	public sector borrowing requirements
PSCR	Public Supply Contracts
PWCS	Public Works Contracts
SSA	standard spending assessment
TUPE	Transfer of Undertakings (Protection of Employment)

ONE

Introduction

Background and purpose of the research

The UK is at the forefront of public sector reform and achieving effective public sector management. However, public sector management in the UK has not received the same attention from academic scholars as has public administration in the USA and other advanced countries. For these reasons, without hesitation I chose to carry out my study in the UK.

My interest has focused on public service contracting in Britain, and in particular on compulsory competitive tendering, the earliest form of marketisation in British local government. As a foreign student of the British experience, taking an objective standpoint the British case could be of practical service to practitioners, policy makers and academics as well as those engaged in the restructuring of the public sector both in the UK and abroad.

Compulsory competitive tendering, which is a result of the introduction of market mechanisms into the running of public service organisations, represents a major component of the new public management. Since the late 1980s in Britain there has been rapid expansion in the use of competitive tendering, although other approaches, such as internal markets, have also been developed. The focus of this book is on compulsory competitive tendering.

Compulsory competitive tendering in the UK represents a major effort on the part of government to reduce service costs and improve service quality and outcomes. CCT is often characterised as a dynamic process in which many interested parties try to influence the whole process to their own advantage. It has been with us for at least 10 years, and the time is ripe for an investigation of its dynamics. Such an investigation should increase understanding of public service contracting, the most popular form of privatisation, and allow insights deriving from the British case to be applied to other countries in the process of restructuring their public sectors. The conclusions also relate closely to Britain, which in the near future is likely to introduce a Best Value framework in which 'competition' and 'contracting' will remain important elements.

With these goals in mind, the study aims to analyse the determinants of compulsory competitive tendering policy outputs at the local government level in Britain and to examine how these outputs have been made. It does this by relating the CCT implementation process to the main factors affecting CCT outputs. More specifically, the study is based on the assumption that policy output as a general phenomenon cannot be separated from the process of formulating and implementing policy. Many of the major determinants underlying the CCT process remain unexplored and must be examined closely for CCT policy output in local government to be understood more fully.

For many years, it has been traditional for local authorities to provide services to the public by employing staff directly. With the expansion of their functions, local authorities have become spenders and employers on a large scale. Local government activities have expanded not just because of encouragement or legislation from central government; the ambitions of local authorities to expand their role in providing services to their communities has also played a part (Carnaghan and Bracewell-Milnes, 1993, pp 22-3).

Local authorities have employed not only service staff, for example teachers, refuse collectors and social service staff, but also those involved in ancillary support services, such as cleaners. Typically, all the staff, main and ancillary, who are engaged in providing a service have been organised within the same department of the authority. There has always been some use of outside agencies, from both the voluntary and private sectors, for the provision of services, but the dominant approach has been to employ directly the staff necessary to do the work (Walsh, 1991, p 1).

As part of its aim of changing the way in which the public sector is managed, the UK government has been attempting to introduce competition and market processes into local government (along with the National Health Service [NHS] and the Civil Service). The methods adopted have taken a number of forms, but a key approach has been to require competitive tendering for services. This approach was first adopted in local government following the 1980 Local Government Planning and Land Act (Walsh, 1991, p 1).

The political and ideological environment under which policies of privatisation generally, and CCT specifically, developed is an important feature to consider. Until the latter part of the 1970s both the Conservative and the Labour parties were concerned with repairing and thus maintaining the post-war 'settlement', which represented full employment, broad welfare provision and a large public sector, rather than challenging it (Foster, 1991, pp 41-2).

Significantly, the drift towards a broadly monetarist approach to the economy and controls on public expenditure first occurred in 1976 during a Labour administration. Despite a decline in economic growth, successive governments throughout the 1970s had failed to control spending on public services and subsidies. Core services within the welfare state were consuming an increasing proportion of gross domestic product (GDP), and the public sector borrowing requirement (PSBR) rose to unprecedented heights in the mid-1970s, while the banks failed to respond to the need for more external finance. A congruent problem was an apparent failure on the part of governments to devise satisfactory ways to distribute resources 'fairly'. This resulted in public scepticism and antagonism towards the structure and mechanisms of the welfare state and its ability to achieve greater equality (Foster, 1991, pp 42-3). Given this background, it might be argued that, by 1979,

> **Thatcherism was almost an idea whose time had come: the old system was breaking apart, creating the circumstances for a new set of policies to be introduced by a radical government. (MacInnes, 1987, p 43)**

Central elements of Thatcherism included the separation of economics and politics, control of the money supply and government spending, 'rolling back the frontiers of the state', strengthening market forces to 'make markets work better' and promoting an 'enterprise culture' while curbing the powers of trade unions, elements that might appeal to a public disillusioned with state intervention (MacInnes, 1987, p 47).

The 'think-tanks' of the New Right, constituting groups of radical and Conservative academics and politicians (notably the Adam Smith Institute, the Institute of Economic Affairs and the Centre for Policy Studies), pressed hard for legislation on competitive tendering. Such organisations emphasised individualism and lamented the 'dependency culture' imbued with the welfare state. To some extent they were pushing at an open door, particularly when Nicholas Ridley was Secretary of State at the Department of the Environment (DoE) (Fenwick, 1995, pp 18-22; Wilson and Game, 1994, p 325).

The centrally determined character of the competitive tendering policy and the element of compulsion it embodied were its most significant features. Prior to this legislation local authority partnerships with the private sector had existed in some service areas, but had been formulated voluntarily. The 1980 Local Government Planning and Land Act heralded a new development in central and local relations whereby the functions of local authorities as autonomous service providers were undermined by central government dictates and financial scrutiny (Foster, 1991, p 123).

CCT has now been extended to a number of other services by the 1988 Local Government Act, the 1992 Local Government Act and the 1994 Local Government Act. This study deals primarily with the Local Government Act 1988 and the services it defines. This is because, although CCT in local authorities was first introduced by the 1980 Act, the 1988 Act considerably extended the scope of CCT and also tightened the rules governing it. The 1988 Act also gave the Environment Secretary powers to ensure that genuine competition was not being restricted, distorted or prevented. It would have been much more dynamic and complex in terms of the implementation process than the 1980 Act and other Acts. CCT legislation will be discussed in more detail later.

The 1988 Local Government Act requires local authorities to subject a number of services to competition. These are: refuse collection, street cleaning, cleaning of buildings, schools and welfare catering, other catering, vehicle maintenance, grounds maintenance and the management of sports and leisure facilities. Local authorities are only allowed to perform work in these service areas using their own staff if they have won the right to do so in competition. Private companies are allowed to bid for the work. Should the local authority win the right to do the work, it must keep separate internal accounts for these services. Meeting these competitive requirements presents local authorities with a major management challenge. Accordingly, competition has led to major changes in the way local authorities manage themselves (McShane, 1995, pp 63-8).

The provisions of the 1988 Local Government Act have been compulsory and pressure from government to conform to policy has

4

had the effect of ensuring that the compulsory competitive tendering policy has been developed nation-wide. However, in reality there have been continuing local variations in the output of CCT policy from one authority to another. This is one starting point for the present research, since at this stage the following question arises: why do similar local authorities, when faced with similar policy pressures 'from above', achieve different outputs in the compulsory competitive tendering process?

The continuing local unevenness in the output of CCT policy suggests that many authorities as policy implementors have been able to influence this process in favour of inhouse teams, while others have met the government's objectives more enthusiastically and have promoted the development of the private sector. It follows that local variations in the output of CCT policy reflect the fact that the CCT policy process has not been implemented as expected by the policy maker, central government. From the policy process point of view, the output of CCT policy does not coincide with the assumption of the 'classical' model of policy implementation that, once a policy has been made, the policy will be implemented and the results of that policy will conform closely with the expectations of the policy maker (Smith, 1973, pp 197-8). Instead, it reflects the fact that, as Bardach (1977, p 56) points out, in the process of policy implementation there are a wide variety of 'games' that interested parties can play to impede, frustrate and subvert policies.

In reality, the competitive tendering system, whereby inhouse tenders are submitted in competition with tenders from external contractors, has a number of important implications in relation to the policy process. In particular, unlike those of other countries, the competitive tendering system of Britain is compulsory, which means that local authorities are forced to put the services defined by the Act out to tender. Accordingly, the implications of the competitive tendering system in Britain are more delicate and complex than in other countries.

In the first place, the implementation of CCT has been a dynamic process. As compulsion has been used by central government, CCT has been seen by many councils as interference in the management of local affairs by democratically elected local councillors. This has created antagonism, and some councils appear to have reacted by seeking to frustrate the purpose of the legislation as far as possible (Carnaghan and Bracewell-Milnes, 1993, p 37). In addition, as Painter explains (1990, p 3), the legislation was motivated mainly by the government's general aims of cutting public expenditure, reducing the size of the public sector in the economy and constraining the power of the trade unions. As a result, the implementation of CCT is associated with the interests of many parties, such as trade unions, private contractors, and local authority councillors and officials, resulting in a complex and dynamic process.

Secondly, once the inhouse provider is regarded as a bidder in the competitive tendering process, the client and contractor side of the local authority (inhouse or DSO[1]) become interested parties and so can no longer be expected to take an objective view in making the final decisions relating to a particular service and contract. This is because, unlike with private contractors' employees who when they lose one contract will be moved on to another, the switch from inhouse to external provision signals the end of public sector employment for most of the direct labour force (Asher, 1987, p 11). It is for this reason that the unions have fought. A study of CCT by Walsh and Davis (1993, p 9) points out that the relationships between client and contractor were generally good, whether the contractors were internal or external to the authority, but that there were a significant number of cases of poor relationships. It can be assumed that the CCT process can become a difficult one from an organisational point of view. The manner in which it is undertaken depends to a large extent on the viewpoint of individual local authorities.

Thirdly, although in principle the competitive tendering process means that there is no presumption in favour either of external contractors or of the inhouse service, in practice this has not been the case. The previous government has been accused of changing the rules of competitive tendering to the advantage of private contractors, while some local authorities sympathetic to inhouse bids have been accused of favouritism. The final selection has often not centred on the tender offering the most efficient, effective and economic services (Carnaghan and Bracewell-Milnes, 1993, p 52; Goodwin, 1994, p 18).

These components of the competitive tendering procedure indicate that there is considerable scope for various factors, including political, organisational and demographic factors, to influence the CCT process and its final output. The outputs of tendering in any one local authority may not be the result of the contract being awarded to the most cost-effective tender, but could be influenced by various determinants at the local level, such as the manner in which individual local authority management has dealt with conflicting pressures from central government or private contractors.

How the different factors in the process interact with each other affects whether a service is privatised (contracted out to a private company) or kept inhouse. Mediating factors in force at the local level mean that the results of contracting out will vary from authority to authority.

The process of privatisation is a highly contested one in localities where the impact of privatisation policies comes to the fore. Two consequences flow from this. First, government-imposed privatisation is unlikely to be universally accepted by members of the localities on which it is imposed; and second, a local variation of privatisation is likely to develop as an output of such a contested process. The nature of the tendering system presupposes that the outputs are the result of a contested process and not simply of an argument about cost-effectiveness and/or social consequences.

Although the phenomenon of privatisation has generated a large research literature in the 1980s and 1990s, most of it has explored privatisation and CCT from an economic perspective. Much of this research has been guided by public choice theory, which argues the superior cost-efficiency of private over public service delivery. In addition, most of the literature has been prescriptive rather than empirical. Although policy output studies have not been entirely neglected, they have generally been a secondary consideration to economic analysis.

While the existence of local variation in CCT output is acknowledged in the literature, there has been a distinct failure to explain systematically what determinants affect it and how they relate to it. This makes an examination of CCT policy output which associates the output with the dynamics of the policy implementation process particularly important. One possible reason for this lack of attention in the research literature to the significance of the variables that shape the linkage between CCT policy implementation and policy output is that most researchers on CCT and contracting out have tended to focus on the economic and social consequences, together with the ensuing diversity of industrial relations surrounding the process (Goodwin and Pinch, 1995).

Another reason is the absence of a coherent power-based theory from nearly all the previous research. While researchers have frequently invoked public choice theory to select certain economic variables, they have generally avoided theory when researching the dynamics of the CCT process. If research is informed by power-based theory, then more of the dynamics of the CCT process will be revealed. This asymmetry in the literature needs to be corrected.

There are a number of key questions which CCT policy output study still needs to answer. Why does a centrally-imposed privatisation policy manifest an uneven development across England? What determinants affect the output of CCT policy and how has the output been made in the CCT implementation process? To answer these questions it is necessary to identify the main determinants of the output of CCT policy and examine the question of how these are associated with the dynamics of the policy implementation process.

This study draws on the theory of policy output and policy implementation in order to understand the major determinants of the CCT output. It uses the theory of the politics of transaction costs to investigate their state of play in local government. The proposed theories provide a coherent and valuable means of assessing organisational outputs – in this case, CCT policy output.

Whether CCT is a desirable policy or not is not a focus of this study. The objectives are to:

- address the key question of how local authorities in England can achieve different levels of privatisation (different levels of CCT output);

- examine how the CCT process, which was imposed mainly by central government, may be influenced at the local level;

- suggest some of the implications of the experience of privatisation policy for local government services.

Scope of the research and methodologies

The research employs two main methodologies: path analysis and case study analysis. Data is used for two time-points, 1991 and 1994, to enable a dynamic perspective on the research question: What factors affect the output of CCT? Analysing data for two time-points minimises the danger of an unusual year being selected, and also aids the exploration of changes and dynamics in CCT output patterns over time.

There are two reasons why the particular years 1991 and 1994 were chosen. First, 1991 was the year of greatest activity in the first round of the CCT implementation phase. There was a three-year period for bringing in CCT, which commenced on 1 August 1989. Partly to give authorities time to prepare for the changes, and partly so as not to overwhelm private contractors, the Act provided for a phased introduction of CCT. Competition was phased in over a 30-month period, from August 1989 to August 1991 for shire counties and shire districts, during which different authorities were required to put the various services out to tender at six-monthly intervals (Walsh, 1991, p 10; Wilson and Game, 1994, p 328). The year 1991 was the politically dynamic one in the CCT process, since it was in a real sense the last year of the first round. Hence it is assumed that the CCT process of 1991 has many implications from the policy point of view. Second, 1994 was the year many local authorities renewed their contracts via the CCT process. Following the passing of the Act, the Secretary of State issued a consultation paper (*Competing for quality*, 1991) on contract periods and then decided to set minimum and maximum periods. The minima are three, four or five years, while the maxima are five, six or seven years, depending on the activity. A Local Government Management Board study found that contract lengths are near the low end of the permitted ranges (Carnaghan and Bracewell-Milnes, 1993, p 96). Very similar averages are reported by the Institute of Public Finance (McGuirk, 1992). This indicates that in the year 1994, three years after 1991 in which many contracts were established, many local authorities were required to renew their contracts. The experiences that local authorities had of CCT in 1994 can provide insights relating to the CCT process.

Data from 296 non-metropolitan districts in England is analysed spatially to account for local variations in CCT output. The reason the non-metropolitan districts were chosen for the analysis is as follows. In England, in terms of service jurisdiction, the non-metropolitan counties (39), metropolitan districts (36) and non-metropolitan districts (296) are dissimilar. For example, the former two sets of authorities have responsibility for the two main services, the education and social services, whereas the latter does not (Byrne, 1994, pp 50, 502-3). A sample in which all authorities have the same pattern of legal duties is needed to maintain statistical consistency. Taking into account the fact that data on some local authorities is missing or unavailable the non-metropolitan districts are better in terms of statistical validity, in that the number of districts in the sample is much higher than that of the non-metropolitan counties or metropolitan districts. Furthermore, the non-metropolitan districts are composed of urban and rural districts and scattered across England, so reflecting the general trends and geographical characteristics of England.

Path analysis is used to examine the main determinants of CCT policy output. Path analysis is a form of causal modelling that has become a popular analytical tool in the social sciences. It represents a method of studying patterns of causation among a set of variables and the direct and indirect effects of variables. Path analysis is not a method of discovering causes, but a method applied to a causal model formulated by the researcher on the basis of knowledge and theoretical consideration in order to analyse correlations among a set of variables (Kerlinger and Pedhazur, 1973, pp 305-6).

This study deals primarily with the seven manual services (refuse collection, street cleaning, cleaning of buildings, grounds maintenance, vehicle maintenance, catering services, and sports and leisure management) defined in the 1988 Act. As was discussed earlier, the 1980 legislation meant that local authority direct labour organisations (DLOs) would operate on a more commercial footing, keeping separate accounts for the different areas of work, and would be required to make a surplus equivalent to a rate of return on a capital sum of 5% (Shaw et al, 1994, p 201). Also, the 1980 Act subjected only two services (construction and maintenance work on buildings and highways) to tender. However, the 1988 Act extended the scope of CCT and also tightened the rules regulating it, leading to more dynamic and complex relationships between the parties involved.

The 1992 and 1994 Local Government Acts are also important for CCT. The 1992 Act, following the 1991 consultation paper *Competing for quality*, extends the compulsory tendering regime into technical and professional work. It also tightens the grip of competitive tendering in the services covered by the 1980 and 1988 Acts by seeking to outlaw what the government defined as various anticompetitive practices on the part of local authorities (Wilson and Game, 1994, p 337). However, the contract start date for 'white collar services' defined in the 1992 Act is October 1995, which is beyond this study's research period. Likewise, the services defined in the 1994 Act are also excluded from the analysis.

At the time of writing, a Labour government having come to power in May 1997, CCT has accordingly been changing in terms of policy direction and nature. As will be described later, the Best Value framework established by the Labour government is at a preparatory stage at the time of writing. It will be explained briefly later but will be omitted from the study.

The case study methodology is used to explore how the determinants of CCT output are associated with the CCT process and how they interact with each other to produce the output. This involves collecting documentary information and carrying out interviews with local government officers. For this purpose, four local authorities were selected. These are not a statistically representative sample of all local authorities, but were selected to ensure that two main dimensions are taken into account: party control and extent of DSO use.

The extensive primary and secondary source material on competition available both in the UK and other countries will also be used. This includes government reports and circulars and academic studies.

Objectives

Both theoretical and empirical conclusions are derived from this research. Because the study discusses and analyses a variety of games that interested parties involved in the CCT process can play to divert resources, deflect goals, resist initiatives and dissipate energies, especially in the context of sustained 'top-down' pressure on local authorities from central government to privatise, it can contribute to the development of strategies for constructing a better policy implementation system.

In theoretical terms the study represents an attempt to integrate case studies on policy output and policy implementation into a more general conceptual framework. In order to do this it was necessary to relate the policy output and its implementation process to some of the other elements found in policy research. Specifically, policy output as a general phenomenon cannot be separated from the process of formulating and implementing the policies concerned. To do this, the views of a diverse group of participants and observers, including policy makers, bureaucrats and social scientists, on the policy process need to be considered. In short, this study will contribute to an exploration of the politics of policy implementation.

This study suggests that future research on privatisation may benefit from a multidisciplinary approach. Because the privatisation debate involves complex economic, political and sociological dimensions, it is imperative that researchers become conversant with literatures which extend beyond their fields of specialisation. Theories drawn from one discipline will typically explain only part of the privatisation phenomenon; multiple theories are needed, from a variety of disciplinary perspectives, to capture the forces operating in privatisation. The use of policy output theory and the theory of transaction costs represents a starting point for such a multidisciplinary approach; theoretical and empirical dialogue across disciplines is likely to enhance our knowledge of the privatisation phenomenon in local government.

Analysis of the determinants of the output of CCT in local government should provide more information for policy makers, local councillors, local government employees and private companies involved in CCT. Such knowledge should facilitate a greater understanding of how the CCT process works. This study also identifies the way in which the outputs of the contested process are generated. The research should also foster an understanding of when CCT is and is not a feasible alternative to public production, despite the cost savings that may be suggested by competition proposals. It should help to explain why similar local authorities, when faced with similar policy pressures 'from above', achieve different outputs in the competitive tendering process.

The research should help countries interested in CCT or other centrally-imposed policies to introduce and implement them effectively. To design and implement policies successfully it is necessary to anticipate the actual performance of the central government. This, in turn, requires analytical procedures that outline the main features of the political, bureaucratic, economic and other contextual settings within which specific policy proposals will be considered. These procedures should also allow reliable judgements to be made about whether the setting is hospitable or inimical to the proposed policy. This research will provide an analytical framework which will calibrate the scale and complexity of the settings and suggest the types of relationships that can exist among the different actors within the setting.

Organisation of the material

Chapter Two reviews the historical background to privatisation and competitive tendering in Britain, and elaborates the major concepts underlying theoretical considerations of competitive tendering problems in general. Specifically, it reviews previous work on privatisation and the competitive tendering of public services both in Britain and in other countries. More importantly, it divides studies of privatisation and the competitive tendering of public services into a number of categories and emphasises the need for policy output studies of privatisation to be undertaken.

Chapter Three presents the analytical model for path analysis and research methodologies. Drawing on the argument put forward in Chapter Two that studies of privatisation should explore more fully policy output and policy process, this chapter presents an analytical framework capable of identifying the main factors determining the output of the CCT process, DSO output. This analytical framework indicates that DSO output can be influenced by several basic but critical components. The chapter describes in detail each of these components and proposes hypotheses in relation to the output of the CCT process. Next, it sets out the methodological approaches via which the research analyses the main determinants of the output of CCT using path analysis. It then describes how the variables, dependent and independent, are defined, operationalised and obtained using the information acquired.

Chapter Four presents the findings of the path analysis, identifies which main factors affected the DSO output in 1991 and 1994, compares the result for 1991 with that for 1994, and emphasises the need for case studies to examine how the main factors affecting DSO output interacted with each other.

Chapter Five presents transaction cost theory as a potential means of analysing how the above factors are associated with the DSO output. It proposes a politics of transaction cost framework which can describe and analyse the main features of the political and bureaucratic settings within which CCT policy proposal has been implemented, with relation to its output, and which can also classify the types of relationships that can exist among different interested parties within these settings. The application of the politics of a transaction cost framework reflects an attempt to discover more fully the state of play of the main determinants in the CCT process.

Chapter Six presents the analytical framework for the application of the politics of the transaction cost approach to the actual CCT of the four local authorities, and outlines the research methodologies employed for the case studies.

Chapter Seven deals with findings from the case studies of the four local authorities. The case studies were based mainly on interviews with the four chief officers in each sampled local authority and a lawyer. Each interview is based on structured and open-ended questions read from a pre-designed questionnaire (see Appendix A). The respondents, as chief officers, were key participants in the decision-making process within each of the four non-metropolitan districts. The lawyer selected for the interview, like the chief officers, took part in the whole CCT process, in her case as a legal consultant, and therefore was conversant with the interaction and interplay between central government, local government and the private sector. The respondents represented distinct and sometimes divergent perspectives, since they had different backgrounds and different points of view regarding CCT. Additional data sources included inter-office memoranda, reports to councillors, minutes and tender documents relating to local government's evaluation of the contracting option. This data is also analysed to obtain more detailed information about the CCT process. More importantly, this chapter explores the relationships and dynamics operating between the main interested parties involved in the CCT process. It summarises the results of the detailed comparisons between the four local authorities to provide an overall picture of the issue.

Chapter Eight concludes the study. It provides an overview of the research by summarising the research questions, theoretical background, analytical framework, hypotheses, methodological approach, and results and findings. It highlights the contributions the study has aimed to make to this field and outlines the implications of its findings for theory and policy.

Note

[1] Direct service organisations are the staff employed by the authority itself to deliver services, and form the contractor side of the authority, operating on a trading basis with client departments (Walsh, 1991, p 4).

TWO

Privatisation and compulsory competitive tendering

Introduction

This chapter examines the privatisation of local government services from the theoretical and historical point of view. It argues that the CCT process is open to considerable influence from mediating forces, which implies that tendering outputs are far from uniform. A review of the literature on the privatisation of local government services reveals that very little academic attention has been paid to policy output. The chapter analyses the limitations of previous work on CCT, and argues for a more detailed and rigorous investigation of the phenomenon. It concludes that further study of CCT output is required to understand more fully what determinants have been involved in the output of the CCT process and how these have operated.

Privatisation of local government services in Britain: an overview

The welfare state: postwar consensus

Since many regarded the 1945-51 governments as having created the welfare state (Hill, 1993c, p 1), it is appropriate to look primarily at the political history of the provision of British local government services since 1945.

After the Second World War and throughout the 1950s and 1960s, a form of collectivism operated in Britain. The period saw the expansion of government, the setting up of the welfare state and the nationalisation of essential industries and a commitment to full employment. This consensus, which lasted up to around 1970, meant a commitment by both the Labour and the Conservative parties to a mixed economy and the welfare state. It also bound the Conservative Party to collectivism and to an approach to economic development and social policy which rendered its programmes little different from those of many European social democratic parties (Girvin, 1988, p 15). The period saw not simply an increase in the size and scale of local government, but an increasing tendency to assume that newly developing public services should be provided by local authorities. The assumptions underlying the reform discussion of the late 1960s and early 1970s entailed a growing and continually increasing role for local authorities (Kerley, 1994, p 107).

Rise of the New Right

The ideological basis for the development of the market approach to public service provision came from the ideas of the New Right theorists. The New Right espouses traditional liberal forms of thinking, emphasising the efficacy of the market as a mechanism for ensuring efficient production and distribution (Walsh, 1995, p 58).

From the turn of the 1970s, the technical arguments of von Hayek (1986) and public choice theorists such as Niskanen (1971) were given enhanced prominence by critics who insisted that the basic contradictions of the welfare state had manifested themselves in the immediate and profound crisis that was occurring. According to the New Right, the role of the state should be the neutral one of enabling people to pursue their own idea of the good, rather than of promoting any particular form of social organisation (Walsh, 1995, pp 58-9).

When Margaret Thatcher came to power in 1979 she began a process of sweeping away the old consensus ideas. The new approach was initially more evident in statements on economic and industrial policy than in what was said about social policy (Hill, 1993c, p 123). Thatcher began with the 1980 Local Government Planning and Land Act, which opened direct labour organisations (DLOs) to competitive tendering for certain services, then sold off a comprehensive list of state assets.

Successive Thatcher governments favoured a radical reconstruction of the social and political order in favour of capital accumulation and the parties of the Right, and focused increasingly on the need for local authorities to be efficient. According to Gamble (1988), this was a project constructed around the themes of 'the free economy, including withdrawal from social responsibility through the denationalisation of social welfare and the privatization of public services'. Thatcherism epitomised such policy moves by attacking social programmes, cutting public expenditure and embarking on a series of measures designed to revive capital accumulation and free enterprise. The postwar social democratic consensus was overthrown and the New Right precepts were put into practice (Asher, 1987, pp 247-51; Goodwin, 1994, pp 2-3; Hill, 1994, pp 28-42; McShane, 1995, pp 36-40).

Central elements of New Right philosophies provide an insight into the ideological objectives of privatisation and, in broad terms, offer a critique of the growth of British government in its advocacy of a 'minimal state' and free market capitalism. Economic crises during the 1970s exposed Keynesian economic theories to challenges from 'supply-side' economists. These economists put forward competing theories about the role of public expenditure and in so doing popularised the idea that the public sector's claim on resources was an unfair one and merely served to constrain the private sector of the economy. Attacking Keynesian ideas at their root, this implied that public spending, instead of stimulating the economy, was in fact a drain on it and an obstacle to economic growth (Foster, 1991, pp 44-5).

Bosanquet (1983) conceives the main component of New Right philosophy in terms of a model of society and the economy which embraces the idea that both have an inherent tendency towards order and growth. 'Natural' social and economic institutions, for example the labour market, will automatically distribute resources in everyone's best interests. Consequently, government planning is regarded as a disruption of this natural order. Likewise, government intervention, which organised groups (such as trade unions) may demand as a means of protecting themselves from the effects of growth and change, will lead to an increase in public expenditure and loss of economic efficiency. The notion that costs involved in the processes of growth and change could be shared collectively by public intervention is rejected by the New Right, which cites the inadequacies of the welfare state as an example of the failures of such a policy (Foster, 1991, pp 45-6; Sword, 1992, pp 19-22; Walsh, 1995, pp 58-64).

The New Right philosophies are reflected in government policies on privatisation including contracting out, with their emphasis on efficiency, market mechanisms, the limiting of public expenditure and the role of organised groups (such as trade unions) (Carnaghan and Bracewell-Milnes, 1993).

A key feature of the British welfare state and local government services in the 1980s and 1990s lies in the dominance of top-down restructuring, which has to be understood with reference to the changing national economy. In general terms, 'restructuring' involves a process of change in the welfare state system and the provision of local government services. Key elements of the Thatcherite restructuring have been the privatisation of nationalised industries and public sector monopolies, commercialisation in local government and healthcare activities, and the rationalisation of organisational structures to increase efficiency (Goodwin, 1994, pp 2-3). The Thatcherite project mirrored a New Right programme of institutional reform, imposing new rules and a new culture to help capital accumulation and individual freedom to flourish (Gamble, 1988).

Privatisation

Today more than ever, central and local government managers are searching for alternative means of providing goods and services at lower cost, while keeping quality concerns in check. Across the world, new forms of governance are continually being created from both traditional and non-traditional bases. In Britain, throughout the terms of the Conservative governments of the 1980s and mid-1990s, privatisation developed to become the cornerstone of public sector policy. From tentative beginnings, privatisation policies flourished to become the main element of political strategy, reversing the post-1945 growth of 'collectivism' in general and socialism in particular (Carnaghan and Bracewell-Milnes, 1993; Goodwin, 1994; Hill, 1993c).

The term 'privatisation' can be said to have gained wide currency in recent years, but its meaning remains a focus for contention (Pinch, 1989). It is an ambiguous term because of the multiple forms the phenomenon takes as well as the multiple motives likely to be involved (Barnekov et al, 1989, p 125; Hill, 1993c, p 130). According to Marsh (1990, pp 459-80), there is no single definitive description of the process of privatisation. In the simplest sense, privatisation is "the act of reducing the role of government, or increasing the role of the private sector in an activity or in the ownership of assets" (Savas, 1987, p 3). The widest, and best, definition of privatisation is that given by Asher (1987, p 4), who describes it as "an umbrella term that has come to describe a multitude of government initiatives designed to increase the role of the private sector". Asher also points out that in its most literal sense, it refers to the transfer of state ownership in nationalised industries to the private sector. This wider definition of privatisation has come to be accepted by most writers, who have realised the many different forms privatisation may take.

Privatisation can include various forms of alternative service production and delivery schemes (Schafritz and Hyde, 1978, p 129). Some of these, such as voluntarism and self-help, rely on citizens to help with the performance of tasks, in lieu of government workers or other agents being used (Lowi, 1979, p 67). Other forms, such as subsidies, tax incentives and voucher systems, involve alternative monetary arrangements between local and central government (Hanke, 1987, p 13). Contracting out and franchise agreements are mainly concerned with switching service provision from the government to other outside providers.

Stubbs and Barnett (1992) provide one of the clearest ways of understanding privatisation (Figure 2.1). They envisage privatisation as a process which involves some degree of shift (whole or in part), either of ownership or of funding arrangements, to the private sector.

In the figure, denationalisation refers both to the selling-off of nationalised industries and to the gradual withdrawal of services from comprehensive public provision. 'Commercialisation' introduces charges for a public service, thereby substituting customer fees for tax finance. 'Contracting out' is the provision of a service through the use of private contractors. In this case, the state remains the funder, but not the provider, of the service.

Theoretically there are five main goals associated with privatisation. The most frequently cited objective is to enhance or alter the use of limited resources by limiting or reducing the cost of providing services and goods for public consumption - especially in those instances where

Figure 2.1: Forms of privatisation

		Funding	
		Public	*Private*
Provision	*Public*	State control	Commercialisation
	Private	Contracting out	Denationalisation

Source: Stubbs and Barnett (1992)

private enterprise is both established and strong and where government is assured of more effective services at a lower cost (Denhardt and Hammond, 1992, pp 236-7). Secondly, privatisation is often used to modify or limit the role of government so that it 'governs' more and 'produces' less (Denhardt and Hammond, 1992).

Following the same line of reasoning, a third objective is to allow government to meet responsibilities that may otherwise be ignored, mismanaged or abandoned because they are too costly. The last two objectives consist of reducing the debt burden and limiting tax rate increases. These objectives frequently relate to situations where the cost of government operations exceeds the available resources (Denhardt and Hammond, 1992).

As has already been stated, privatisation is the act of lessening the traditional role of government (and thus, political forces) in certain areas. In view of the distinctions made earlier, this would mean that political authority affects some, and even many, of the processes and behaviours that occur within organisations. What is clear is that, in all cases, privatisation is an expressly politically-motivated process, and the arguments for it reflect the New Right philosophy of economic freedom, efficiency and the role of the market while condemning union power and public spending.

Relationships between privatisation, contracting out and CCT

Privatisation can include various forms of alternative service production and delivery schemes. The most commonly used privatisation option is contracting out. This involves a binding agreement by which a government pays a private firm or outside entity to provide all or part of a specific service (Goodwin, 1994, p 31). According to Asher (1987, p 7), the term 'contracting out' describes the situation where one organisation contracts with another for the provision of a particular good or service. She states that it is essentially a form of procurement, in the sense that contractors may be considered 'suppliers', but in common usage it has come to refer more specifically to the purchase of an end product which could otherwise be provided 'inhouse' by the purchaser.

In the private sector, contracting out is a common and growing phenomenon and is sometimes referred to as 'outsourcing' (Asher, 1987, p 8). The commercial reasons for contracting out vary, but generally include cost-effectiveness, lack of inhouse expertise, and the need for increased flexibility to respond to changes in market conditions (Asher, 1987).

The process by which private contracts are usually awarded is known as competitive tendering. The most common form of competitive tendering involves private contractors competing against one another either for contracts which had previously been in private hands and had expired (for example, catering concessions at sporting events) or for contracts which had not previously existed (for example, contracts for building the M25 orbital motorway around London). However, since the time of the Thatcher Government a different form of competitive tendering has become popular in Britain (Asher, 1987, p 10). This is where private contractors can compete against the inhouse teams.

As a result of increasing emphasis on the efficiency of core budget services, many recent competitive tendering exercises have involved services previously provided by a direct labour force. In most of these cases, the inhouse workforce has been asked to compete against interested private sector bidders. Where the inhouse force has offered the most cost-competitive alternative, it has generally retained the service and the contract price has become its budget. In cases where a private firm has proved cheaper than the inhouse service, the direct labour organisation has often been disbanded and the winning firm has assumed day-to-day control of services. This particular form of competitive tendering, in which an inhouse team competes against private contractors for a service it previously provided, is at the centre of the debate. It is the only type of tendering exercise that can lead to switches from one type of labour to another, a possibility that provokes a number of delicate questions (Asher, 1987, pp 10-11).

Competitive tendering is also one of the policies that comes under the commonplace heading of 'privatisation' (Carnaghan and Bracewell-Milnes, 1993, p 22). More specifically, it is one of the many dimensions of privatisation (Butler, 1988; Pirie, 1988). However, it is distinct from the other policies − contracting out, the sale of assets and the use of charges − in that it is the source of the provision that is in question, not its financing. Competitive tendering is the offering of tenders by several potential suppliers in competition with one another. In other words, competitive tendering is the process by which various contractors are invited to tender for the provision of a contract, this usually being awarded on the basis of some specified criteria such as least cost, highest quality, or greatest flexibility (Goodwin and Pinch, 1995, pp 1397-8). Compulsory competitive tendering can be defined as a competitive tendering policy which is forced on a local authority by central legislation.

Competitive tendering and contracting out for the provision of government services are related but distinct phenomena. Contracting out may be the result of competitive tendering, but both also occur independently of each other (Carnaghan and Bracewell-Milnes, 1993, p 30). Most competitive tendering for local government services does not result in contracting out, and when contracting out is used it is not always as a result of competitive tendering. When competitive tendering does not necessarily involve contracting out, since an internal department within the parent organisation may bid for, and win, the contract, such contracts are often said to be won inhouse and this process has been termed 'contracting in' or 'market testing' (Goodwin and Pinch, 1995, p 1398).

Parker and Hartley (1990, p 12) rightly observe that competitive tendering falls far short of complete privatisation since officials still determine what is supplied, and services are still funded out of taxation. Consequently it does not (especially in the absence of bids for alternative levels of service) introduce consumer choice and 'allocative efficiency'.

Background to CCT

Compulsory competitive tendering is usually thought of as being a recent Conservative innovation, whereas in fact there has been a long tradition in local authorities of companies from the private sector being invited to tender for contracts. These contracts have, for example, involved the supply of stationery, computer systems and other projects. Competitive tendering dates back to the 1950s, when local authorities used the private sector to carry out specific services (Sword, 1992, p 3).

When the Conservatives were elected to government in 1979 they were keen to reduce inflation, public expenditure and the public sector borrowing requirement. As local authority cash was a large part of public expenditure they had to find a way of controlling it. Introducing market forces into the supply of local authority services was one way they saw of doing this. This would simultaneously 'roll back the frontiers of the state' and control local authority expenditure, which was large and getting larger (Hill, 1993c, pp 123-30; Hill, 1994, pp 28-42; McShane, 1995, p 36; Prowle and Hines, 1989, pp 3-5).

Some Conservative local authorities had already been conducting experiments in allowing private enterprises to bid for local authority services and the message was relayed to all local authorities that the government wished to see these experiments continue. This was known as the period of voluntarism and limited compulsion - from 1980 to 1985. What followed were the Conservatives' first attempts at compulsion (Sword, 1992, p 3).

Limited compulsion

The first formal move to initiate compulsory competition for local authority services was the introduction of the 1980 Local Government Planning and Land Act. This Act dates back to 1975, when the Chartered Institute of Public Finance and Accountancy (CIPFA) published a report entitled *Direct works undertakings accounting*. This was the report of a CIPFA working group charged with examining the accounting practices of direct labour organisations and the means by which performance could be measured against financial results. This CIPFA report was the catalyst for the debate on the future of work to be carried out by the DLOs which was to continue for the next five years. Within five months, the Labour government of the day had established a departmental working group charged with investigating the organisation and operation of DLOs and considering the recommendations contained in the CIPFA report (Carnaghan and Bracewell-Milnes, 1993, p 27; McShane, 1995, pp 25-6).

In 1976, the Labour Government issued a Green Paper proposing a reform of local authorities' direct labour organisations and suggesting competitive tendering (Carnaghan and Bracewell-Milnes, 1993, p 27). In spite of the government's commitment to establish a financial objective supported by charging, tendering and accounting requirements for the future operation of direct labour organisations, no legislation was introduced by the Callaghan administration. In spite of the early recognition of the necessity of legislation, and the fact that the content of any legislation was identified at an early stage, the departmental working group appointed in October 1975 did not report until August 1978 (Foster, 1991, pp 41-3; McShane, 1995, pp 25-6).

In November 1978, the Parliamentary Under-Secretary of State at the Department of the Environment (DoE) stated that future legislation on DLOs would be designed to improve their accountability and create conditions in which they could become more fully comparable with private contractors. In 1978, a working party of local authority, district audit and DoE representatives produced recommendations regarding the use of competition. The May 1979 general election prevented the Labour Government from introducing legislation, but the new Conservative Government issued a consultation paper outlining its own proposals, which were later embodied in Part III of the 1980 Act. This came into operation on 1 April 1981 in England and Wales, and on 1 April 1982 in Scotland (Carnaghan and Bracewell-Milnes, 1993, pp 27-38; McShane, 1995, pp 25-8; Walsh, 1991, p 9).

Part III of the Act required local authorities to adopt competitive tendering for a proportion of construction and maintenance work on buildings and highways. Local authorities were only allowed to carry out such work by direct labour if they had won the right to do so in competition. Where they won work, they were required to keep a trading account and to make a trading surplus at least equivalent to a rate of return on capital of 5% (Walsh, 1991, p 9).

Voluntarism

Aside from the limited compulsion related to DLOs, there was a movement of competition and privatisation on a voluntary basis in the 1980s. However, interest in both contracting out and competitive tendering grew slowly during the early 1980s (Carnaghan and Bracewell-Milnes, 1993, p 31; Walsh, 1991, p 9).

According to one survey, in the year to March 1985 only about 11% of councils in Britain appeared to have contracted out the provision of any services (39 out of 346 survey respondents). The great majority of councils (about 78%) had neither contracted out any services during the year nor considered doing so (Carnaghan and Bracewell-Milnes, 1993, pp 31-2).

Voluntary subjection of services to competition had covered some services, including professional services in some instances, but had largely related to refuse collection, cleaning, catering and environmental services. However, as Walsh points out (1991, p 9), the majority of authorities had not taken up competitive tendering on a voluntary basis. Those that had voluntarily subjected services to competition had not normally done so on an extensive basis, and contracts had normally been small.

NHS experience

Compulsory competitive tendering and the contracting out of services in the NHS preceded the local government initiative. An examination of its application and effects within the NHS provides an insight into the origins of CCT. It is also of interest to examine in what ways a technical/policy option has come to assume an ideological function, following on from the previous discussion.

The NHS, as created in 1948, was very much a monument to faith in social equity and social engineering. The contracting out of ancillary services has been present in the NHS since it was founded (Goodwin, 1994, p 13). In the 1950s, it was used at a time of full employment to overcome recruitment difficulties, particularly in the contracting of managerial and operational staff in key areas. Little is known of the full extent of contracting out in this period but it seems to have been quite limited and based in the south-east (Asher, 1987).

The 1960s saw a growth in contracting out in the NHS. This growth, documented by Asher (1987), was especially marked in the cleaning, catering and laundry service sectors. The 1970s saw a significant downturn in public sector contracting out, particularly in the NHS (Asher, 1987).

Following the election of the Conservative Government in 1979, as much public sector work as possible became subject to competition and contracting out to the private sector was encouraged "wherever practicable and sensible" (National Audit Office, 1987). The government realised that mandatory contracting out of ancillary services would cause major industrial disruption, so the preferred form of contracting out was via competitive tendering (Asher, 1987; Goodwin, 1994).

During the early 1980s, the Conservative government moved decisively and quickly towards a system of competitive tendering for NHS ancillary services. This development was encouraged by a favourable ideological environment but, more importantly, by strong political lobbying by private contractors and New Right ideologists and organisations, as well as Conservative Party members (Asher, 1987). Among the influential New Right authors and institutions at the time were members of the Adam Smith Institute. Especially important was a paper by Forsyth (1982) which highlighted the advantages that privatisation and contracting out could bring to the NHS. Similarly, the Institute of Directors presented a paper which argued that privatisation was the obvious and most desirable strategy for breaking public sector unions. The Tory Reform Group and the Bow Group are on record as having demanded wholesale contracting out, arguing that competitive tendering was a soft option (Asher, 1987, pp 98-102).

According to Goodwin, strong political compulsion lay behind the policy of competitive tendering. Goodwin also states that progress towards a central directive on competitive tendering was aided by the lack of significant political opposition. At that time, the unions themselves were in disarray and came up with no nation-wide policy actions until after compulsory competitive tendering was introduced in September 1983 (Goodwin, 1994).

The introduction of mandatory competitive tendering in the NHS was conducted in an ad hoc manner, and attracted criticisms which were expressed most forcefully by administrators responsible for its implementation. They were critical of the timing, cost and implications of the policy and its emphasis on efficiency as opposed to quality and level of service (Foster, 1991).

Leedham argues that pressures from various interests played a major role in the development of the contracting out policy for the NHS:

> **Pressures that have shaped the development of contracting out policy for the NHS have been far greater than the need to test efficiency ... Powerful interest groups, political ideology and the practicalities of power relations transformed the policy from a technical option to serve a more haphazard ideological function. (1986, p 11)**

Evaluating the success of government policy in the area of privatisation is extremely difficult since government objectives are not always clear. However, it is estimated by the government that in the UK as a whole the drive to test NHS support services in the market has brought savings of more than £626 million during a period of seven years (Carnaghan and Bracewell-Milnes, 1993, p 116). Many surveys (CQBB, 1991; Cubbin et al, 1987; Hartley and Huby, 1985; Milne, 1987; National Audit Office, 1987; Sheaff, 1988) point out that yearly savings from competitive tendering in the NHS were estimated at more than 20% of the previous cost of the services before they were put out to contract. Increased workloads, redundancies, poorer wages and conditions and a significant trend towards the use of part-time rather than full-time labour account for most of these savings (Carnaghan and Bracewell-Milnes, 1993; Foster, 1991).

However, in assessing savings, a number of factors should be considered. Most notably, government figures do not include costs relating to the actual tendering process, which are quite significant administratively; neither do they include transaction costs incurred when implementing a new contract. Because of this the 'savings' argument should be regarded with a degree of scepticism (Griffith et al, 1987, p 168). Griffith et al maintained that the 'inefficiency' attributed to public services often refers to the perceived potential for increasing the exploitation of working people. In their study of CCT in the NHS, they claim that the 'savings' achieved, while running into millions of pounds, are bogus:

> **Counterbalancing any gains have been the losses through redundancy payments, administrative burden, lower morale, industrial action, increased exploitation and unemployment and, for some Districts at least, lower standards. (1987, pp 168-9)**

On the other hand, they state that the available evidence does not allow them to reach a conclusion as to whether competition has resulted in genuine gains in efficiency, and that it is impossible to say whether there has been significant 'over-manning' in the NHS domestic departments (Griffith et al, 1987, pp 170-2).

It is true to say that the NHS experience of compulsory competitive tendering contributed to its application to local government services. However, as will be discussed later, the competitive tendering rules for the NHS are less onerous to the inhouse organisation than is the case in local government. The NHS inhouse unit only needs to be cheaper than the private contractor to win the contract and survive. The local authority DSO not only needs to be cheaper than the private contractor but to survive must also earn its target rate of return. This inconsistency between government departments is rather surprising (Prowle and Hines, 1989, pp 7-8).

Progress towards compulsion

It appears that limited compulsion, voluntarism and the NHS experience of compulsory competitive tendering mentioned above provided an insight into progress towards compulsion. This section addresses the main Acts associated with CCT for the seven manual services which are within the scope of this study.

1988 Local Government Act: The failure of voluntarism and limited compulsion was a blow to the government. By 1987, only 350 contracts had been awarded to the private sector (Walsh, 1991, p 126), so only a small step had been taken towards the government's goal of reducing the role of local government in the services it provided. Local authorities were not responding to the government invitation to contract out, and even those contracts which were awarded fell short of what was expected. These results led the government, in February 1985, to propose in a consultative paper, *Competition in the provision of local authority services*, to extend competition to a number of local authority services. The paper proposed that competition should be extended to refuse collection, street cleaning, catering, cleaning of buildings, ground maintenance and vehicle maintenance. A Bill was introduced in June 1987 and received Royal Assent as the 1988 Local Government Act in April 1988 (Carnaghan and Bracewell-Milnes, 1993, pp 40-2; Kerley, 1994, pp 107-19; Walsh, 1991, p 10; Walsh and Davis, 1993, pp 30-1).

The 1988 Act defines authorities and also sets out seven defined activities which were to be the subject of CCT (Table 2.1). (In Scotland, 'local authority' means a regional, island or district council, or any joint board or joint committee within the meaning of the 1973 Local Government [Scotland] Act.)

The management of sports and leisure facilities was added to the list by Parliamentary Order in November 1989. There were some exemptions

Table 2.1: List of services subject to CCT under the 1988 Local Government Act

Services	Details
Refuse collection	Household and commercial waste
Cleaning of buildings	All buildings except police, children's and old people's homes
Other cleaning	Mainly street cleaning
School and welfare catering	School meals, meals-on-wheels
Other catering	Staff canteens, functions
Ground maintenance	Excludes research and plant survival work
Vehical repair and maintenance	Excludes police/fire vehicles
Sports and leisure management	Sports centres/playing fields, swimming pools

Source: Sword (1992, p 7)

from the legislation. Competition was not required where the gross cost of the service in the previous year had been less than £100,000. In addition, there were exemptions for emergent services and where the work was performed by staff for whom the defined activity was only a small part of their total activities (Carnaghan and Bracewell-Milnes, 1993; Walsh, 1991).

If the local authority wishes to perform the activity by direct labour, it has to subject the work to competition. It must invite at least three companies to tender from those who express an interest. The authority's own staff, normally organised in a direct service organisation, are required to tender on the same basis as the private sector companies. The extension of competition for local authority services interacts with a number of other pieces of local government legislation, notably the Education Reform Act 1988 and the Local Government and Housing Act 1989 (Walsh, 1991, p 11).

The 1992 Local Government Act: In the third stage, all the regulations involved in the 1988 Act were then further tightened by the 1992 Local Government Act. CCT was extended to other areas, including other manual services, and theatre, library and arts management. Professional services such as legal, architectural, financial and engineering services were also included. The extension of the latter, in particular, raises complex issues about how to reconcile cost and quality, a matter which has not yet been adequately resolved. While the local authority is not under an obligation to accept the lowest tender, cost can be seen as the most important consideration since many other issues are excluded as being 'non-commercial' (Bailey, 1997, pp 180-1; Wilson and Game, 1994, pp 325-7). In short, the 1992 Act created a new power for the Secretary of State to make further regulations specifying and enforcing what is deemed to be 'anticompetitive', which goes beyond the provision relating to 'non-commercial' matters in the 1988 Act (McShane, 1995, p 82).

The 1994 Local Government Act: The fourth stage is provided by Part II of the 1994 Deregulations and Contracting Out Act, which makes provision for the contracting out of the functions of ministers and officeholders and, in Section 70, local authorities. This aimed to remove the remaining statutory obstacles to the use of private contractors, and to overcome the general presumption against delegation in so far as it had not been overcome by Section 101 of the 1992 Local Government Act (Bailey, 1997, pp 180-1).

Best Value as an alternative to CCT

In 1997, the Labour government introduced the Best Value framework as an alternative to CCT. Although the Best Value framework following CCT is strictly outside the scope of this research, it should be mentioned simply to aid understanding of the general context of privatisation policy in Britain.

Since Labour came to power in May 1997 the main direction of CCT has been changing. The Labour government is planning to introduce Best Value as an alternative to CCT. In June 1997 the Department of the Environment, Transport and the Regions[1] issued 12 Principles of Best Value which will form the basis for pilot schemes in local authorities. These statements spell out the broad content and process of Best Value (UNISON, 1997, p 3). They make it clear that Best Value represents a duty that local authorities owe to local people, both as taxpayers and users, and that it is intended to apply to all local authority services. They emphasise that the quality of services, as well as their cost, matters, and that although there will be no compulsion to put services out to tender, there should be no presumption that services should be delivered directly if other, more efficient means are available. Competition will continue to play an important role (LGA, 1998).

Since the autumn of 1997, the government has been implementing 30 Best Value pilot projects. These are intended to be two-year projects, and are subject to monitoring and evaluation by consultants (LGA, 1998).

There is currently no agreed definition of 'Best Value'. The government's consultation paper sets out objectives and principles. Its proposals incorporate five key objectives and 12 principles. The five key features (LGA, 1998) are:

- corporate perspective

- continuous improvement

- performance targets

- transparency

- audit and clarification

The 12 Principles of Best Value (LGA, 1998) are:

- accountability

- effectiveness

- applicability to all services

- competition but not compulsion

- competition alone is not enough

- government standards

- performance targets

- performance information

- audited evidence

- public information

- Secretary of State's power to intervene

- last-resort powers of Secretary of State

The concept of Best Value is ambiguous, and this could lead to major problems in legal definitions and practical application. However, what is notable about Best Value is that two of the 12 principles refer to the role of competition, which will not be compulsory, and that competition alone will not be enough to demonstrate Best Value.

The government has drawn up a timetable for the Best Value framework (Table 2.2). At the time of writing the government is committed to introducing primary legislation to establish the duty and framework of Best Value as soon as Parliamentary time permits. In the meantime, it will continue to explore ways in which the principles of Best Value can be put into effect through secondary legislation and guidance where this is consistent with the purposes of the extant primary legislation (LGA, 1998).

Comparison of the privatisation policies of Britain and of other countries

CCT differs from policies adopted by other countries within the European Union and the USA in that the central feature of the policy is compulsion.

Table 2.2: Best Value timetable

Best Value	
October 1997	Selection of 30 Best Value pilots
1998-99	Monitoring of Best Value pilots
1999	Best Value legislation
2000	Abolition of CCT and start of Best Value
CCT	
1997	Circular Part I, 1988 Act, conduct of CCT and withdraw Circular 5/96
1997-98	Review of Part II, 1988 Act – workforce matters
1998	Review of trading powers under 1970 Local Authorities (Goods and Services) Act

Note: adapted from *Best Value - A strategic approach* (UNISON, 1997, p 4)

This makes it quite likely that the nature of competition and of the CCT policy process in British local government will be different from in other countries, where there is no compulsion in privatisation policies and where the influence of competition, if any, is not significant (Council of Europe, 1993, p 9; Kane, 1996, p 51).

In a 1990 survey of council services in France, Denmark, Canada and the USA, David Green states:

> **In all the countries and practically all the towns and cities visited 'competition' was a live and emotive subject. Nowhere, however, was it yet being enforced by central government as it is here, save in respect of those instances where funds were being provided by central government or 'State' for use at County or City level on behalf of the others.... But the real difference between competition here and elsewhere is its imposition in Britain by Central Government on Local Government via a legalistic framework. Even in France where much of local government is controlled from the centre ... there was no hint of such an approach on the horizon. Competition began and ended with the authorities themselves. (1990, ss 8.1-8.6)**

The compulsory nature of competition associated with British local government ensures that the policy is enshrined in a legislative framework and subject to regulation by the centre. The need for compulsion inevitably introduces rules, some of which are bound to be restrictive, as well as causing additional work and antagonisms (Carnaghan and Bracewell-Milnes, 1993, p 142). Arguably, this denotes a trend towards centralisation and also implies that the complexities of the CCT process may be compounded, particularly in relation to the interaction of the main parties to a contract. In short, CCT creates complex relationships between purpose-specific organisations in fragmented environments. John (1994) states that this centralising element in government policy only really emerged in the later 1980s and is continuing into the 1990s. Experience of CCT to date has seemed consistent with this hypothesis. However, since Labour came to power in May 1997 the main policy direction of CCT has been changing. For this reason, the main comparisons made will be limited to CCT prior to Best Value.

The voluntarist/limited compulsion experiment of the early 1980s could not be regarded as being designed to increase government control, since the Government afforded local authorities the opportunity to experiment with competitive processes. However, the legislative framework for CCT has been widened by the implementation of the 1988, 1992 and 1994 Local Government Acts. This does seem to imply creeping centralisation given that local authorities were first coerced to compete for manual services, and are now being faced with the prospect of competition for professional services (Kane, 1996).

It could be argued that the centralisation argument surrounding CCT is strengthened when the organisational effects of the policy are considered. In many cases, CCT has forced local authorities to alter their internal organisational arrangements to take account of a purchaser–provider split.

To understand more fully the nature of competition in British local government, it is useful to make a comparison with other European countries' experience of marketisation policies at the local level. Shaw and Fenwick (1995) argue that CCT is atypical from a comparative viewpoint, since from the outset the policy contained an element of compulsion, which cannot be found in the marketisation policies adopted in other European countries.

Germany has had some limited experience of contracting for the cleaning of buildings, slaughterhouses and refuse collection. In Germany, it is common knowledge that local authorities are considering further privatisation measures, with an emphasis on the field of sewage disposal, where it is intended to transfer facilities which so far have operated in the framework of local budgets either to owner-operated municipal enterprises or to private enterprises (Council of Europe, 1993, p 28; Walsh, 1991, p 7).

Sweden does not have any legislation obliging the municipalities to employ a tendering procedure, but they do have the option of doing so, to various extents and in various fields of activity. The view of the Swedish Government is that contracting out may be appropriate for services such as refuse collection and street cleaning. There is some experience of contracting in Sweden, primarily on the part of small authorities, largely in order to cope with difficulties in recruiting staff (Council of Europe, 1993, p 52; Walsh, 1991, p 7).

In The Netherlands extensive use is made of competition, with about 60% of municipalities using private companies for services such as cleaning and grounds maintenance (Walsh, 1991, p 7). The development of the contracting out of local service provision in The Netherlands has been documented in some sources (Braunig, 1992; Shaw and Fenwick, 1995; Snape, 1994).

The immediate contrast with the experience of the UK is that municipalities in The Netherlands have enjoyed a great deal of autonomy with respect to the development of management strategies. This was despite the fact that the centre-right Lubbers coalition governments of the 1980s favoured reducing the size of the state and redeveloping the structure of the public sector. The nature of competition in the municipal authorities was to a large extent dependent on a wider programme of organisational renewal suited to the needs and context of the particular authority, as witnessed in the approach adopted in Tilburg (Braunig, 1992).

Apart from the stipulations of the EC directives there is no requirement in current Danish legislation for local authorities to resort to competitive tendering. However, many local authorities decide voluntarily to invite tenders. It is estimated that in Denmark about 15% of all public sector cleaning is contracted out. There is an interesting arrangement in Aarhus, the second largest Danish city, where domestic refuse collection is carried out by a non-profit society which has a 25-year concession from the council (Council of Europe, 1993, p 23; Kane, 1996, pp 54-5).

Ireland is an example of another European country where some change has taken place in the management and provision of local services. In contrast both to the UK and The Netherlands, privatisation of local services has not been advanced (Barrington, 1991). However, it is more widespread than was previously thought (Kane, 1996). The late 1980s witnessed an increase in privatisation, particularly of refuse collection services (Kane, 1996).

While competitive tendering is widely used in the USA, its use varies considerably from one authority to another. A survey by the International City Management Association in 1985 found that contracting operated with regard to 12% of library services, 30% of tree maintenance, 10% of crime prevention and control and 24% of data processing (Rehfuss, 1989). The experience of contracting in the USA is highly variable, with some jurisdictions using it much more widely than others (Walsh, 1991, p 8). In the USA what is noticeable is that all contracting is voluntary, not being mandated by state or federal law.

From this it can be seen that Britain stands alone in its pursuit of a centralist position which promotes compulsory competition for local government. In a detailed survey of competitive tendering in the European Community, Digings (1991, p 16) also states that the UK is the exception in making competitive tendering obligatory. In the other countries of the Community, in the majority of cases contracts tend to be let to private contractors for purely pragmatic reasons, with no ideological undertones; although there are exceptions, it generally remains a fundamentally unpoliticised issue. In short, the British approach is novel, and has been ideologically driven by a government intent on centralisation and regulation (Kane, 1996). It follows that the processes of competitive tendering and contracting out in Britain differ from those of other countries in many respects.

Review of the literature on privatisation

Recent decades have seen a consistent move towards public service privatisation (Moe, 1984). Numerous studies have been written on privatisation, competitive tendering and contracting out. These studies have focused on a variety of issues. Some evaluate the pros and cons of privatisation, competitive tendering or contracting out while others examine the social and economic consequences that may discourage local authorities from privatising. Competitive tendering, privatisation and contracting out are closely related to each other, and it is difficult to divide the literature on them clearly according to the subject.

Although contracting out and/or the competitive tendering system are implemented in the UK and many other countries, and although studies on them have been conducted in many other European countries and in the USA, this literature review focuses primarily on UK studies, referring only briefly to those undertaken in other countries. As has already been explained, competitive tendering and contracting out are not the same. Nevertheless, they are closely related to each other, and so studies on them should be dealt with together. Accordingly, this literature review covers studies on both competitive tendering and contracting out.

General review

The works on competitive tendering and contracting out published to date cover many different aspects of privatisation. However, a particularly disappointing feature of the literature has been its reticence in dealing with the local variations in output of the competitive tendering process. While writings on the subject of contracting out and competitive tendering have been numerous, they have been confined to chapters or sections of chapters in books, articles in journals, and small booklets produced by politically motivated bodies. Goodwin's (1994) work *Privatisation and the NHS* provides almost the only substantial output study on contracting out in the NHS. Walsh and Davis (1993) and Walsh et al (1997) also touch on the output of CCT, but only via passing references.

One reason for the lack of output studies of CCT is that competitive tendering has been a very emotive issue, with the result that considerable efforts have been made both to credit and discredit the economic rationale of the policy and to highlight the social consequences of competitive tendering for local government officials and for standard of service. Consequently, variations between local authorities in output have been neglected. The lack of output studies on contracting out and competitive tendering will be clear from the following typology of the literature.

Earlier studies of contracting out and competitive tendering can be broadly classified into the categories shown in Table 2.3. The aim of such classification is to understand the general trends of such research.

As Table 2.3 shows, the literature on contracting out and competitive tendering can be classified according to two main criteria. One of these is the approach the research adopts. The literature on competitive

Table 2.3: Matrix of the literature on contracting out and competitive tendering

	Political	Practical	Analytical
UK (local government services)	Type I	Type II	Type III
UK (other services)	Type IV	Type V	Type VI
Other countries	Type VII	Type VIII	Type IX

tendering can be broadly divided into three categories according to the approach it adopts: *political, practical* and *analytical.* The *political* category denotes that the research addresses the pros and cons of competitive tendering and contracting out. *Practical* research deals with how to implement contracting out and competitive tendering successfully. The research aims to identify the conditions under which expected outcomes from contracting out and competitive tendering may be assured. In brief, this research seeks to investigate the implications for management practice. *Analytical* research analyses empirically the practice or system of competitive tendering and conceptualises the competitive tendering process as a dynamic process. The strength of the analytical approach lies in the combination of a contextual and processual view of strategic change allied to a multilevel and dynamic appreciation of competitive tendering.

The second criterion is whether the research deals with the UK or other countries. The literature on the UK is subdivided into two categories: UK local government services, and that on other UK bodies such as the NHS and the Civil Service.

A combination of the two criteria gives nine literature types.

Research of Type I is primarily concerned with identifying the pros and cons of competitive tendering from the political point of view, and at the same time dealing with the issues of UK local government services. This literature has developed alongside the introduction of competitive tendering following the 1980 Local Government Planning and Land Act and the 1988 Local Government Act. Political and ideological support for competitive tendering has come from a variety of sources, such as public choice theorists and the New Right, while arguments against it have come from the three sources of "conservatism, socialism and bureaucracy" (Carnaghan and Bracewell-Milnes, 1993, p 33).

Even if the tendering process did not lead to contracting out and the tender was won by the inhouse bid, proponents of competitive tendering argued that the local authority would be under great pressure to become more efficient. Making cuts in the existing workforce so that it would become efficient was also likely to weaken the position of local union organisations in ensuring ratepayers got a 'value for money' service (Shaw et al, 1992).

Opposition to competitive tendering centred on the likely redundancies that would result if the contract went to the private sector, the downward pressure on wages and conditions of service, the likelihood of lower standards if the service was contracted out, and the diminution of the "services on the basis of need" ethos prevalent in local government (Pyper, 1990).

Literature of Type I deals mainly with why the government chose the competitive tendering and contracting out policy, and what are the advantages and the arguments against. According to the literature on the pros and cons of competitive tendering and contracting out (DoE, 1985; John, 1990; Minogue and O'Grady, 1985; Pyper, 1990; Spencer, 1984; Stoker, 1988; Walker and Moore, 1983), the advantages of competitive tendering and contracting out are:

- generally lower cost
- tighter financial control
- reduced management 'load'
- clear service standards
- 'competitive' ethos

Meanwhile the disadvantages of CCT are:

- less direct control
- less flexibility in use of DLO staff
- increased overheads (letting the contract, maintaining performance)
- risk of exploitation once the DLO is disbanded

The characteristics of Type I studies are as follows: first, they are not based on empirical research but on theoretical, normative and ideological discussion; secondly, they are concerned to support or oppose competitive tendering and contracting out either politically or theoretically, without empirical evidence. In other words, most of the literature on the pros and cons of contracting out and competitive tendering has been published by interest groups and is highly partisan.

Type II comprises literature in which the focus of the examination of competitive tendering is on identifying recommended ways of implementing it successfully, the main emphasis being on local government services. Some scholars (Audit Commission, 1989; Beresford, 1987; Frater, 1988; Local Government Training Board, 1987; Jennings, 1987; Prowle and Hines, 1989; Talbot, 1986) have suggested the conditions under which expected outcomes from contracting out can be assured.

For example, three major conditions crucial to any contracting arrangements are suggested by Talbot (1986):

- fair competition;

- contracting officials will be rational decision-makers who are motivated to adhere to the goal of maximising cost savings, along with ensuring adequate service performance;

- the government should play an effective 'watchdog' role and the contracting officials should continuously monitor contractor service performance to ensure that the activities conform to the specifications of the contract.

The literature in this category usually lacks an underlying conceptual framework to arrive at its prescriptions. Empirical studies have not been conducted, nor are they available to justify the guidelines.

Type III comprises literature which aims to analyse the practices or system of contracting out and competitive tendering and to deal with issues concerned with UK local government services. This study falls into this category so it will be discussed in more detail. Type III literature can be further categorised using four themes: the economics of contracting out; industrial relations and contracting out; the impact of contracting out on management; the policy output of the competitive tendering process.

Much of the evidence presented either to prove or disprove the value of competitive tendering is tendentious, produced by those concerned either to promote or oppose competition (Walsh, 1989). For example, *Public Service Review,* published by proponents of competition, regularly contained lists of the savings that had been made by local authorities that had introduced competition.

The economic arguments (Audit Commission, 1993; Walsh, 1991; Walsh and Davis, 1993) in favour of competitive tendering and contracting out are highly controversial and have created a great deal of interest. Proponents of contracting out point to efficiency gains and cost savings deriving from competition between rival suppliers. Walsh was one of the leading scholars on competitive tendering and contracting out but was neither an opponent nor an advocate. He could see the benefits of those policies, but also problems, because of the inadequacy of the analysis on which they were based (Stewart, 1996). In one detailed survey of 40 panel authorities carried out by INLOGOV, Walsh and Davis (1993) concluded that competition had led to an average overall reduction in service cost of 6.5%, the range being from an increase in cost of 62.4% to a reduction of 49.7%.

However, the literature on financial effects has many weaknesses. For example, Walsh and Davis, in their 1993 study, provide empirical evidence in support of scholarly arguments that significant transaction costs are involved in CCT. They found that the costs of preparation for compulsory competitive tendering in local government were 7.7% of the annual contract value. These costs were largely associated with the preparation of specifications, for example the measurement of sites on which work is to be done, and the costs of letting contracts. They argue that privatisation by contracting out has less appeal than private–private contracting owing to the higher transaction costs incurred in public–private contracting, especially the costs of preparing documents and monitoring activities.

The main problem with the Type III literature is that the results of such inquiries are often contradictory. Little information is given on how they are arrived at. There is no statement of the difference between short- and long-term implications, or the relationship between capital and revenue expenditure savings (Walsh, 1989, p 42). Little information is given about how savings are achieved. Equally, the focus by the trade unions on the failure of contractors to adequately deliver the service says little about the failure of the public service, and ignores the successful contracts.

The true economic performance of the competitive tendering initiative in the UK will, no doubt, remain a controversial issue for some time. While contracting out has produced 'savings' on the cost of the service provided per se, it is almost certain that the government's estimates of savings have exaggerated the benefits (Key, 1987). What is disappointing in this literature is the lack of a detailed economic analysis of the implementation of competitive tendering in local government services, other than from cases specially selected to further political arguments.

The literature in this category on industrial relations issues deriving from the competitive tendering policy is mainly concerned with the responses of the trade unions in local government. The two important studies which examine the UK experience of the privatisation of local government services and industrial relations, Rainnie (1994) and Foster (1993), both argue that there have been major changes in the industrial relations of local government, and that these continue. Rainnie says that the industrial relations lessons (for trade unions) to be drawn from CCT are contradictory. He also emphasises that the overwhelming success of inhouse bids in tendering for contracts represents a victory for a strategy of keeping contracts inhouse rather than outright opposition to privatisation per se. This, in part, can be put down to the success of a campaign aimed at painting a picture of the private sector as bad employers, inefficient and incapable of delivering high-quality services. Foster (1993) suggests that, after initial opposition, unions have not resisted organisational change, instead concentrating on influencing local political opinion and the process of CCT, and limiting potential damage to their members.

Walsh (1991) notes the lack of serious industrial unrest accompanying the introduction of CCT in local government, arguing that most problems were solved via a process of consultation and negotiation.

The literature dealing with the management issue primarily covers the impact CCT has on the essence of public management, how the client–contractor split should be retained, and how local government management has to face challenges in managing contracting.

Kerley (1994) points out that local authorities have undoubtedly done a great deal of soul-searching in recent years, reassessing the composition, culture and method of the organisation of local governments. He also addresses challenges which local authorities had previously ignored. Fenwick (1995) reveals the need to address a number of problems associated with the impact of CCT on management. This involves a focus on staffing levels and skills, communication and command chains and questions of efficiency, accountability and the distribution of power. Walsh (1991) and Walsh and Davis (1993) argue that CCT requires new levels of management information, together with the skills to put it to effective use and the development of formal communication networks to implement change.

Shaw et al (1994) analyse the organisational implications of CCT and highlight how officers and councillors viewed the changing nature of management within local authorities in the period following the award of the first service contracts. In particular, they examine the different reactions to the development of a more commercial approach to the management of services, and end by assessing the specific impact of CCT in the context of other important changes in local government.

Literature on the final theme in this category, output studies of CCT and contracting out in local government services in the UK, is scant. Asher (1987) uses case studies of three local authorities to provide some research results concerned with the output of competitive tendering. However, her main concern is to address the policy output of competitive tendering before the introduction of the 'compulsory' system under the 1988 Act so her book does not deal with CCT under the 1988 Act.

Painter (1991) and Adonis (*Financial Times*, 1991) both present some evidence for regional variations in the privatisation of local government services during the first round of compulsory competitive tendering. Other studies (Shaw et al, 1994; Walsh and Davis, 1993) which have dealt with the output of competitive tendering generally lack a conceptual framework based on established theory. The studies on this theme are conducted from a geographical, rather than from a policy science, point of view.

Literature of Type IV which is concerned with the other UK services, including the NHS and the Civil Service, discusses the pros and cons of competitive tendering. As with Type I, most of the literature in this category is partisan and has been published by interest groups such as the Adam Smith Institute and the Tory Reform Group.

Three representative publications in support of contracting out in the NHS have come from the Adam Smith Institute in London: *Privatisation*, by Pirie (1985), *Reservicing Britain* (1980) and *Reservicing health* (1982), both by Forsyth. A fourth pamphlet which advocates tendering and contracting out in the health service was published by the Tory Reform Group in 1984: *High noon in the National Health Service*. Two pamphlets presenting opposing views are *Public or private* and *Privatisation: Who loses? Who wins?* (LRD, 1983). Less partisan views on the issues surrounding contracting out and competitive tendering can be found in *Contracting out and the public sector* (RIPA, 1984).

The arguments in favour of contracting out in the NHS have stimulated a great deal of interest and argument. Proponents (Department of Health,

1989; Domberger et al, 1987; Forsyth, 1980; Parker and Hartley, 1990) point to efficiency gains and quality service. For example, a pamphlet written by Michael Forsyth, then a Conservative member of Westminster City Council, argued strongly in favour of using private contractors to provide 'hotel services' to the NHS (Pirie, 1985, p 90). Forsyth also put forward the ideological reasons for contracting out, on the basis that the less governments do, the better.

Literature of Type V aims to identify the successful conditions for contracting out and implementation of such a policy in the other UK services. One of the guides to contracting out in the NHS is *Quasi-markets and social policy* (Le Grand and Bartlett, 1993, pp 19-34). Le Grand and Bartlett specify the conditions the NHS will have to meet if such contracting out is to succeed, and go on to make a preliminary empirical assessment of the extent to which these conditions appear to be met in practice. The conditions concern *market structure, information, transaction costs and uncertainty*, and *motivation and cream-skimming*. However, scholars rarely put forward empirical evidence concerning the results of contracting out in relation to theoretical conditions.

Type VI analyses the practices of the NHS. As with Type III, which is concerned with local government services, this literature can be subdivided into the same four categories. The first deals with the economics of contracting out in the NHS, which has received much attention. For example, in a survey by Hartley and Huby (1985), the evidence from contracting out in the NHS suggested yearly savings from competitive tendering averaging 26%, the range being from potential savings of 68% to extra costs of 28%. In the Health Service, the cost-savings and efficiency gains have received much advocacy (Domberger et al, 1987; HPSS, 1991; National Audit Office, 1987; Parker and Hartley, 1990), often in articles or publications by those groups with a partisan interest in the matter, such as Right-wing activists.

Proponents of contracting out by competitive tendering have tended to point to the substantial international evidence to support their view that contracted out services lead to significant savings for local taxpayers. The main argument in favour of competitive tendering in the NHS is that savings made can be used for direct patient care (Goodwin, 1994, p 21).

However, critics and opponents of contracting out show that savings produced to date in the NHS are only a fraction of expenditure on support services. The Radical Statistical Health Group (1987) pointed out that the amount of money saved does not include a variety of other 'hidden financial costs'. Such hidden costs include the administrative work required to draw up specifications and the inhouse tender and the time spent by managers negotiating and consulting with staff and unions (Goodwin, 1994, p 22). Other works (Joint NHS Privatisation Research Unit, 1990; LRD, 1984) also indicate that the hidden costs of redundancy payments and early retirement and the costs of mid-contract failures by private firms have also been neglected in studies on cost savings.

The studies of industrial relations in the competitive tendering process in the NHS (the second sub-category of this literature type) generally record a high degree of conflict between health authority management and trade unions. The majority of these articles were produced in the period 1984-85, when disputes over compulsory competitive tendering were at their zenith (Goodwin, 1994). Specific topics discussed include the dispute over the tendering of domestic cleaning at Barking Hospital in Redbridge, Essex (Ball, 1984; Caudrey, 1984; Hyde 1984a; Sherman 1984a), and the well-researched trade union resistance to contracting out policies at Hammersmith hospital (Huws and DeGroot, 1985; Sherman, 1984b) and also at Addenbroke's hospital in Cambridge (Hyde, 1984b). The articles and reports documenting disputes such as these provide valuable examples of differing attitudes to privatisation on the part of both health service managers and trade unions.

The studies on the impact of competitive tendering on management, the third sub-category, deal mainly with patterns of health authorities management. For example, Sheaff (1988) suggests that one of the most significant consequences of competitive tendering appears to have been a tightening of managerial control over employment, together with a shift towards greater local bargaining. Bach (1990) states that health authorities management can be attracted by the increased flexibility that contracting out can provide. However, he points out that the term 'flexibility' is also used as a euphemism for desired changes in work organisation, and implicitly to indicate a reduction in trade-union influence over working practices.

The final subset of this literature type, output studies on contracting out in the NHS, bears little resemblance to that on local government services. The earliest statistical evidence that can be used to examine the output of competitive tendering in the NHS is the work of NHS

Unlimited (1984). Compiled by the Labour MP Frank Dobson, this work is a collection of quotations revealing widespread disquiet among health authority managers concerning the viability of compulsory competitive tendering. Further evidence suggesting a geography to contracting out appears in the early study of Mohan (1986), which reveals that the spread of competitive tendering (as opposed to actual privatisation via contracting out) has been very uneven across England. Goodwin (1994) also examines spatial variations through examining the incidence of contracting out across England and Wales from 1985 to 1991. Geographers have also looked at the issue of contracting out in relation to the restructuring of health services in specific localities. Pinch and Witt (1988) discuss the subcontracting of services in the context of the restructuring of health services in Southhampton, and Townsend (1987) in the context of the rationalisation of the labour force in Middlesbrough.

Research of Type VII discusses the pros and cons of contracting out and competitive tendering and is also concerned with other countries. In the academic literature, public choice theorists have offered a theoretical foundation for a favourable view of public service contracting out. Despite several divergences in subject, methods and emphasis, these scholars (Niskanen, 1971; Ostrom and Ostrom, 1977; Savas, 1977) have concentrated primarily on analysing specific services and the structure by which they are supplied, with less concern for the voting and demand mechanism. Using a neoclassical economic framework, these scholars argue that the competitive marketplace produces goods and services efficiently, whereas monopolies, whether public or private, tend towards both inefficiency and unresponsiveness.

However, as might be expected, counter-arguments have also been put forward. The arguments against the contracting out of public services have been identified by various studies. Some argue that purchasing services from one or a few private contractors on a continuing basis can produce cosy relationships that may cause corruption, erode competition and quality control, and lead to higher costs and lower-quality services (DeHoog, 1984b; Donahue, 1989). Others say that private sector autonomy, which is essential for creativity and flexibility, may suffer (DeHoog, 1984b; Kramer and Grossman, 1987; Sharkansky, 1980). Excessive government control may create private sector dependence on government contracts, which may reduce the benefits to be gained from a self-supporting organisation (NAPA, 1989).

A further argument is that accountability is not easy to maintain (DeHoog, 1984b; Johnson and Douglas, 1991). Lessened sensitivity to citizens' needs and desire to increase profits may result in poorer service. Governmental control of quality of service is more difficult, and more monitoring will be needed.

Johnson and Douglas (1991) argue that distribution of the functions of provision and production of public services between government and the contractor is prone to be mismanaged. DeHoog (1984b; 1985) says that the growing reliance on the use of private organisations makes the creation and implementation of coherent public policy an even more formidable task for government agencies.

That contracting out may not work equally well in all service areas, owing to the difficulties of measuring the outputs and inputs of certain services, is another counter-argument (DeHoog, 1984b; 1985). Opposition by unions and city workers may be a forceful impediment, says Donahue (1989). Finally, competition is not easy to achieve (Donahue, 1989).

Research of Type VIII focuses on countries other than the UK, mainly the USA, to identify the conditions under which contracting out is to be implemented successfully.

DeHoog was one of the earliest researchers, and is probably the most prolific writer, on the subject of how contracting out should be implemented (the process and procedures involved). In her 1984 studies, she offered three alternatives to the public choice perspective drawn from the disciplines of economics, political science and organisation theory. She then elaborated on three major conditions which were assumed by contracting out proponents and which are critical in any contracting arrangements (1984a; 1984b). First, competition in the contracting system, both in the contracting environment and in the government's contracting procedures, is essential for successful contracting out. Second, it is assumed that contracting officials will be rational decision makers who adhere to the goal of maximising cost savings during the contracting processes. Third, an effective watchdog and oversight function must be exercised by government. Contract officials need to monitor a contractor's work continuously to ensure that it conforms to the requirements of the contract.

Many other scholars and institutes (Cooper, 1980; Ferris, 1986; Hunt, 1984; ICMA, 1989; Kettl, 1988; NAPA, 1989) have also suggested desirable ways in which to ensure expected outcomes from contracting out.

Finally, literature of Type IX analyses the practices of contracting out and is concerned with other countries. Like Types III and VI, this literature can also be subdivided into four categories.

The first category is concerned with the economics of contracting out. There are numerous research works (such as Chi et al, 1989; DeHoog, 1984a; Ferris and Graddy, 1994; Hilke, 1992; Korosec, 1994; NAPA, 1989; Rehfuss, 1989; Savas, 1982, 1987, 1992; Sullivan, 1987; Van Dyke, 1990) which analyse empirically the economics of contracting out worldwide. Most research indicates that contracting out public services can save money. However, some research (such as Ferris and Graddy, 1994) argues that the contracting out of public service provision is not always as efficient as might be expected, emphasising the high transaction costs involved. Local government decision makers should also consider the implications of the production costs involved.

Most of the literature in the second sub-category, industrial relations in other countries, has focused on the potential for conflict between municipal management and organised labour based on the relative strength of unions and their ability to influence policy (Korosec, 1994, p 8). This is probably because in all countries except the UK, the competitive tendering policy is based on the voluntary system, not a compulsory system.

Much of the literature (for example, Chandler and Feuille, 1991; Ferris, 1986; Hirsch, 1995; Korosec, 1994; Sharp, 1990) cites evidence which illustrates that trade unions may have an effect on the decision to contract. Sharp, for example, has noted that:

> **... in communities with strong public sector labour unions, there is likely to be strong resistance if city government attempts to privatise services, because the labour practices of private sector providers may seem like reversals of the gains that organised labour has toiled for over the years. (1990, pp 116-18)**

In his 1995 research, Hirsch also attempts to discover if unionisation affects the decision to contract out.

Chandler and Feuille (1991) draw on a 1989 survey of 1,256 cities nation-wide, to widen the focus on labour-management relations and the role of public unions in municipal decisions to contract out. They select the sanitation service as the unit of analysis for their investigation because of the relatively high levels of unionisation involved and the widespread use of public and private providers to deliver this service. They examine labour-management practices and decisions to contract out from 1973 to 1988.

The third sub-category concerns the impact of contracting out on local government management in countries other than the UK and includes studies by Johnson and Douglas, 1991; Kolderie, 1986; Van Dyke, 1990. Van Dyke (1990), for example, is interested in the changes in "organisational structure, management practices, personnel administration, inter-organisational culture, and technical know-how" as a result of contracting out. Kolderie also argues that a major problem a government encounters in contracting out is to determine who decides what services are to be provided.

The fourth sub-category is concerned with output studies of competitive tendering. Scholars have observed that only since the late 1980s has empirical research reached beyond cost studies comparing public and private service delivery to examine the determinants of contracting decisions (Chandler and Feuille, 1991; Hirsch, 1995). This rather limited research has been conducted principally by economists, although some work has been conducted by political scientists and labour relations experts. On the whole, this research has utilised cross-sectional survey data to test a variety of hypotheses relating to decisions to contract out. It has focused largely on exploring local government variation in contracting decisions.

Interestingly, the development of this research has followed a discernible pattern. The earlier works typically included numerous hypotheses and variables derived from public choice theory and supportive cost studies (Ferris, 1986; Ferris and Graddy, 1986; McGuire et al, 1987; Miller, 1988; Morgan et al, 1988). Economic incentives and cost-related issues reflect the emphasis of this approach. Although these earlier studies also examine politics in relation to contracting decisions, the emphasis seems to be upon economic considerations rather than political ones in explaining contracting decisions. However, recent work in the USA has given greater attention to the political factors. Political frameworks have been used in at least two studies (Hirsch, 1995; Korosec, 1994).

Although a substantial literature now exists on the analysis of privatisation in other countries, political scientists do not seem to be well represented and their research studies have largely been confined to the areas of the economic savings incurred from contracting out, successful conditions for it to occur and its impact on management. However, with few exceptions little attempt has been made to explain, within a theoretical framework, the main determinants of the output of CCT policy and the dynamics of the CCT implementation process relating to its output.

Conclusions drawn from the literature review

This review does not purport to provide a comprehensive list of all the research conducted up until now, nor to evaluate all studies in detail. The taxonomy of the literature on competitive tendering and contracting out is undoubtedly incomplete. Its categories inevitably partially overlap, and the specific examples presented under each heading can only hint at the broad array of studies that each category subsumes. Nevertheless, the taxonomy may prove useful in so far as the categories demonstrate the characteristics of research on competitive tendering and contracting out carried out in the fields of politics, public administration, economics, and so on. The main purpose of the categorisation of the literature on competitive tendering is to make it clear that output studies of competitive tendering have been relatively lacking, and not based on solidly established theoretical frameworks.

Analysis of the literature reveals a number of characteristics. Much of the research on competitive tendering in local government services in the UK was guided by public choice theory which argued the superior cost efficiency of private over public service delivery. Although politics was not entirely neglected in these studies, it was generally a consideration secondary to economic analysis.

Output studies of competitive tendering in local government services in the UK have been relatively limited. The reason for this is that in the UK most of the research on competitive tendering has focused on theoretical and ideological discussion of the pros and cons, and on identifying the economic savings made by competitive tendering and examining the conditions under which it is to succeed. These studies also lack a conceptual framework based on a systematic theory undergirding their arguments.

The literature review also reveals that scholars rarely present empirical evidence regarding the results of competitive tendering, or identify a systematic link between the actual outputs and the dynamics of the policy implementation process.

Much of this literature on the output of competitive tendering is in the form of case studies only. Although rich in detail, these studies often do not allow generalisations to be made which would offer solutions to practitioners facing problems in implementing the competitive tendering system. For this reason, this research study will use quantitative analysis and examine the particular situations in selected local authorities to then make such generalisations.

In other countries, especially the USA, the policy output associated with competitive tendering and contracting out has been largely unexplored in the literature up until recently, due to an emphasis on an economic approach derived from public choice theory. Some of the research employing the political approach also has limitations, in that it deals primarily with the relationship between management and labour unions as a determinant of the output of competitive tendering.

The need for CCT output studies

Competitive tendering policy output is worthy of far more attention and consideration in the UK than it has received in the literature to date. As was stated earlier, it is mainly economists who have taken an interest in the financial savings incurred by competitive tendering since its introduction, especially as an explanation for its growth. Although political scientists have also addressed this question, the approach they have adopted is mostly political and partisan, implying that few, if any, analytical studies with special reference to the output of competitive tendering have been conducted. As a result, little attempt has been made to identify the main factors influencing the output of CCT policy, and the dynamics behind the CCT policy process in relation to its output in the UK.

A number of output studies have been conducted by geographers from the geographical perspective, rather than the policy science point of view. These two viewpoints differ significantly in that the former focuses mainly on the spatial variations in the policy output of competitive tendering process while the latter is primarily concerned with identifying the dynamics of policy process, including the policy implementation process and policy output. The policy science point of view aims to examine empirically the actual determinants of the policy output and to investigate how these are related to the dynamics of the competitive tendering process and how they influence the policy output. This study adopts the policy science point of view for three key reasons.

Firstly, because this approach can supply knowledge about the inner workings of the local authorities and about why certain authorities have certain levels of DSO output. The reality of CCT is that there is rarely consensus in local authorities as to how the process should proceed because of the many interested parties that are involved. A grasp of the power relations within the authorities is important to gain an understanding of their apparent attitude to CCT.

Secondly, through understanding the exact way in which the environmental or resources attributes of local authorities affect policy implementation and policy output, it is possible to identify the necessary conditions under which central-government-initiated policy or local government policy may be implemented successfully.

Thirdly, academic explanations fail to capture how the CCT process works at the local level and the way in which the outputs of the contested process are generated. This aspect has also been largely ignored by the researchers. The output study of CCT presented here can provide useful information as to what factors have affected public policy output and in what way. Such a question is far from being of merely academic interest, but is rather one of critical importance to communities, service user groups, local councillors, officers, and private contractors and workers, who have to confront the effects of spatially fragmented privatisation initiatives on levels of service provision and employment conditions.

The limitations of the studies of CCT output indicate the need to identify generalisations that can be made about the output of competitive tendering in the UK and to examine how this changes from local authority to local authority. A more sophisticated explanation of the trends is required to answer the main questions that arise from an appreciation of the literature: What are the main factors affecting the CCT output at the district level? In what ways do these main factors affect it when local authorities are faced with similar policy pressures 'from above'?

To provide an insight into the dynamics of the process this policy output study needs to explore the ways in which the main factors in the process of competitive tendering interact. This will require the powers and roles of the key participants to be considered when examining tendering outputs. Accordingly, the next chapter explains the analytical framework and methodologies used in the study to identify objectively the main factors involved in the DSO output.

Note

[1] The Department of the Environment became the Department of the Environment, Transport and the Regions when the Labour government took office in 1997.

THREE

Analytical framework and research methodology: path analysis

Introduction

The main purpose of this study, as was indicated earlier, is to investigate what factors affect CCT output[1] and in what ways. The term 'CCT output' might sound somewhat strange to a UK reader; 'output of privatisation' or 'effects of privatisation' are the more commonly used terms. All three terms may be used interchangeably. The term 'CCT output' is used in this study to highlight the fact that policy output has been generated by the CCT policy itself.

The indicator DSO output is used to measure the dependent variable, CCT output. DSO output means the distribution of tenders between the DSO and private contractors: that is, the proportion of tenders won by the DSO during the CCT process. It indicates the percentage of the total value of work that is undertaken by the DSO following the competitive tendering process. The term 'DSO output' will be used to refer to the percentage of the total value of work undertaken by the DSO since this term more accurately and concisely describes the nature of the variable.

The questions that this study aims to answer have already been stated: What determinants influence the output of CCT policy? In what ways do these factors affect CCT policy output?

This chapter deals with the analytical framework and methodology associated with the first purpose of this research, which is to identify the main factors affecting the DSO output in the CCT policy process. The chapter aims to provide an analytical framework for empirical analysis, based on the literature review of policy output studies. The model used is itself a literature-based framework, specifically developed for this research but potentially useful in the field as a whole. It puts forward the research questions and hypotheses investigated in the study and addresses the research methodology used in the analysis. The research is to a certain extent exploratory and theory-building in nature, and seeks to contribute to the theoretical literature on the subject.

The analytical framework synthesises findings from the literature on the policy process of local government and its relationships with policy output, and deals with indicators for measuring variable and data-related limitations. The next section describes the procedure for the analysis.

Analytical framework and hypotheses

Background

In this study, the analysis identifying the main factors of DSO output in the CCT policy process is primarily based on the system model. This implies that public policy is best understood by considering the operation of a political system in its environment and by examining how such a system maintains itself and changes over time (Ham and Hill, 1993, p 39; Hansen, 1981, pp 28-32).

Taking this perspective, this study highlights the relationships between public policy output and the social, economic and political variables of local government. Fortunately, other political scientists (Boaden, 1971; Easton, 1965; Ham and Hill, 1993; Newton and Sharpe, 1977) have worked on this issue of uniting public policy with its environments. In Ham and Hill's terminology (1993, pp 9-10), policy output studies are studies of policy outputs which seek to explain why levels of expenditure or service provision vary between areas and take policies as dependent variables in an attempt to understand them in terms of social, economic, technological and other factors. The model used in this study is an adapted version of the 'political system' described by Easton (1965).

Since 1963, when Dawson and Robinson (1963, pp 265-89) published their study on the determinants of welfare policies in the United States, students of public policy have been preoccupied with the question of the relative importance of socioeconomic and political variables as determinants of public policy. Dawson and Robinson's conclusion that socioeconomic factors are the major determinants of public policy has been substantiated by several later studies of other areas of public activity in different institutional and political settings. Although some studies (Chakravorty, 1996; Ferris, 1986; Hirsch, 1982; McGinnis, 1994), in particular American ones, have demonstrated that socioeconomic factors have a significant effect on public policy decisions, the general conclusion to be drawn from this research, particularly that carried out in Britain and some European countries, is that the political variable, party political control, is a more powerful determinant than are socioeconomic variables (Barnett et al, 1990; Headey, 1978; Hill and Bramley, 1990; Newton, 1976; Page et al, 1990).

These conflicting arguments have incited a considerable amount of research, most of it aiming at restoring the importance of political factors as policy determinants. In discussing the question of the relative importance of 'politics' and 'economics' as policy determinants, Dye points out:

> **It is a useful question, despite its oversimplification, if it inspires serious modelbuilding, thoughtful specification of policy-relevant variables and their relationships to each other, careful testing of hypotheses, and then reformation of the original models on the basis of the results achieved. (1976, p 653)**

Although some efforts have been made to refine the models of analysis, most studies so far have been based on the general theoretical approach, where a simplified version of Easton's general system model has provided the framework within which the variables have been structured (Newton, 1981, p 23).

Discussions of the findings have focused mainly on the range, reliability and validity of the variables – both dependent and independent – used in these studies (Fry and Winters, 1970). Far less attention has been paid to the inter-relationships between variables and their relative importance in public policy output. Since the late 1970s, serious attempts have been made to revise and refine the models of analysis. One such attempt (Lewis-Beck, 1977) has used path analytical techniques based on causal models of the relationships between environmental variables underlying government public policy. Lewis-Beck has suggested that research efforts to date have failed to assess accurately the relative importance of environmental variables for public policy, largely because they have relied on statistical techniques that are inadequate for the task (Lewis-Beck,

1977, pp 559-60). Lewis–Beck says that to make accurate assessments of the relative importance of socioeconomic and political variables, and their relationships, it is necessary to specify the underlying causal structure and estimate its parameters. He suggests the use of "effect coefficients" which combine the direct and indirect effects of causal variables. To discuss the causal model in more detail it may be useful to consider the conventional formulation of the Eastonian approach to policy analysis. Despite slight differences as to its precise formulation, the underlying model developed in most studies of public policy process may be outlined as in Figure 3.1.

According to this model, both socioeconomic and political factors exert a direct impact on public policy (linkages c and b). In addition, socioeconomic variables influence public policy indirectly via the political variable (linkages a and b) (Hansen, 1981, p 28).

Although the major elements of this model – the three sets of variables – may be regarded as a crude approximation to Easton's model, the way in which the elements are related differs in at least one important respect from Easton's formulation: only relations (a) and (b) seem to be in accordance with the model: the direct relationship between socioeconomic variables and public policy is not a part of it. It is also difficult to conceive how such environmental characteristics may produce policy output directly. In traditional Easton system models, inputs arise out of the environment, taking the form of demands and supports (Ham and Hill, 1993, p 13), are aggregated in some fashion, and impact on the political system (Hansen, 1981, p 28). Figure 3.2 sums up Easton's

Figure 3.1: Conventional system model

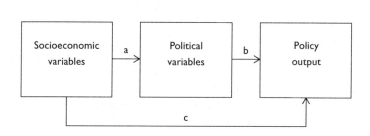

Source: Hansen (1981, p 29)

Figure 3.2: Simplified Easton model (adapted from Easton's system model)

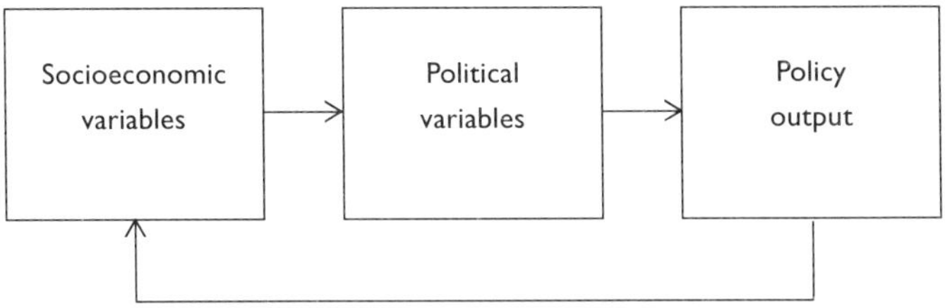

Source: Ham and Hill (1993, p 13)

formulation and reflects his basic idea that the political system is a mechanism for transforming demands into "authoritative allocation" (Ham and Hill, 1993, p 14). According to Easton's model, public policies are constructed by political bodies, and a social problem has at least to be perceived by the decision makers in order for them to effect the decision.

From this point of view, it is not acceptable that socioeconomic variables directly affect public policy. However, unlike in Easton's theory, there has been a tendency to interpret these relationships as a causal chain; both socioeconomic factors cause political factors, which in turn give rise to public policy, but they also influence public policy directly (Aiken et al, 1987; Ferris, 1986; Hansen, 1981, pp 28-9; Page et al, 1990; Schoford, 1978).

In Figure 3.1 the linkage (c) implies that changes in the socioeconomic environment automatically lead to changes in public policy. In the real world some environmental variables might affect policy output directly or indirectly. Policy areas where decisions are made according to a set of fixed standards or decision-making criteria based on certain environmental characteristics do exist. In particular where local governments are strictly regulated by central government, it might be expected that there is little leeway for the exercise of discretion on the part of the decision makers. This means that some environmental variables can influence public policy directly without going via a political variable (Hansen, 1981, pp 29-30; Lineberry and Sharkansky, 1978, pp 11-13).

It seems more reasonable to treat the relationships between political and environmental characteristics as inter-related factors on which public authorities may act than to consider the political variable only as a mechanism which other environmental variables should pass through to affect the policy output. The decision process is affected by factors surrounding the policy process and these include political and other environmental variables. This model interprets these relationships of variables as a causal chain, and assumes that there are direct and indirect causal links between environmental variables and policy output.

Hypothetical causal relationships

There is a substantial body of work on the behavioural determinants of local government policy output, drawn from a variety of intellectual disciplines, including economics, political science and organisational theory (for example, Barnett et al, 1990; Danziger, 1976; Ferris, 1986; Sharpe and Newton, 1984; Tiebout, 1956). Such research has mainly (but not entirely) focused on expenditure or revenue. Also, it has rarely been concerned specifically with CCT or privatisation policy, in spite of the fact that since the early 1980s CCT or privatisation policy has played a major role in British local government service provision. Much of the literature concerning local authorities in the UK deals with overall expenditure levels, fiscal decisions or budgetary decision making.

In the meantime, as was discussed in Chapter Two, most of the literature on CCT has taken a descriptive, institutional and political approach. This has concentrated on changes in government policy, the response of local authorities and public unions to CCT and the savings from competition. Much less attention has been paid to the determinants of CCT policy output.

It also seems that there is no generally agreed method of assessing the impact of factors affecting policy output (Page et al, 1990, p 44). This study addresses an array of environmental and contextual factors, including economic, political, demographic, strategic and organisational factors and DSO proportion (DSO output), primarily employing the system theory. In the absence of a comprehensive theory, it is necessary to create hypothetical causal relationships for analysis according to the purpose of the research.

Figure 3.3 shows a hypothetical framework for the analysis of DSO output. The elements shown have mostly been dealt with in the field of policy analysis and organisational analysis. However, they are supplemented and adjusted in line with the purpose of the research, and the inter-relationships between variables posited are to a certain extent

Figure 3.3: Hypothetical causal relationships for the analysis of DSO output

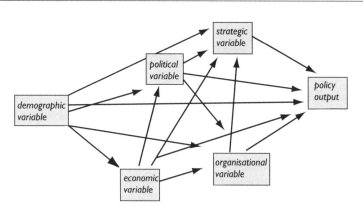

intuitive and exploratory. The following section discusses the anticipated role of these variables on DSO output, touching upon the theoretical expectations and empirical findings.

Any comprehensive analysis of DSO is incomplete by definition if the policy situation is not included with the other contextual variables. For this reason, this analytical framework also deals with the strategic variables associated with the policy situation, which other studies in the literature on policy output studies have not considered. The analytical framework has the following characteristics.

• The framework applies conventional output analysis techniques, and modifies them for the DSO output analysis. The most important part of this framework lies in its attempt to widen the range of possible explanatory factors and approaches well beyond the bounds of conventional studies. The aim is to develop causal and comprehensive environmental factors, and to examine their effects on DSO output.

• This approach explains the local variation in DSO output as the consequences of the interaction of the major forces in the local authority environment rather than as the product of explicit local choices (Danziger, 1978, p 81). The framework regards environmental variables as crucial determinants external to the boundaries of its policy system.

- The approach has a strong empirical orientation. It emphasises the effects of environmental variables on DSO output and attempts to identify the causal relationships of environmental variables behind CCT policy.

- The nature of the relationships between variables in the framework is to a certain extent intuitive and hypothetical.

Despite these characteristics, this framework is open to some criticisms. Basing the analytical framework on the causal relationships can be attacked on methodological grounds, such as the inability of correlation methods to discriminate between causal models, and the problems for regression models posed by multicollinearity (Danziger, 1978, pp 82-3). Secondly, it has been alleged that study which comes about from analysing causal relationships often produces findings that are disappointing in terms both of the correlation found and the percentage of variance explained (Sharpe and Newton, 1984). Third, and most seriously, this approach might be attacked for its weak or non-existent theoretical base. It is often claimed that there is no articulated theory which links the policy outputs to the environmental inputs (Sharpe and Newton, 1984).

Many of these criticisms can be rebutted. While some early studies were perhaps methodologically naïve, most recent work is usually sensitive to such issues and aware of the difficulties in moving from statistical relationships to implications of causality. The framework for this study was made after consideration of these contentious issues.

Variables and hypotheses

This section deals primarily with the variables and hypotheses directly associated with the final dependent variable, DSO output. The other working hypotheses concerned with the mediating variables are briefly discussed in the section on page 75, entitled 'The model'.

Dependent variable

The dependent variable in this analysis is the output of CCT policy, or DSO output, which is the percentage of the total value of work that is undertaken by the DSO for 1991 and 1994. Ranging between 0 (perfect external production of service) and 100 (perfect inhouse production), DSO output is a result of competitive bidding and contractual agreements.

Independent variables

The decision to choose one alternative over another is not always easy. Public sector decision-making is complicated by the fact that, unlike private entities (which seek self-serving alternatives), public organisations are supposed to choose alternatives taking environmental (independent or explanatory) factors into account (Newton, 1981). Each public sector decision is based on a range of differing circumstances and actors. Organising the various main attributes underlying the DSO output into an integrated model provides a starting point for understanding why and how these outputs are achieved as they are. By definition, this model is a simple representation of the real world of CCT policy (Korosec, 1994, pp 92-3).

The environment is made up of individuals, groups and organisations with values and interests, operating alone or together over time (Hill, 1993a, p 39). The independent variables in a study of public policy ought to be selected on the basis of a thorough study of a particular public policy (whether it is a regulatory, distributive, or redistributive policy) and actual decision-making behaviour in the individual local authorities. However, for this study time and resources have rendered such a procedure unfeasible. Also, availability of data has restricted the number of variables (for example, the degree of unionisation) which can be used. Instead, a set of independent variables believed to be relevant to CCT policy analysis has been selected. For this reason the model could reflect the author's academic concerns rather than the general interests of local decision makers.

Figure 3.3 represents a graphical illustration of how the theories contained in this chapter are integrated to form the model used in this research. It breaks the independent variables down into five general categories (political, economic, organisational, strategic and demographic) and suggests that under certain circumstances, the DSO output will be higher than under other circumstances. Each of these issues will be discussed in more detail in the following sections.

Political variable

Studies of local policy variation have paid little attention to general political theories of policy making. The specific question of the theoretical role of political parties in local policy decisions has been similarly neglected (Boyne, 1996a, p 233).

The political factors tested in the policy output studies were derived from an earlier phase in the literature of American State Government, notably the work of Key (1956), Lockard (1963) and others. In this literature it is claimed that the key factors affecting the type of policies pursued were characteristic of the state political system. It was assumed that party colour can be an important determinant of local policy output. It is implied, among other things, that what local governments do is a direct reflection of their party ideology or party colour.

However, some scholars (Boyne, 1996a; Bulpitt, 1967; Dearlove, 1973; Fried, 1975; Green, 1959; Jackson, 1965; Oliver and Stanyer, 1969) have argued that party colour has little or no effect on policy output. Fried's summary of the findings of almost four dozen such studies, covering 12 countries, is one such example:

> **Political variables have relatively less direct and independent impact than socio-economic variables. In many, probably most cases, some socio-economic variable has been found more useful in explaining the variance in outputs than any political variable. Somehow, the nature of the socio-economic environment seems more important than the nature of community politics in shaping community policies. (1975, p 71)**

Boyne (1996a, p 232) also points out that 50 studies which tested the impact of political parties on local policy variation in the UK all suggest that political variables are insignificant in a majority of cases.

Despite these arguments, no one would wish to deny that it is highly likely that political factors are crucial in affecting policy output. There is substantial evidence of a significant link between political factors and the overall scale of council activity (Barnett et al, 1990; Cameron, 1978; Foster et al, 1980; Headey, 1978; Hewitt, 1977; Kleinman et al, 1990; Page et al, 1990; Peters, 1974). Foster et al, for example, conclude that, on balance, there is a political effect in UK local politics, a finding subsequently reinforced by the work of Sharpe and Newton (1984). Page et al also point out that the direct effects of party on local policies have increased quite dramatically since 1979.

Drawing on existing research (Barnett et al, 1990; Hansen, 1981; Kleinmann et al, 1990; Sharpe, 1981) reveals three main political variables to consider:[2] degree of unionisation, the interest groups involved, and the composition of the political party.

The degree of unionisation of local government officials and the attitudes of interest groups towards a particular policy are important (Korosec, 1994, p 7). These variables might be crucial determinants of policy output at the local level. However, data regarding these variables is difficult to obtain. The relationship between political party composition and the activity of trade unions in a local authority is strong (Cross and Mallen, 1987, p 103; Stoker, 1991, p 43) so by including the political party composition as an independent variable, the analysis will also broadly reflect the effect of the activity of trade unions in the policy process. Including both variables in the same analysis usually causes a problem of multicollinearity because of the high correlation between the two.

It is difficult to quantify the role of interest groups engaged in the policy process. Hence this study deals only with political party composition as a political variable. Political party composition has been used as a crucial factor in studies of local politics (Boyne, 1996a; Page et al, 1990). This research will attempt to discover if the political affiliation of elected local councillors is related to local variation in DSO output.

Many tests of political party effects are based on the assumption that different ideologies will be reflected in different scales of government policy, as measured, for example, by spending, staffing and taxation. For example, it is expected that privatisation issues will reveal that there is more reliance on CCT by Conservative administrations than by Labour administrations, due to the fact that, ideologically, the Conservatives prefer less government spending through the policy of privatisation, organisational efficiency, and so on.

Even if party distinctions are used in their purest form, you would still expect to see a difference in DSO preferences for Labour and Conservative administrations. It is accepted that most Conservative-controlled local authorities might be generally averse to directly employed labour, DSO, because CCT has been introduced and implemented by Conservative governments since 1979 when Margaret Thatcher came to power. In general, competition was viewed by the Conservative government as essential to organisational efficiency and effectiveness (Boyne, 1996b, p 704).

By contrast, Labour councils are essentially supportive of directly employed labour. Hence, the Labour Party has put forward a number of proposals to replace the legislation on CCT (Carnaghan and Bracewell-Milnes, 1993, p 36). It might be assumed that Labour politicians are reluctant to allow any changes if these entail redundancies or loss of earnings or benefits for council workers (Carnaghan and Bracewell-Milnes, 1993, p 33).

Most studies merely hint at this assumption, but others are more explicit (Ashford et al, 1976; Boaden, 1971). For example, Boaden states that the traditions of gas and water socialism together with Conservative concern for the ratepayer suggest the major divisions between the parties (Boaden, 1971, p 31). Similarly, Ashford et al note that "Labour and Conservative councillors have different attitudes towards the extraction of private wealth in order to provide public services and benefits" (Ashford et al, 1976, p 5). It is reasonable to expect that this choice will also affect CCT. Party ideology is generally thought to influence not only the overall scale of local authority activity, but also the scale of each service.

Similarly, in a study of privatisation of local government services in the USA, Hirsch (1995, p 237) puts forward the argument that purely on the basis of ideology privatisation might seem to be favoured more by Republicans than by Democrats, and hypothesises that Conservatives generally view privatisation in a more favourable light than do Liberals.

In the light of this argument, it can be assumed that different ideologies will be reflected directly in different scales and patterns of local governmental activity. International City Management Association (ICMA) studies published in 1984 and 1989 in the USA noted that many key issues came into play when a government was deciding whether to privatise certain service delivery functions. Among the issues discussed were the factors of political forces, availability of providers, the overall size of the government, legal constraints, service delivery area, and the ability to promote competition. Of these, political support was one of the most crucial variables in influencing the success or failure of the privatisation policy (ICMA, 1984; 1989).

The ICMA studies suggested that in those instances where elected officials and officers successfully campaigned for and engendered support (both internally and externally) for the privatisation policy, the policy was implemented smoothly. The idea that elected officials need to 'engender' support suggests that contracting out is sometimes not perceived to be the best option for a particular local government.

In discussing the political variables, it is necessary to consider the following issues: left versus right, seats and control, and time-lags. Many studies of local policy variation test only for the effect of the Labour Party, but some studies acknowledge that this is a narrow operationalisation of the concept of party politics and many other party variables have therefore been tested (Boyne, 1996a). For example, Ashford et al (1976) and Boyne (1987) have run separate statistical analyses of Labour seats and Conservative seats to test the relative policy effects of these parties. The reason for including Labour and Conservative seats in the same analysis is that the local authority activity will be examined more analytically by combining measures than by examining Labour or Conservative seats alone (Sharpe, 1981, pp 1-12).

All the measures of party strength in the empirical studies are based either on the percentage of council seats held by a party, or on a dichotomous variable which indicates whether a party is in overall control of a council. The choice between these measures reflects the author's view regarding the policy implications of the size of the ruling party's majority (Boyne, 1996a, p 234). There are conflicting views on this issue in the empirical studies. Boyne argues for seats as a measure of party strength: the higher the percentage of party members on the council, the greater will be the likelihood that party affiliation will be an important factor. In this study the operationalisation of the political variable is based on the percentage of council seats occupied by a party. However, considering that in the UK a party needs more than 50% membership of an authority to be sure of influencing policy, the concept of overall control will also be taken into consideration in the discussion of the party effects on policy output.

A number of studies recognise that their policy variables may be influenced by historical as well as contemporary forces. Some studies attempt to deal with this problem by measuring party strength over a longer time period. For example, Oliver and Stanyer (1969) measure seats over a 10-year period because of the influence of previous investment decisions on expenditure in the year in question. Similarly, Ashford et al (1976) measure seats over 19 years in an attempt to allow for the cumulative effect of political influence. Sharpe and Newton (1984) also measure party control over a period between three years and 17 years in order to relate policy output to party effect. In this study, these longitudinal measures of party effect are also considered because the effects of the party which previously held a majority may live on for some time, thus obscuring the party effect at any given point in time.

In view of the theoretical arguments above, it can be hypothesised that local variation in DSO output is conditioned by the prevailing political attitude of the local authority councillors to CCT. The following *political hypothesis* is suggested for this study:

- the local authorities with a higher proportion of Labour councillors will have a higher level of DSO output, while the local authorities with a higher proportion of Conservative councillors will have a lower level of DSO output.

Organisational variable

Within a government, there are many attributes of the organisation itself which may explain how and why decisions are taken as they are. One of the more basic issues which may be expected to contribute to the decision-making process is past experience (Korosec, 1994, p 102). This variable will differ due to the range of past experiences that different organisations may observe or encounter.

Organisational past experience is a significant issue in relation to contracting out (Korosec, 1994). Korosec (1994, pp 103–6) argues that whether or not an organisation has had experience violating the laws or regulations on contracting out in the past can influence any subsequent contracting out. Bouttes and Hamamdjian (1997, pp 81–2) also indicate that incentive schemes, that is, rewards and sanctions, are an important part of the contractual arrangements. In other words, if a local authority has had experience of having violated the laws on contracting out in the past and been sanctioned against its practices, the authority may be more inclined to change its previous attitude towards contracting out and to comply with the laws on it in the following contract, and perhaps even to think about accepting it in other applications. This is because as local governments learn more about the contracting system they create their own perceptions of and attitudes towards it and learn how to deal with the system and use it to their advantage.

As Korosec argues (1994, pp 92–4), laws and regulations have a direct effect on the decision-making process, because they attach legal restrictions or mandates to what citizens can obtain from government. This is especially true in the realm of contracting out and competitive tendering. Laws are created to set guidelines for how local authorities must or must not act during the process of contracting out and competitive tendering. A code of sanctions is included to provide backing for the laws.

It is clear from Plunkett and Attner's (1994, pp 439–40) discussion of leadership and its power bases that there are two types of motivation: positive versus negative. A positive style includes status, praise, financial rewards, recognition, responsibility and opportunities for advancement.

By contrast, a negative style incorporates coercion in the form of sanctions/fines, suspensions, termination, and the like. Negative leadership styles are based on the assumption that the subordinate (in this case the local authority) will either willingly or reluctantly comply with the laws or regulations after it is sanctioned by the manager's disciplinary powers. It is expected that a local authority which has been sanctioned by central government in relation to anticompetitive practices would be more willing to comply with CCT, leading to a high degree of privatisation, or a low level of DSO output.

For example, under the 1988 Local Government Act, the Secretary of State has powers to issue notices to local authorities which fail to tender in an adequately competitive fashion. A notice issued under Section 13 of the 1988 Act is a request for an explanation of the apparent sanctions issued against local government. If the minister remains unsatisfied in the light of the explanation provided, a notice may be issued under Section 14 of the 1988 Act, ordering that the contract be retendered (Atkins, 1996).

In the light of the discussions above, it is expected[3] that the more experience a local authority has had with sanctions issued by central government, the more willing the local authority will be to accept CCT in the future, leading to a lower DSO proportion. This is mainly because the local authority's experience of having violated the laws on contracting out and having consequently been sanctioned means that the local authority should be in a worse situation politically or financially, leading to the assumption that in its subsequent competitive tendering of services the local authority is more likely to strive to comply with the policy.

In the UK, the 1988 Act specifically prohibits councils from introducing any such anticompetitive considerations in drawing up contracts, inviting tenders or making or terminating contracts (Carnaghan and Bracewell-Milnes, 1993, p 44). If a local authority has ever been sanctioned by central government in the past, it is likely to act at present or in the future in a way which complies with competition principles, in order to avoid burdensome sanctions were it to violate the competition rules again. This should lead us to expect a high level of privatisation.

This study hypothesises that the more experience a local authority has had of sanctions (against anticompetitive behaviour) since the introduction of CCT, the more likely it is to comply with CCT principles in the future. This leads to the assumption that the local authority which has been sanctioned is more likely to accept CCT principles and finally to make efforts to follow the rules of competition. The *organisational hypothesis* proposed is:

- the more experience a local authority has had of sanctions (against local government) issued by central government, the lower the DSO output of the local authority will be.

Economic variable

Fiscal dependency (or independency, or constraint) is not a new issue facing local authorities, either in developed or underdeveloped countries. However, in these times of fiscal restraint and changing relationships between central and local government, fiscal dependency can become an important determinant of contracting out (Ferris, 1986; Hepworth, 1990; Korosec, 1994).

The fiscal environment under which local governments operate has been worsening in recent years in many countries, including the UK and the USA, with a reduction in intergovernmental grants and central attempts to shift programmatic responsibilities to the local level. As a consequence of declining fiscal fortunes, local governments are increasingly trying to manage with limited resources (Ferris, 1986, p 293).

Korosec (1994), Ferris (1986) and Stubbs and Barnett (1992) are among researchers who have suggested that fiscal dependency (or independency) may encourage (or discourage) privatisation of local government services. One hypothesis related to this study is that the greater the fiscal independence of the local authority, the less privatisation there will be. This hypothesis is expected to be supported for the following reasons.

First, in cases where resources are sufficient (a situation of no fiscal pressure), local authorities may be less willing to consider alternative service delivery as a means of providing needed goods, or of providing more goods and services for less money. Although CCT policy is implemented compulsorily by central government, if a local authority has sufficient financial resources, it is less likely to be interested in external provision, the one purpose of which is to save public expenditure.

Second, fiscal dependency (or independency) is related to the relationships between central and local government. Within an organisational exchange framework, Pfeffer and Salancik (1978, p 43) observe that "for continuing to provide what the organisation needs, the external groups or organisations may demand certain actions from the organisation in return". The power–dependence theory may help to explain the financial dependency between central and local government.

Rhodes (1979; 1981; 1986) offers a power–dependence model of central–local relations explored through organisation theory, and has argued that both central and local authorities possess resources of several types which can be used against other actors. These include hierarchical, political, financial, legal, constitutional and information resources.

Pfeffer and Salancik (1978, p 43) also note that "the exchanges between central and local government may involve monetary or physical resources, information, or social legitimacy". Although critical resources may appear to take a variety of forms, resources must be: important to the dependent organisation or group; under the significant control of the supplying organisation or group, with no or few alternative suppliers available to the dependent organisation or group.

Wilson and Game (1994, pp 110-11) show that both central departments and local authorities have resources which each can use against the other and against other organisations as well. They maintain that central government has resources to:

- exert control over legislation and delegated powers;

- provide and control the largest proportion of local authorities' current expenditure through the Revenue Support Grant;

- control individual authorities' total expenditure and taxation levels by 'capping';

- control the largest proportion of local capital expenditure;

- set standards for and inspect some services;

- have a national electoral mandate.

By contrast, say Wilson and Game (1994, p 111), local authorities also:

- have resources to employ all personnel in local services, far outnumbering civil servants;

- have, via both councillors and officers, detailed local knowledge and expertise;

- can control the implementation of policy;

- can decide their own political priorities and most service standards, and how money should be distributed among services;

- have a local electoral mandate.

From the power-dependency theory point of view, local authorities with lower fiscal independence are more likely to accept central-government-initiated policy, particularly in relation to financial resources. They are less likely to act independently of central government, leading us to expect that they cannot act independently of it.

It is generally accepted that there is no single objective indicator to measure fiscal independence. Byrne (1994, pp 300-1) states that local authorities in the UK derive their income from three main sources:

- the rents and fees they charge for services (such as car parks, bus fares);

- grants or subsidies which they receive from central government (such as housing subsidies);

- local taxation (the rates or council tax).

Grants account for the highest proportion of local government income. Hence, the proportion of grants involved in local authority income can be a good indicator of fiscal independence.

In England, a formula has been introduced which will determine grants to local authorities (Hepworth, 1990; Hill, 1993c, p 143; Wilson and Game, 1994, pp 144-8). Local government expenditure in England is financed both by local taxation and by grants from central government, so that local authorities' activities are tightly constrained by statutory controls from the centre (Hill, 1993c, p 142). The way in which the grants system works is complex and closely linked with central control over local taxation. Nowadays, it leaves local authorities very little room for local manipulation of their resources.[4]

This implies that central government is not able to manipulate financial resources in such a way as to provide special advantages to local authorities that central government wishes to favour. One of the main purposes of the formula is to control the abuse of grants used by central government. In theory, central government does not have enough discretionary power to manipulate the distribution of grants to the local authorities it wishes to favour. Accordingly, the proportion, of grants contained in local authority income is not an appropriate indicator of fiscal independence.

In this study, the proportion of community charge (for 1991) and council tax[5] (for 1994) in local government income is used to measure fiscal independence. Although this might be debatable, in reality the proportion of local government income made up of community charge for 1991 and that made up of council tax for 1994 are indicators that allow assessment of the fiscal independence of local government.

In view of the arguments above, it is assumed that the local authorities which have low fiscal independence are more likely to conform to central government policy than those with high fiscal independence. Accordingly, the following *economic hypothesis* is proposed:

- the greater the fiscal independence of a local authority, the greater will be the DSO output of the local authority.

Strategic variables

Strategic variables are those variables which interested parties involved in the policy process can use strategically and to their advantage. In this research, contract size, contract period and geographical location fall into this category. These variables have been ignored in previous literature on the analysis of privatisation.

The role of the private sector in affecting the output of the tendering process has been greatly underestimated,[6] and yet this has had a fundamental impact on the local variation of DSO output. Most debates on tendering outputs have tended to examine such issues as local authority–trade union relationships, and economic savings, as was discussed in Chapter Two. Private companies are considered subservient in decision making and are regarded as passive beneficiaries of government policy rather than as active participants influencing local competitive tendering processes.

The private sector is fundamental to DSO output, for the simple reason that there has never been a law compelling firms to bid for contracts. This is important because private companies can choose which contracts to bid for, so can restrict their bids to contracts which offer the best returns.

Private companies may prefer some geographical regions to others. The reasons may include whether there is sufficient local labour to undertake the work, and whether some regions are aggressive towards private companies. Consequently there may be a lack of interest on the part of the major contractors in certain geographically remote areas such as the far north.

Carnaghan and Bracewell-Milnes (1993, p 143) point out that private contractors are reluctant to tender for the provision of government services if they find that the time and money spent in submitting tenders is rarely successful. Partly as a result of this, in some areas of the country competition is more theoretical than real.

Private sector providers can choose to concentrate only on local authorities which welcome them in the short term. Alternatively, they can choose sites for their strategic importance: for example, a company may have won contracts in other nearby locations (Walsh et al, 1997). As Key (1987) reasons, the output of the competitive tendering process supports the hypothesis that it is the preference of private sector contractors that has fashioned the extent of contracting out rather than the extent of union resistance to tendering policy.[7]

Bids for services can also be influenced by the contract's size and duration (Adam Smith Institute, 1990; Carnaghan and Bracewell-Milnes, 1993; Stubbs and Barnett, 1992; Walsh, 1991; Walsh and Davis, 1993; Walsh et al, 1997). These factors influence the decision to submit because they influence the expected return. More specifically, the transaction costs, in terms of time and expense in preparing the submission, must be compared. Contract size is related to the capability of the private sector. If the contract is too big for the private company to provide the service, small firms will find it impossible to bid for a large contract[8] (Walsh et al, 1997).

A study of the behaviour of Bay Area Rapid Transit (BART) contractors in the USA showed that when BART reduced the size of each bid package considerably, many more bids were submitted per solicitation than otherwise would have been (Gaver and Zimmerman, 1977). Apparently, more small firms are available to bid on these small contracts.

The same is true of contract period. If this period is too short, private sector contractors very often have to bear the costs of preparation for tender, leading to transaction costs on the part of private providers. This can also play a role in the CCT process as a strategic variable (Walsh et al, 1997).

It would be reasonable to expect that contracts of short duration are less attractive to large firms, although possibly they may be more attractive to small ones. Small contracts may interest large firms if they are considered to be an introduction to other contracts coming up at a later date. However, in general, the more valuable the contract the more attractive it is to firms (Walsh et al, 1997). To examine the strength of this argument this study explores the bidding strategies and preferences of the private sector. The size and duration of the contract are considered in order to allow a full understanding of the CCT process. In line with the above argument the following *strategic hypotheses* are proposed:

- DSO output will be affected by the private sector's geographical choice.

- DSO output will be affected by contract size.

- DSO output will be affected by contract period.

Demographic variables

Sharp (1990) and others (Adam Smith Institute, 1990; Boyne, 1995; Korosec, 1994; Le Grand and Bartlett, 1993) have suggested that demographic factors relating to local government may also play a role in contracting out. There are two demographic variables, population size and population density (degree of urbanisation). Korosec, for example, suggests that "a government in a major metropolitan area will have the greatest number of alternative contractors or prospective providers" (Korosec, 1994, p 11). Many more services are made available by private agents in metropolitan areas than in rural areas, since metropolitan areas offer more opportunities for contracting out, or more developed local economies to work with.

Contractors may not be willing to venture out into rural areas to bid on contracts, because they may believe that there is not much work to be found in those areas; this is known as service creaming (Le Grand and Bartlett, 1993, pp 31-2). The contracting system will be most likely to be used in urban areas where there is more opportunity to bid frequently and regularly on proposals. Also, in rural areas the points to be serviced are dispersed and so service provision takes longer than in urban areas, which are clustered. Therefore, from the provider point of view, urban areas are preferable.

Unlike those in urban areas, local authorities in rural areas will have trouble finding suitable private contractors if they cannot attract a large enough pool of contractors for competitive bidding. The number of viable contractors directly affects the competitive nature of the bidding process because the more bidders there are, the more pressure there is for the lowest possible bid. In this connection, the more pressure there is towards low bids, the lower the likelihood that the competitive bidding process will result in a DSO win.

A research project carried out by Sharp suggests that:

> **Smaller governments located far from metropolitan areas**
> **are likely to have the greatest difficulty in locating a private**
> **contractor. Even if an isolated local authority is able to**
> **locate a contractor, little price competition is likely.** (1990,
> p 115)

Sharp contends that the demands of a local authority directly relate to the number of suppliers. Smaller authorities typically do not have many different demands to meet due to the small scale of their operations, while larger local governments typically have more demands to serve. The greater the needs of local government, the better the earning potential becomes for contractors.

As contractors become aware of this potential, they may be more likely to enter the marketplace. As the pool of contractors increases, the result may be more competitive pressures among the various agents. This research suggests that the larger a local government, and the more urban the location, the lower the DSO output is, owing to the greater number of contractors the local authority can attract. In line with the above argument the following *demographic hypotheses* are proposed:

• The more urban a local authority, the lower the DSO output will be.

• The larger the population of a local authority, the lower the DSO output will be.

These are the basic hypotheses assumed in terms of how the environmental variables are related to the dependent variable, DSO output. Based on this generally assumed relationship, working hypotheses will be proposed in the following section, taking account of the direct and indirect relationships of variables applied in the analysis, and of how they affect DSO output.

As shown above, the hypothesis building between the dependent and independent variables is exploratory and experimental in nature because little previous research on the output of competitive tendering policy has addressed these relationships.

Research methodologies

Path analysis

Path analysis employed in this study is an extension of multiple regression analysis, which provides a means of examining the total association between DSO output and other independent variables. The model is based on the same assumptions as multiple regression, and therefore can be considered as a series of multiple regression models. However, the path model approach offers certain advantages over regression models so far as testing the influence of political, economic, strategic, organisational and demographic variables is concerned.

Path analysis was developed by Sewall Wright as a method for studying the direct and indirect effects of variables. Path analysis is not a method for discovering causes, but a method applied to a causal model formulated by the researcher on the basis of knowledge (Kerlinger and Pedhazur, 1973, p 305). In cases where the causal relations are uncertain, the method can be used to discover the logical consequences of any particular hypothesis with regard to them. It is useful in testing hypotheses rather than in generating theory (Kerlinger and Pedhazur, 1973).

The model, the indicators, the data and their limitations

The model

Figure 3.4 shows the hypothesised causal model, founded on theoretical discussion of the analysis and the general hypotheses suggested earlier. In this study, the proposed hypotheses for the dependent and independent variables regarding CCT policy are examined empirically. The constructs in the hypothetical framework are operationalised using measurement statements, as shown in Table 3.1. Path analysis is applied to explore the empirical strength of the relationships suggested in the hypotheses.

However, the hypothetical relationships between the mediating variables (except those between DSO output and the main independent variables) are to a certain extent experimental and exploratory.[9] The reported results are intended as preliminary empirical observations conducive to further theoretical development, marking a continuation of a journey begun by this analysis. While the model is not suggested as being better than those used in previous research,[10] it includes variables related to the hypotheses which can then be later explained by theory. A

Figure 3.4: Hypothesised causal model

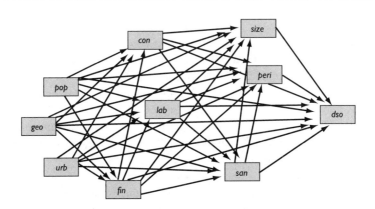

Notes: *pop* = population size; *urb* = degree of urbanisation; *geo* = geographical location; *fin* = fiscal independence; *con* = proportion of Conservative Party councillors; *lab* = proportion of Labour Party councillors; *san* = number of sanctions issued against local government; *size* = size of the contract; *peri* = period of the contract; *dso* = DSO proportion of total value of work.

brief theoretical discussion of the working hypotheses constructed follows. The hypotheses mentioned in the previous section are also incorporated.

Urban researchers (Haworth et al, 1978; Hirsch, 1982) analysing urbanisation and urban growth have identified population size and degree of urbanisation as being positively and significantly related to the fiscal independence or fiscal power of a local government. It is generally accepted that there is a very strong relationship between population size, degree of urbanisation and fiscal independence.

Every commentator on urban inequality has argued for a very strong association between geographical location (north/south, east/west, white region/non-white region and so on) and the fiscal independence of local government (Chakravorty, 1996; Cheshire and Carbonaro, 1996). Hence:

- H1: Fiscal independence (*fin*) is directly and positively affected by population size (H1a) and degree of urbanisation (H1b). Fiscal independence is also affected by geographical location[11] (H1c).

Table 3.1: Research hypotheses

Hypothesis number	Independent variable	Dependent variable	Assumed impact
1a	*pop*	*fin*	+
1b	*urb*	*fin*	+
1c	*geo*	*fin*	+ or −
2a	*pop*	*con*	−
2b	*urb*	*con*	−
2c	*fin*	*con*	+
2d	*geo*	*con*	+ or −
3a	*pop*	*lab*	+
3b	*urb*	*lab*	+
3c	*fin*	*lab*	−
3d	*geo*	*lab*	+ or −
4a	*pop*	*san*	+
4b	*urb*	*san*	+
4c	*fin*	*san*	+
4d	*lab*	*san*	+
4e	*con*	*san*	−
4f	*geo*	*san*	+ or −
5a	*pop*	*size*	+
5b	*urb*	*size*	+
5c	*fin*	*size*	+
5d	*lab*	*size*	+
5e	*con*	*size*	−
5f	*san*	*size*	−
5g	*geo*	*size*	+ or −
6a	*pop*	*peri*	+
6b	*urb*	*peri*	+
6c	*fin*	*peri*	+
6d	*con*	*peri*	+
6e	*san*	*peri*	+
6f	*lab*	*peri*	−
6g	*geo*	*peri*	+ or −
7a	*fin*	*dso*	+
7b	*lab*	*dso*	+
7c	*san*	*dso*	−
7d	*pop*	*dso*	−
7e	*urb*	*dso*	−
7f	*con*	*dso*	−
7g	*size*	*dso*	−
7h	*peri*	*dso*	−
7i	*geo*	*dso*	+ or −
8	*lab or con*	*dso*	+ or −

It is acceptable to hypothesise that political party composition is affected by population size and degree of urbanisation. The pattern of the effect of demographic variables on the political variable varies from one country to another. In the UK, it is assumed that the less urban and the smaller the population of a local authority is, the more Conservative it will be (Byrne, 1994, pp 150-4; Hampton, 1987, p 120; 1991, p 128; Stoker, 1991, pp 40-9).

The economic variable does appear to have a significant relationship with the political variable. The economic variable seems to be no less powerful than the other environmental variables in the multiple regression analysis.

Next, it is important to discuss the different ideological and policy preferences of local political parties in relation to financial independence. Stoker (1991, pp 40-1) points out that one of the characteristics of policy making in Conservative-controlled local authorities is to hold back spending and keep down the local rates or community charge. In a similar vein, in a study of American party politics, Beck and Sorauf (1992, pp 168-9) maintain that, for the most part, Democrats support more government spending while Republicans support less. Lineberry's work (1989, p 286) also examines government spending and involvement in citizens' lives on these same ideological bases.

Political scientists studying voting behaviour point out that social and economic factors such as social class, income level, degree of education can be important determinants of political ideology. In terms of political theory, it is generally accepted that the higher the income level of residents in a local authority area, the more likely it is that they will support the Conservatives. Sharpe and Newton (1984, p 177) support this argument, stating that Labour authorities are generally poor and that their purchasing power seems to be relatively low.

In view of these arguments, it is hypothesised that in the UK, local authorities with high fiscal independence are more likely to have a high proportion of Conservative local councillors. It is generally accepted by political scientists that the political party composition of local authorities varies according to geographical location (Painter, 1995). Hence:

- H2: The proportion of Conservative councillors (*con*) in the total number of councillors in local government is directly and negatively affected by population size (H2a) and degree of urbanisation (H2b), as well as directly and positively affected by fiscal independence (H2c).

The proportion of Conservative councillors is also affected by geographical location (H2d).

The characteristics of Labour Party councillors are understood to be opposite to those of Conservative Party councillors mentioned above. Often coming from working-class backgrounds and with a history of active involvement in the trade union movement, these councillors have pioneered innovations and developments in welfare services (Goss, 1989).

It is expected that in the UK the more urban the local authority and the bigger its population size, the higher will be the proportion of Labour councillors (Byrne, 1994, pp 150-4; Hampton, 1991, p 128; Stoker, 1991, pp 40-9). Because of the ideological characteristics of Labour or the Liberal Democrats, it is theoretically assumed that a local authority with a high level of financial independence is likely to have a low proportion of Labour councillors. In accordance with the hypothesis made above, it is hypothesised that the proportion of Labour councillors varies according to geographical location. Hence:

- H3: The proportion of Labour councillors (*lab*) out of the total number of councillors in local government is directly and positively affected by population size (H3a) and degree of urbanisation (H3b), as well as directly and negatively affected by fiscal independence (H3c). The proportion of Labour councillors is also affected by geographical location (H3d).

It is assumed that in a situation where the population size, degree of urbanisation and fiscal independence of a local authority are high, the local authority can effectively resist a policy imposed from above without fear of sanctions. Power-dependence theory (Wilson and Game, 1994, pp 110-12) implies that the local authority which has sufficient resources might be more powerful in negotiating or bargaining with central government. Accordingly, it is assumed that a local authority with high population size, high fiscal independence and a degree of urbanisation should receive more sanctions from central government during the CCT process.

As regards the relationship between the sanction and political party composition, it is understood that the Labour Party tends to resist the Conservative-initiated policy CCT, whereas the Conservative Party tends to comply with it, leading us to expect that prior to 1997 Labour councils were more likely to incur sanctions issued by central government than Conservative councils.

As Sharpe and Newton (1984) note, a policy has differing effects in different regions, which means a local authority should have different attitudes towards a policy, considering its negative or positive effects on the local authority. It is hypothesised that the number of sanctions issued against a local authority by central government can vary according to geographical location. Hence:

- H4:The number of sanctions (against anticompetitive behaviour) issued against the local authority (*san*) is directly and positively affected by population size (H4a), degree of urbanisation (H4b), fiscal independence (H4c) and proportion of Labour councillors (H4d), as well as directly and negatively affected by proportion of Conservative councillors (H4e). The number of sanctions issued against local government is also affected by geographical location (H4f).

Considering the scale of economy and the local authority's ability to make arrangements for a large contract, it is hypothesised that in a situation where the population size, degree of urbanisation and fiscal independence of the local authority are high, the contract size will be relatively big. Furthermore, the size of the contract will have a significant impact on the cost of the monitoring procedures. Hence, it is hypothesised that contract size is associated with the capability of the local authority to implement the contract effectively.

Since CCT was introduced, it has been noted that contract size has been used to influence the local authority's chances of winning the contract (Walsh et al, 1997). One way of using it includes packaging work in a way that makes it unattractive to private bidders and operating default systems which are penal (Walsh and Davis, 1993), leading them to give up tendering for work.

From the perspective of small businesses, contract size strongly affects ability to compete, and thus the success of the small firm depends on the size of the contract that the local authority is putting out (Abbott et al, 1996). In view of this, Abbott et al hypothesise that authorities controlled by the Conservatives will be more favourable to small businesses, allowing them to win more CCT work. Considering that the Labour Party has been politically reluctant to embrace CCT, it is hypothesised that Labour-controlled councils preferred larger contracts, whereas Conservative councils preferred small ones.[12]

As regards the relationship between contract size and sanctions, it is assumed that a local authority which has experienced the sanctions issued by central government is more likely to make the contract smaller, because the setting-up of too big a contract is regarded as a strategy employed by a local authority to prevent private contractors from tendering for it. In addition, it is hypothesised that contract size is associated with geographical location, because it can also be affected by regional factors. Hence:

- H5: The size of the contract (*size*) is directly and positively affected by population size (H5a), degree of urbanisation (H5b), fiscal independence (H5c) and proportion of Labour councillors (H5d), as well as directly and negatively affected by proportion of Conservative councillors (H5e) and the number of sanctions issued against the local authority (H5f). The size of the contract is also affected by geographical location (H5g).

As Sharp (1990, p 115) has noted, whether the location of a local authority is urban or rural affects its ability to prepare and implement the contract. As the population of a local authority increases and the local authority becomes urban, it is assumed that there will be a corresponding increase in the period for which the contract runs.

As regards the relationship between political party composition and the contract period, the period for which the contract is let can influence the level of competition. A shorter contract period may, owing to high start-up costs, discourage competition for the inhouse tender (Prowle and Hines, 1989, p 98). It is hypothesised that Labour councils prefer a shorter contract, whereas Conservative councils prefer a longer contract.

As regards the relationship between the contract period and the sanctions issued by central government, it is expected that a local authority which has experienced sanctions issued by central government is more likely to make the contract period longer because private contractors prefer a longer contract to a shorter one. This is because a longer contract can lower the transaction costs incurred.

As with contract size, it is hypothesised that the contract period differs according to geographical location. Hence:

- H6: The period of the contract (*peri*) is directly and positively affected by population size (H6a), degree of urbanisation (H6b), fiscal independence (H6c), proportion of Conservative councillors (H6d) and the number of sanctions issued against the local authority (H6e), as well as directly and negatively affected by proportion of Labour councillors (H6f). The period of the contract is also affected by geographical location (H6g).

The main hypotheses relating to DSO output, the final dependent variable, have been discussed in the section 'variables and hypotheses (pp 60-74). These main hypotheses are as follows:

- H7: DSO output (*dso*) is directly and positively affected by fiscal independence (H7a) and proportion of Labour councillors (H7b), as well as directly and negatively affected by the number of sanctions issued against the local authority (H7c), population size (H7d), degree of urbanisation (H7e), proportion of Conservative councillors (H7f), the size of the contract (H7g) and the period of the contract (H7h). DSO output is also affected by geographical location (H7i).

Some scholars argue that political party effect on the policy output is crucial, while others underestimate this effect. Stoker (1991, p 37), in particular, characterises the development of local government in the post-war period in the UK as involving a shift from an apolitical climate to one of intense 'politicisation'. This study advances the hypothesis, based on Stoker's study, that the variable most crucial in affecting DSO output is political party composition. Hence:

- H8: DSO output is more strongly affected by the political variable (the proportions of Labour or Conservative councillors) than by any other variable.

These hypotheses are based on the view that, rather than seeing political, organisational, economic, strategic and demographic variables as in some sense distinct or opposed, it is better to view them as interdependent and mutually reinforcing. It is not a question of 'Do political variables, for example, explain more or less than economic ones?' but rather 'What combinations of environmental variables are associated with what types of CCT output patterns?'

The hypotheses and the intercorrelationships between the variables, and as a result the analytical framework, put forward in this study are exploratory and experimental in that they are based primarily on the researcher's knowledge and intuition and on his theoretical examination of the existing literature. One of the main reasons for this is that there have been few studies on the relationships between the political and socioeconomic variables associated with contracting out.

The hypotheses and intercorrelations, and the assumed impact of the variables, are illustrated as a hypothesised causal model in Figure 3.4 and Table 3.1. In this hypothesised causal model, *pop*, *urb* and *geo* are exogenous variables, whose variability is assumed to be determined by causes outside the causal model, whereas other variables are endogenous variables whose variation is explained by exogenous and endogenous variables in the system. Correlations of exogenous variables are treated as 'given' and cannot be decomposed. When exogenous variables are correlated among themselves, these correlations are treated as 'givens' and remain unanalysed (Kerlinger and Pedhazur, 1973, p 309).

According to this model, political, economic, organisational, strategic and demographic factors have a direct impact on DSO output. These variables influence DSO output indirectly via a number of intermediate variables. For example, population size has an impact on DSO output both directly and indirectly via the number of sanctions issued against local government.

This model also shows that population size, geographical location and degree of urbanisation are posited as simultaneous, direct and linear influences on the proportion of Conservative councillors, fiscal independence, the proportion of Labour councillors, the number of sanctions issued against local government, the period of the contract, the size of the contract, and DSO output.

The data, the indicators, and their limitations

Data regarding the variables applied in this study were acquired primarily from *Local elections in Britain* (Local Government Chronicle Election Centre, 1994), *Local government comparative statistics* (CIPFA, 1991c; 1994c), *Direct service organisations statistics* (CIPFA, 1991a; 1994a), *Finance and general statistics* (CIPFA, 1991b; 1994b), *Regional trends* (Central Statistics Office, 1995), *The municipal yearbook* (Clements, 1991; 1994; 1996; 1997) and *The contracts handbook* (Davis-Coleman, 1995a; 1995b; 1996). The data regarding DSO output proportion, the dependent variable, are taken from *The contracts handbook* as described later in Table 4.2. The book includes eight specific service delivery areas which the 1988 Local Government Act stipulates local authorities should put out to tender, and also covers all contracts which were made for local authorities. This is one of the best available sources of data on DSO proportion, not only because the data set is one of the few public data sets available on CCT, but also because it covers many of the independent variables associated with this current study.

The model used here was designed to examine the variations in the percentage of DSO output (the dependent variable) by means of nine independent variables. The universe for path analysis for 1991 includes 215 local authorities, since 81 local authorities had no experience of competitive tendering in 1991.

The second path analysis uses the same independent variables, although 146 local authorities were used in the computations because the other 150 had not opened services to competitive tender in 1994. The indicators, variables (including dummy variables[13]) and data sources included in the analysis are explicated in Table 3.2.

Various specific terms and phrases are used in this study. These terms were defined conceptually as shown in Table 3.2. For the purposes of clarity and precision, the main terms are operationally defined below.

Definition of terms

- *DSO output* relates to the proportion of the total value of the works undertaken by the DSO in eight areas – refuse collection, cleaning of buildings, other cleaning (such as street sweeping), schools and welfare catering, other catering, grounds maintenance, vehicle repairs and maintenance, and management of sports and leisure facilities.

- *Political party composition*[14] refers to the proportion of Labour and Conservative councillors among the total number of councillors in the local authority.

- *Population size* refers to the population (number of people) of the local authority.

- *Contract period* relates to the duration of the contract, and *contract size* refers to the value of the contract.

- *Fiscal independence*[15] is the degree to which the local authority has financial autonomy.

- The *degree of urbanisation* is determined by dividing population size by the size of the area.

Table 3.2: Overview of variables and indicators used in the analysis

Variables	Indicators	Name of indicators in text and tables	Operationalisation	Years covered	Data sources
Dependent variable	DSO output	dso	Percentage of the total value of work that is undertaken by the DSO	1991, 1994	The contracts handbook
Political variable	Political party composition	con lab	Conservative councillors/total number of local councillors Labour councillors/total number of local councillors	1991, 1994	Local elections in Britain
Economic variable	Fiscal independence	fin	Council tax/SSA* (1994), Community charge/SSA (1991)	1991, 1994	Finance and general statistics The municipal yearbook
Strategic variables	Contract size Contract period Geographical location	size peri geo†	Size of the contract Period of the contract Eight regions	1991, 1994	The contracts handbook Regional trends
Organisational variables	Sanctions issued against local authority	san‡	Number of sanctions issued by central government	1991, 1994	The contracts handbook
Demographic variables	Population size Degree of urbanisation	pop urb	Population size Population/acre	1991, 1994	The municipal yearbook

Notes: * SSA= Standard Spending Assessment; † dummy variable applied; ‡ dummy variable applied.

- The *number of sanctions* issued against a local authority is a term used to specify the experience of local government with regard to anticompetitive behaviours in the CCT process. It is measured by the number of anticompetitive behaviours recorded by central government since the introduction of the 1988 Act. In this study, a dummy variable[16] was introduced to compute the number of anticompetitive behaviours on the part of local government.

- *Geographical location* is a term used to signify the location of a local authority. In many cases, official statistics (*Regional trends*, *Social trends*) divide England into eight regions, namely North, Yorkshire and Humberside, North-West, West Midlands, East Midlands, East Anglia, South-West and South-East. However, it is possible to classify English regions in various ways and this study follows *Regional trends* in this respect. In order to measure the effect of geographical location on the dependent variable, the dummy variable is introduced. The reference category for the geographical location is the North region, which implies that the North is a standard for comparison by regions (Table 3.3).

Some of the hypotheses suggested for the analysis are likely to be debatable.[17] The sanctions issued against a local authority for being anticompetitive are a case in point. As was mentioned earlier, the sanctions taken against a local authority by central government are more likely to be a consequence of the authority's favouring the DSO than to be a cause of it. However, if the causal relationship between the two variables, the sanctions and the DSO, is considered over a lengthy continuous period of time (from 1988 to 1994, for example), it can also be hypothesised

Table 3.3: Dummy variable for geographical location

Region	dum2	dum3	dum4	dum5	dum6	dum7	dum8
North	0	0	0	0	0	0	0
Yorks and Humberside	1	0	0	0	0	0	0
North-West	0	1	0	0	0	0	0
West Midlands	0	0	1	0	0	0	0
East Midlands	0	0	0	1	0	0	0
East Anglia	0	0	0	0	1	0	0
South-West	0	0	0	0	0	1	0
South-East	0	0	0	0	0	0	1

that the variable, the number of sanctions, can play a role as a cause, as well as being a consequence of high or low DSO output. In this analysis, since DSO output is fixed as the final dependent variable, only the role of the variable, the number of sanctions, is considered as a cause of high or low DSO output.

This apart, data availability has to some extent guided the selection of variables. Some variables are conceptually problematic, not simply because of the difficulty of obtaining adequate data, but also because the definitions vary according to context. Also, the data sets for the two years 1991 and 1994 are limited to 215 and 146 respectively out of a total of 296 non-metropolitan districts in England, because the other non-metropolitan districts had not opened services to competitive tendering in the two years in question.

Despite these problems and the range of possible misinterpretations of the results of the analysis, the present study should add to existing knowledge about variations in local government CCT policy output in England, for the following reasons:

- the results of the study by path analysis can contribute to an understanding of how the policy output has been made;

- the methodology has not before been employed in the field of CCT in the manner proposed in this study;

- the whole set of indicators used has not been used before;

- the study compares data for two years, 1991 and 1994, thus ensuring a dynamic perspective on the research questions.

Analytical procedure

The analysis is processed according to the steps indicated in Figure 3.5.

The data from the different sources (as shown in Table 3.2) is analysed using path analysis. A brief introductory discussion of path analysis follows. More detailed expositions of the history, rationale, and mechanics of path analysis can be found in Frankfort-Nachmias and Nachmias (1996, pp 448-51).

Path analysis gives insights into the causal ordering of variables in a system of relationships. The first step in path analysis is to specify descriptive statistics and intercorrelationships among variables. From the correlation matrix, it is possible to obtain correlation coefficients for

Figure 3.5: Analytical procedure

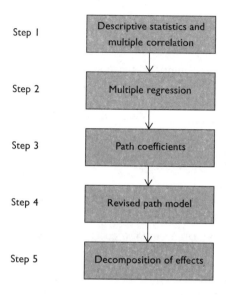

both the dependent variable and the independent variable, and measure the strength of linear association between any two variables. The correlation matrix also provides information about multicollinearity and other statistically-related problems between variables in multiple regression analysis (Kerlinger and Pedhazur, 1973, pp 306-9).

The next step is to find out the regression coefficients using multiple regression analysis. Path coefficients between independent and dependent variables were represented by standardised regression coefficients. The standardised regression coefficient reflects the impact of a one-standard-deviation change in the independent variable on the dependent variable – again measured in standard deviation (Kerlinger and Pedhazur, 1973). This direct effect measures that part of the total relationship between two variables which is not transmitted through other mediating variables.[18] By contrast, the indirect effects are those influences that are transmitted through mediating variables from the exogenous variable to the endogenous variable (Kerlinger and Pedhazur, 1973).

The significance of path coefficients and the overall significance of individual relationships can be examined by conducting a t-test, and by examining coefficients of determination (R^2), respectively. The t–test indicates whether or not a path coefficient differs statistically from zero, that is, whether or not a hypothesised linear relationship holds. The coefficient of determination indicates the amount of variance in the dependent variable which is accounted for by the variables entered in the path or structural equation (Kerlinger and Pedhazur, 1973, pp 309-10).

The next step is to draw a revised path diagram supported by analysis. In the originally hypothesised path diagram (Figure 3.4), the theorised causal relationships are represented by uni-directional arrows linking two variables. The path diagram in Figure 3.4 shows 21 paths emanating from population size, geographical location and degree of urbanisation, which are exogenous variables. The strength of the three variables' individual influence is denoted by the value of the path coefficient associated with each path.

Likewise, *fin,* for example, is postulated as affecting *con, lab, san, size, peri* and *dso.* The path diagram proposed is simplified into a revised path diagram. The revised path diagram demonstrates revised causal relationships of variables after insignificant paths are deleted. To simplify the model prior to decomposition, all paths whose coefficients were not statistically significant at the 0.10 level or less were eliminated. This relatively moderate threshold level was chosen so as to avoid conservatism in estimating direct and indirect effects; linkages that had even a slight effect remained in the model for decomposition. The correlations between all pairs of variables were then decomposed into the sum of their direct and indirect effects. A significant relationship between two variables is indicated by a bold arrow (in Figure 4.3) joining them in the path model, while an insignificant effect is indicated by a dotted arrow.

The final step is to decompose the effects of independent variables on dependent variables into direct and indirect effects, leading to an examination of the net effect of each variable on each of the various variables concerned. This allows the direction and strength of the relationship between variables to be understood.

The sum of the direct and indirect effects represents the total meaningful effect of one variable on another. The total effect of direct and indirect paths provides an indication of the adequacy with which the model was specified.

The next chapter applies this analytical framework to actual data in order to investigate the hypothetical relationships put forward in this chapter and to assess the effects of the variables on the DSO output.

Notes

[1] Levy, Meltsner and Wildavsky distinguish different classes of programme effects produced by governmental action in terms of *outputs, outcomes* and, finally, *impacts*. An output is the easiest of the three to measure quantitatively, since it is basically a service actually rendered, usually on an immediate or short-term basis. An output of an educational programme, for example, may consist of the number of children actually receiving instruction. *Outcomes*, the consequences of programmes in human terms, are usually more qualitative and have more long-term implications. An outcome of an educational programme might be measured in terms of children's reading scores, but there are many other outcomes from schooling, and not all of these are measurable in the short run. For example, schools may produce such outcomes as changed study habits, improved self-estimates of ability, and so on. Finally, *impacts* may involve even longer term consequences for society. The impact of schooling may be to produce a literate population and increase society's economic productivity. Often such impacts are quite remote. Impacts are the most difficult effects to measure because the mechanisms by which they are achieved are uncertain and the timescales involved can be very long (Levy et al, 1974, pp 4-8). See Ham and Hill, 1993, pp 12-15.

[2] One of the most favoured measures of party impact that has been employed in output studies outside the USA is the strength of the left-wing parties, Labour, Social Democrat or Communist. Size of Labour majority is the most favoured variable used in British studies for measuring party effect (Sharpe, 1981, pp 5-6). However, in this study the strength of the Labour and Conservative parties was used to measure party effect more accurately. Sharpe and Newton (1984, p 181) choose six independent political variables to measure party effect by regression analysis. These are: turnout, percentage of uncontested seats, percentage of Conservative seats, percentage of Labour seats, years of Conservative control, and years of Labour control.

[3] In terms of causality, sanctions can also be thought of as a consequence of a local authority favouring the DSO rather than a cause of it. However, when we consider the operation of sanctions throughout the time period from the introduction of CCT to 1994, for example, sanctions could function as a cause as well as a consequence. From the organisational point of view discussed above, it can be argued that they are an independent variable influencing the extent of DSO use.

[4] There are different perspectives from the above. Wildavsky (1973) points out that the budgetary process is basically a political one, so that there could be room for central government to steer grants according to its broad intention. Wilson and Game (1994, p 147) also indicate that the whole process of grant distribution in the UK is political. In addition, in practice central government has political and administrative discretion in the area of distribution of grants to local authorities. Stoker (1988, p 170) also underlines the fact that central government may use its general grants to local authorities both as a legitimation for exerting a general influence on local policies and as a method of influencing overall local authority expenditure.

According to Boyne (1996a, pp 716-17), in the UK, previous governments had attempted to influence levels of spending in local government as a whole, but the Conservatives sought to control the spending of individual authorities by manipulating grants, specifying the expenditure required to meet service needs in each local area and capping council spending.

However, the predominant viewpoint is that the formula concerning distribution of grants is complex and closely linked with central control over local taxation. As such, it nowadays leaves local authorities very little room for local manipulation of their resources. Hence, the proportion of grants in local government income is not a good indicator of fiscal independence.

[5] Although the proportion of income from council tax (15.3% in England 1994-95) (CIPFA, 1995, p 45) is low in the financing of revenue expenditure, formal fiscal autonomy or independence can be assessed by the use of the local tax base (Rose and Page, 1982, p 174).

[6] Dunleavy (1980, p 120) argues that the involvement of private firms in public service provision has been almost unstudied, and very little attention has been given to the consequences of interventions in the urban public policy by private corporations.

[7] From the policy point of view, some scholars (Boyne, 1992; Sharpe and Newton, 1984) imply that the pattern of policy implementation and policy output varies across regions. Although this point differs from the argument put forward above from the private contractor's point of view regarding CCT, Key's (1987) view indicates that policy output, DSO output in this study, might vary according to geographical location.

[8] However, there are costs associated with dividing up contracts. These include the loss of economies of scale as well as the additional

administrative costs associated with managing several contracts (McAfee and McMillan, 1988).

[9] In situations where the relationships between variables are unclear for some reason (including lack of previous studies on them), hypothesis making inevitably comes to rely on the researcher's intuition and subjectivity. As a result, the hypothesis is more exploratory in nature and the results of the study are conducive to further theoretical development. The working hypotheses, except the main hypotheses which are directly concerned with the final dependent variable, DSO output, are therefore more exploratory and experimental in nature. For further discussion of the nature of the hypothesis see Kerlinger and Pedhazur (1973), Creswell (1994), Globerman and Vining (1996), Lewis-Beck (1994) and Frankfort-Nachmias and Nachmias (1996).

[10] Crano and Brewer (1986, p 150) emphasise that in no case will the path model allow us to state with certainty that the model we have constructed provides the complete and true specification of the causal parameters of the variables of interest. One reason for this is that there are a great many possible path models that can be constructed from any given set of variables; as the number of variables in the model becomes large, the number of possible structural models becomes astronomically great, and one of these alternatives might explain the set of relationships much more compellingly than the model that was developed originally.

[11] The structure of the hypotheses relating to geographical location is different from that of the other hypotheses in that the former is literally a null hypothesis (concept-oriented, non-directional); while the latter are all operational alternative hypotheses (operational, directional). This is because few studies have been conducted on the relationship between geographical location and the other CCT-related variables. Therefore, the hypotheses concerned with geographical location are only concept-orientated and non-directional. For the nature of the hypothesis, see Creswell (1994, pp 72-5).

[12] Paradoxically, if the contracts were for very small parts of the work, then private contractors may not be interested because of the inherently low profitability (Prowle and Hines, 1989, p 98). However, because too small a contract can cause many transaction costs to the inhouse as well as to private contractors, it is rare for contract size to be too small.

[13] A *dummy variable* is a vector in which members of a given category are assigned an arbitrary number, while all others – that is, subjects not belonging to the given category – are assigned another arbitrary number.

For example, if the variable is gender, one can assign 1s to males and 0s to females. The resulting vector of 1s and 0s is a dummy variable. Dummy variables can be very useful in analysing research data when the independent variables are categorical (such as gender, geographical location, religion). They can be used, for example, in combination with a continuous independent variable or as a dependent variable (Kerlinger and Pedhazur, 1973, p 105).

[14] District councils are divided into wards, but they have a choice over their election cycle. They may either adopt the metropolitan district system, which means that one third of the seats (one per ward) are up for election each year for three years out of four, or alternatively, all the seats can be contested once every four years. Generally, districts in urban areas adopt the metropolitan district system, while rural districts have elections once every four years (LGMB, 1991, pp 16-17).

[15] In order to measure fiscal independence, proportion of community charge (for 1991) and council tax (for 1994) of SSA is adopted. The community charge (poll tax) is a local charge on adults for services provided in the area where they live. The simplified example below shows how community charge is calculated:

- A district council has a net expenditure of £12 million. The county council precept is £30 million. There are 100,000 people on the community charge register.

> **Community charge = (£12 million + £30 million)/100,000**
> **= £420 per person (LGMB, 1991, p 47).**

Council tax is a tax on both the person (like the poll tax) and on his or her property (like the rates); indeed there is division between the two. It is based on the relative value of the property. The amount of tax will vary according to the value of the property, for which purpose houses and flats are to be grouped into eight valuation bands (A to H) (Byrne, 1994, pp 333-4).

[16] The reason for introducing the dummy variable for the variable is not only that the number of sanctions issued against local government by central government is not high (the mean is 0.06 and 0.03 for 1991 and 1994 respectively), but that the total number of local authorities which were issued with sanctions by central government is also small. Therefore, a better way to deal with the variable is to take advantage of the dummy

variable, which tranforms the initial variable's data from actual data to nominal data. That is, the value of the variable, unlike that of other variables, is set at 1 (if the local authority has ever experienced a sanction issued by central government for committing anticompetitive behaviour) or 0 (if the local authority has never been guilty of anticompetitive behaviour). Therefore, in this analysis, two dummy variables, *san 1* for 1991 and *san 2* for 1994, are used. The rationale for using these two dummy variables is as follows:

- *san 1*: 1 if the local authority had experienced a sanction issued by central government against anticompetitive behaviour between 1989 and 1991, and 0 if it had not;

- *san 2*: 1 if the local authority had experienced a sanction issued by central government against anticompetitive behaviour between 1992 and 1994, and 0 if it had not.

[17] Pedhazur and Schmelkin (1991, pp 194-5) indicate that the researcher may have several different hypotheses regarding the same phenomenon, because a hypothesis is a conjectural statement about a relation between two or more variables.
[18] For the role of mediating variables see Creswell (1994, pp 85-9) and Kerlinger and Pedhazur (1973, pp 306-12).

FOUR

Determinants of compulsory competitive tendering output

Introduction

The aim of this chapter is to explain the CCT output of local government in England, and to provide a framework capable of examining the CCT process in a systematic fashion, applying a range of independent variables to the dependent variable, CCT output (DSO output), over time.

There have been many attempts to explain the competitive tendering of local governments both in Britain and in many other countries in Western Europe and North America, but the approach adopted in this research diverges from the main body of the literature and explores a new way of analysing the issue.

Drawing on the analytical framework and research methodologies discussed in the previous chapter, this chapter identifies empirically the main factors affecting DSO output for the two years 1991 and 1994. This analysis does more than simply highlight the links between dependent and independent variables. It tries to demonstrate the extent to which these react on one another, like chemicals heated in a crucible, to form an amalgam of both.

Path model for 1991

Descriptive statistics and intercorrelation of variables

Descriptive statistics and the intercorrelation of all study variables for 1991 are presented in Table 4.1. The mean and the standard deviation of the variables provide descriptive statistics on the variability of the equation. For the dependent variable, *dso*, for example, the mean is 66.02 and the standard deviation is 43.04. This difference suggests that there is much

Table 4.1: Descriptive statistics and intercorrelations of all study variables (1991)

Variable	M	SD	1	2	3	4	5	6	7	8
1 con	0.37	0.20	1.00							
2 lab	0.30	0.27	-0.39**	1.00						
3 fin	2.22	0.53	0.08	-0.03	1.00					
4 pop	101823	42205	0.10	0.26**	-0.12	1.00				
5 urb	8.39	10.57	-0.12*	0.37**	-0.26**	0.36**	1.00			
6 size	457280	563922	-0.18*	0.13	-0.09	0.17*	0.17*	1.00		
7 peri	4.86	0.86	0.01	0.05	0.04	-0.01	-0.04	0.02	1.00	
8 dso	66.02	43.04	-0.17*	-0.34**	0.05	-0.05	0.10	0.13	0.03	1.00

Notes: The number of sanctions issued against the local authority (*san*) and geographical location (*geo*) are treated as dummy variables; * significant at 0.05, ** significant at 0.01; M = mean; SD = standard deviation.

variation to explain here. Two variables – the number of sanctions issued against the local authority and geographical location – are omitted because they are treated as dummy variables.

Correlation analysis confirmed the expectation that *dso* – as measured by the DSO proportion – would be positively or negatively correlated with the suggested environmental variables of local government. As Table 4.1 shows, the correlation coefficients between *dso* and *con* and *lab* are significant. By contrast, the other indicators, *fin*, *pop* and *peri*, were less clearly related to *dso*. Although the descriptive data provides an interesting picture of the correlationships between variables, it does not explain or predict how or why there is variation among the different variables.

Results

The original regression method used was an ordinary least squares (OLS) method. The results of the OLS regression analysis were tested for autocorrelation, heteroscedasticity and multicollinearity.[1] While autocorrelation and multicollinearity were not detected, residual plots suggested that heteroscedasticity was present with many of the independent variables. To correct for heteroscedasticity, a weighted least squares method was employed, using the predicted value of the dependent variable as the weight. Due to the fact that autocorrelation and multicollinearity were neither expected to be nor found to be a problem with this model, no further tests for them were administered.

Summary of path analysis, including adequacy of equations, is shown in Table 4.2. Variables which are not shown in the table were omitted because the effect on the dependent variable was too weak. It can be seen from Table 4.2 that F statistics discovered were statistically significant at the 0.1 level, promoting confidence in the overall validity of the model. The R-squared coefficient, that is, the explanatory power of variables for the equation, was relatively low. As Table 4.2 shows, the standardised path coefficient (beta) from *fin* to *con* (0.10) indicates that a one-standard-deviation change in *fin* results in a 0.10 standard-deviation change in *con*.

Table 4.2: Summary of path analysis (1991)

Dependent variable	F	Prob	R^2	Independent variable	Beta	t	Prob
fin	12.60	0.00	0.08	*dum2*	-0.09	-2.05	0.09
				urb	-0.27	-0.47	0.00
con	16.08	0.00	0.25	*fin*	0.10	1.95	0.05
				pop	0.14	2.54	0.01
				urb	-0.23	-4.0	0.00
				dum5	0.16	2.92	0.00
				dum6	0.17	3.19	0.00
				dum8	0.49	8.74	0.00
lab	32.52	0.00	0.41	*dum2*	-0.10	-2.15	0.03
				dum6	-0.13	-2.62	0.00
				dum7	-0.35	-6.99	0.00
				dum8	-0.46	-8.89	0.00
				pop	0.15	2.91	0.00
				urb	0.45	8.88	0.00
san	20.12	0.00	0.06	*pop*	0.25	4.48	0.00
peri	16.69	0.00	0.07	*dum3*	0.27	4.08	0.00
dso	10.05	0.00	0.16	*size*	0.13	1.87	0.06
				con	-0.25	-3.25	0.00
				lab	0.37	4.85	0.00
				pop	-0.22	-2.87	0.00

The results of the equation for the final dependent variable, DSO output, are as follows. The R-squared value was 0.16. However, as was stated earlier, this equation is not fully specified. Specifically, it does not contain variables which relate to some hypotheses: H7a (fiscal independence), H7c (the number of sanctions issued against the local authority), H7e (degree of urbanisation), H7h (the period of the contract) and H7i (geographical location). The F statistic (10.05) was statistically significant at 0.0001 – thereby giving confidence about the overall validity of the model.

In the analysis for 1991, the direct effect of *geo, fin, urb, san* and *peri* on *dso* is not significant, which indicates that this *dso* does not react directly to variations in *geo, fin, urb, san* and *peri*.

Using the criterion of $p < 0.10$ as the basis for model reduction, the results from the data suggest that the paths from *pop* to *fin, peri* and *size*, from *geo* to *san, size* and *dso,* from *urb* to *san, peri, size* and *dso,* from *fin* to *lab, san, peri, size* and *dso,* from *con* to *san, peri* and *size,* from *lab* to *san, peri* and *size,* from *san* to *peri, size* and *dso,* and from *peri* to *dso* should be deleted, because their effects on the dependent variable were too weak or insignificant. For the equations, the critical t-values were statistically significant at the 90% confidence level.

These results indicate that each independent variable in each equation has a significant impact on the dependent variable. Fiscal independence $(R^2 = 0.08)$ is directly affected by geographical location (*geo*) (*dum2*, Yorkshire and Humberside) and degree of urbanisation (*urb*). The path coefficients from geographical location and degree of urbanisation to fiscal independence are -0.09 and -0.27 respectively, and are both statistically significant at the level of 0.1. Hence:

Equation 1: Y (*fin*) = 2.3426 – 0.0132 x *urb* – 0.2119 x *dum2*
(constant p < 0.000)

The proportion of Conservative councillors $(R^2 = 0.25)$ is determined by fiscal independence, population size, degree of urbanisation, geographical location (*dum5*, East Midlands; *dum6* East Anglia; *dum8*, South-East). The path coefficients from fiscal independence, population size, degree of urbanisation, *dum5* (East Midlands), *dum6* (East Anglia) and *dum8* (South-East) are 0.10, 0.14, -0.23, 0.16, 0.17 and 0.49 respectively. The six paths together explain approximately 25% of the variance in the proportion of Conservative councillors. Hence:

Equation 2: Y (*con*) = 0.1535 + 6.849E − 07 x *pop* − 0.0044 x
urb + 0.0400 x *fin* + 0.0929 x *dum5* + 0.1363 x *dum6* + 0.2092
x *dum8* (**constant p < 0.006**)

The proportion of Labour councillors ($R^2 = 0.41$) is affected by population
size, degree of urbanisation, geographical location (*dum2*, Yorkshire and
Humberside; *dum6*, East Anglia; *dum7*, South-West; *dum8*, South-East).
The path coefficients from population size, degree of urbanisation, *dum2*
(Yorkshire and Humberside), *dum6* (East Anglia), *dum7* (South-West) and
dum8 (South-East) are 0.15, 0.45, -0.10, -0.13, -0.35 and -0.46 respectively.
These six paths together explain 41% of the variance in the proportion
of Labour councillors. Of these six variables, degree of urbanisation is
the strongest (beta 0.45) affecting the variance of the proportion of Labour
composition. Hence:

Equation 3: Y (*lab*) = 0.2506 + 9.437E − 07 x *pop* + 0.01153 x
urb − 0.1216 x *dum2* − 0.1346 x *dum6* − 0.2633 x *dum7* − 0.2666
x *dum8* (**constant p < 0.000**)

The number of sanctions issued against local government ($R^2 = 0.06$) is
only affected by population size. The path coefficient from population
size to the number of sanctions issued against the local authority is 0.25.
Of the variance in the number of sanctions issued against the local
authority 6% is accounted for only by population size. Hence:

Equation 4: Y (*san*) = -0.0873 + 1.556E − 06 x *pop*
(**constant p < 0.02**)

Period of contract ($R^2 = 0.07$) is affected only by geographical location
(*dum3*, North-West). The path coefficient from geographical location to
period of contract is 0.27. The sole path from *dum3* to *peri* explains 7%
of the observed variance in period of contract. Hence:

Equation 5: Y (*peri*) = 60.171 x *dum3* (**no constant**)

The determinants of the final dependent variable, DSO output ($R^2 =
0.16$), are size of contract, proportion of Conservative councillors,
proportion of Labour councillors and population size. The four path
coefficients from size of contract, proportion of Conservative councillors,
proportion of Labour councillors and population size are 0.13, 0.25,

0.37 and –0.22, respectively. These four paths explain 16% of the variance in the DSO output. Of these variables, the effect of the proportion of Labour councillors on DSO output was the strongest (path coefficient, 0.37). Hence:

Equation 6: Y(*dso*) = 62.7885 – 2.1310 x *pop* – 49.29 x *con* + 61.425 x *lab* + 1.105 x *size* (constant p < 0.0000)

The revised model based on Table 4.2, with all estimates of path coefficients, is presented in Figure 4.1. Table 4.3 compares the results of path ananysis with the research hypotheses.

The individual results of each variable suggest which hypotheses were supported and which were rejected.

Hypotheses 1a, 1b and 1c concerned the effect of population size, degree of urbanisation and geographical location on fiscal independence. The results of this analysis show that there is no linkage between population size and fiscal independence, so H1a was rejected. It was hypothesised that the coefficient between degree of urbanisation and

Figure 4.1: Revised path model (1991)

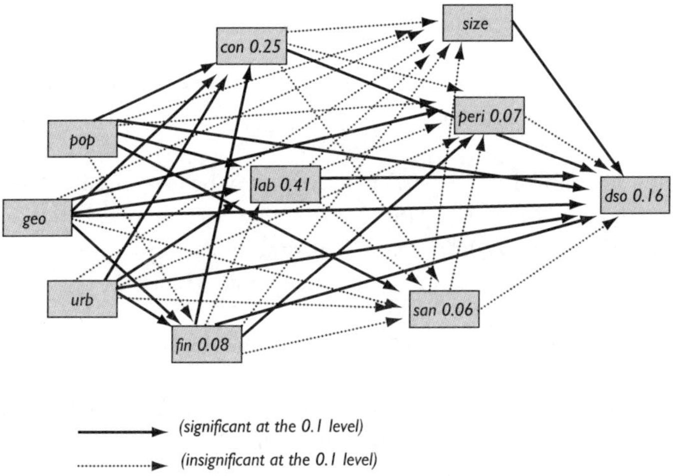

(significant at the 0.1 level)
(insignificant at the 0.1 level)

Table 4.3: Comparison of the results of the equations with research hypotheses (1991)

Hypothesis number	Independent variable	Dependent variable	Assumed impact	Findings in relation to hypothesis
1a	pop	fin	+	rejected
1b	urb	fin	+	rejected
1c	geo	fin	+ or −	supported
2a	pop	con	−	rejected
2b	urb	con	−	supported
2c	fin	con	+	supported
2d	geo	con	+ or −	supported
3a	pop	lab	+	supported
3b	urb	lab	+	supported
3c	fin	lab	−	rejected
3d	geo	lab	+ or −	supported
4a	pop	san	+	supported
4b	urb	san	+	rejected
4c	fin	san	+	rejected
4d	lab	san	+	rejected
4e	con	san	−	rejected
4f	geo	san	+ or −	rejected
5a	pop	size	+	rejected
5b	urb	size	+	rejected
5c	fin	size	+	rejected
5d	lab	size	+	rejected
5e	con	size	−	rejected
5f	san	size	−	rejected
5g	geo	size	+ or −	rejected
6a	pop	peri	+	rejected
6b	urb	peri	+	rejected
6c	fin	peri	+	rejected
6d	con	peri	+	rejected
6e	san	peri	+	rejected
6f	lab	peri	−	rejected
6g	geo	peri	+ or −	supported
7a	fin	dso	+	rejected
7b	lab	dso	+	supported
7c	san	dso	−	rejected
7d	pop	dso	−	supported
7e	urb	dso	−	rejected
7f	con	dso	−	supported
7g	size	dso	−	rejected
7h	peri	dso	−	rejected
7i	geo	dso	+ or −	rejected
8	lab or con	dso	+ or −	supported

fiscal independence would be positive, while in actuality it was negative. Hypothesis 1b was not supported by this finding. However, the relationship between geographical location (*dum2*) and fiscal independence was significant (0.09). Hence, there is support for hypothesis 1c.

Hypotheses 2a, 2b, 2c and 2d examined the influences of population size, degree of urbanisation, fiscal independence and geographical location on the proportion of Conservative councillors. Population size (H2a) was statistically significant, but in a direction opposite to that expected. Hence, the hypothesis was rejected. However, hypotheses 2b and 2c, stating that the proportion of Conservative councillors will be negatively and positively affected by degree of urbanisation and fiscal independence respectively, were supported at the 0.01 level. The results of this analysis also indicate that geographical location is significant in influencing the proportion of Conservative councillors. Hence, hypothesis 2d is supported.

Hypotheses 3a, 3b, 3c and 3d examined whether population size, degree of urbanisation, fiscal independence and geographical location affect the proportion of Labour councillors. The effect of fiscal independence (H3c) on proportion of Labour councillors was expected to be negative. However, the coefficient was instead positive, and not significantly different from zero (t-value of 0.653), so hypothesis 3c cannot be supported by this result. Both population size and degree of urbanisation were statistically significant in determining the proportion of Labour councillors, and the slope coefficients of the two variables were found to be positive, as expected. Therefore, hypotheses 3a and 3b were supported. Hypothesis 3d, stating that the proportion of Labour councillors will be affected by geographical location, was supported. The dummy variable for geographical location (*dum2, dum6, dum7* and *dum8*) was statistically significant in influencing the proportion of Labour composition. Therefore, hypothesis 3d was supported.

Hypotheses 4a, 4b, 4c, 4d, 4e and 4f investigated whether population size, degree of urbanisation, fiscal independence, proportion of Labour councillors, proportion of Conservative councillors and geographical location affect the number of sanctions issued against the local authority. The results of the path analysis show that there are no linkages between the above-mentioned independent variables except the relationship between population size and the number of sanctions issued against local authority. The sole variable, population size, affected the dependent variable significantly and the slope coefficient was positive, as expected. Therefore, only one hypothesis (H4a) was supported.

Hypotheses 5a, 5b, 5c, 5d, 5e, 5f and 5g concerned the influences of population size, degree of urbanisation, fiscal independence, proportion of Labour councillors, proportion of Conservative councillors, number of sanctions issued against the local authority and geographical location on the size of the contract. None of the independent variables was significantly related to the size of the contract. Thus, the findings provide no support for hypotheses 5a, 5b, 5c, 5d, 5e, 5f and 5g.

Hypotheses 6a, 6b, 6c, 6d, 6e, 6f and 6g examined whether period of contract is affected by population size, degree of urbanisation, fiscal independence, proportion of Labour councillors, proportion of Conservative councillors, number of sanctions issued against the local authority and geographical location. In this analysis only one variable, geographical location, was statistically significant whereas the other variables were insignificant. Hence one hypothesis, H6g, was supported.

Hypotheses 7a, 7b, 7c, 7d, 7e, 7f, 7g, 7h and 7i concerned whether the final dependent variable, DSO output, is affected by fiscal independence, proportion of Labour councillors, the number of sanctions issued against the local authority, population size, degree of urbanisation, proportion of Conservative councillors, the size of the contract, the period of the contract and geographical location. Proportion of Labour councillors, population size and proportion of Conservative councillors were significant in the analysis and the slope coefficients of these were as expected, thus providing support for hypotheses 7b, 7d and 7f. The size of the contract was also statistically significant; however, the slope coefficient was the opposite of that expected. Therefore, hypothesis 7g was rejected. The other five independent variables were not significant at the 95% confidence level. Hypotheses 7a, 7c, 7e, 7g, 7h and 7i were rejected.

Hypothesis 8 examined whether the political variable is the strongest factor affecting the final dependent variable, DSO output. As expected, the political variable, proportion of Labour councillors, was the strongest factor determining DSO output (beta 0.37). Therefore, hypothesis 8 was supported.

Table 4.4 shows how the total effects of the independent variables are made up. One advantage of path analysis over conventional regression analysis is the ability to extend the multiple regression equation treatment to a network of equations involving more than one equation (Kerlinger

Table 4.4: Decomposition of path coefficients (1991)

Dependent variable	Independent variable	Direct effect	Indirect effect	Total effect
fin	dum2	-0.09	0.00	-0.09
	urb	-0.27	0.00	-0.27
con	fin	0.10	0.00	0.10
	pop	0.14	0.014	0.154
	urb	-0.23	-0.023	-0.253
	dum5	0.16	0.016	0.176
	dum6	0.17	0.017	0.187
	dum8	0.49	0.049	0.539
lab	dum2	-0.10	0.00	-0.10
	dum6	-0.13	0.00	-0.13
	dum7	-0.35	0.00	-0.35
	dum8	-0.46	0.00	-0.46
	pop	0.15	0.00	0.15
	urban	0.45	0.00	0.45
san	pop	0.25	0.00	0.25
peri	dum3	0.27	0.00	0.27
dso	size	0.13	0.00	0.13
	lab	0.37	0.00	0.37
	con	-0.25	0.00	-0.25
	pop	-0.22	0.10	-0.12
	urb	0.00	0.10	0.10
	fin	0.00	0.02	0.02
	dum2	0.00	-0.04	-0.04
	dum5	0.00	0.05	0.05
	dum6	0.00	-0.05	-0.05
	dum7	0.00	-0.13	-0.13
	dum8	0.00	-0.17	-0.17

and Pedhauzur, 1973, p 305). The estimation of path coefficients also makes it possible to decompose the observed empirical correlation or covariance between any two variables into two components: direct and indirect effects. A direct effect is posited to exist if a single arrow connects two variables. When two variables of interest are connected only via other intervening variables – in other words, the relationship is represented by compound paths with no direct path between the two variables of interest – the effect is deemed to be indirect (Kerlinger and Pedhazur, 1973, pp 314-15).

As Table 4.4 shows, the direct and indirect relationships between the dependent and independent variables are complicated. With regard to DSO output for 1991, the political variable (*con* and *lab*), one strategic variable (*size*) and one demographic variable (*pop*) are directly related to it, while another strategic variable (*geo*), the economic variable (*fin*) and another demographic variable (*urb*) are indirectly related. These relationships can be expressed in simple diagrammatic form (Figure 4.2).

As Figure 4.2 shows, DSO output (*dso*), the final dependent variable, is directly affected by *pop*, *con*, *lab* and *size*, and indirectly affected by *pop*, *geo* and *urb* through the mediating of *con* and *lab*. In other words, DSO proportion is a function of population size, proportion of Conservative and Labour councillors, contract size, geographical location and degree of urbanisation. Of these, the political variable, proportion of Labour councillors (*lab*), has the greatest total effect on *dso* (0.37). It is accepted that where there is a high proportion of Labour councillors, a low proportion of Conservative councillors, a large contract size and a low level of population size, there will be a higher level of DSO output.

Figure 4.2: Simple relationships (1991)

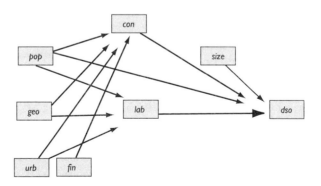

Summary

The hypothesised path model for 1991 performs reasonably well. Some of the estimated relationships are significant at the 0.1 level. The model accounts for 16% of the variation in DSO proportion, which is the percentage of the total value of work that is undertaken by the DSO. This is a reasonable fit for a cross-sectional local-government-level analysis.

Despite the aggregate nature of the study and the corresponding imprecision of some of the variables, the analysis provides evidence for the analytical model of DSO output presented here. It was found that for each of the equations, the two variables, the number of sanctions issued against the local authority and the period of contract, did not either directly or indirectly affect DSO output. This finding suggests that for the 1991 data set, these two variables were not associated with the variances in DSO output. Other variables were significant in the various equations. The size of the contract, the proportion of Labour councillors, the proportion of Conservative councillors and population size directly affected DSO output, whereas degree of urbanisation, fiscal independence and geographical location indirectly affected it.

Perhaps the most noticeable results are those associated with the political variable, the proportion of Conservative councillors and the proportion of Labour councillors. The political variable was initially expected to be one of the strongest variables associated with the percentage of DSO output, and so it proved.

Another thing to notice is that degree of urbanisation, fiscal independence, population size and geographical location (*dum2*) were each found to be significant factors which affected DSO output indirectly. These results tell us that in 1991, DSO output was affected, in part and indirectly, by the demographic variable (*urb*), the strategic variable (*dum2*) and the economic variable (*fin*).

Generally speaking, the results for 1991 indicate that the choice of internal over external production of local government services is less common where the local authority has a high degree of Conservative party composition, where the population of a local authority is large and where the size of the contract is small. In terms of the strength of the variables associated with DSO output, opposition from Labour councillors is the most frequently noted obstacle to attempts to privatise (Carnaghan and Bracewell-Milnes, 1993). These analysis results support the general perception of CCT.

Path model for 1994

Descriptive statistics and intercorrelation of variables

Table 4.5 shows the descriptive statistics and intercorrelations of variables for 1994 which were applied in this study. The strongest correlation between variables is 0.45 (between *pop* and *size*) and the weakest 0.03 (between *dso* and *peri*). For the final dependent variable, DSO output, the mean is 53.52, which is lower than that for 1991 (66.02), and the standard deviation is 45.52. The DSO proportion for 1994 was relatively strongly related to proportion of Labour councillors, *lab*, as with 1991, and also the correlation coefficient between the proportion of Conservative and of Labour councillors (−0.36) was weaker than that for 1991 (−0.39).

As regards the relatively weak relation between the Conservative and Labour councillors for 1994 compared to that for 1991, it appears that the proportion of Liberal Democrat councillors has increased. Since the proportion of Liberal Democratic councillors was not included in the path analysis, its effect on DSO output will be discussed in a separate section.

Results

The equations for 1994 were created to test the same propositions as were applied in the analysis for 1991, using the data for 1994. The

Table 4.5: Descriptive statistics and intercorrelations of all study variables (1994)

Variable	M	SD	1	2	3	4	5	6	7	8
1 con	0.36	0.20	1.00							
2 lab	0.28	0.26	-0.36**	1.00						
3 fin	2.16	0.93	0.12*	-0.10	1.00					
4 pop	102881	44279	0.11*	0.23**	-0.14*	1.00				
5 urb	8.44	10.67	-0.16**	0.37**	-0.21**	0.39**	1.00			
6 size	345547	448352	-0.08	0.33**	-0.18*	0.45**	0.36**	1.00		
7 peri	4.55	1.98	-0.12	0.17*	-0.05	0.06	0.08	0.26**	1.00	
8 dso	53.52	45.42	-0.10	0.23**	-0.14	0.12	0.17*	0.11	0.03	1.00

Notes: * significant at 0.05, ** significant at 0.01; M = mean; SD = standard deviation.

relationships of the independent and dependent variables used in the analysis for 1994 were the same as those for 1991. The 146 local authorities were included in the computations for the analysis for 1994.

An ordinary least squares method was employed for the initial regression run, and as before the results were tested for autocorrelation, multicollinearity and heteroscedasticity. While there were no problems associated with multicollinearity and autocorrelation, heteroscedasticity was detected, as with 1991; so to solve the problem weighted least squares models were used.

Table 4.6 shows the results of the tests of path coefficient significance for 1994. As in the 1991 path model, using the criterion of $p < 0.10$ as

Table 4.6: Summary of path analysis (1994)

Dependent variable	F	Prob	R^2	Independent variable	Beta	t	Prob
fin	9.24	0.000	0.06	urb	-0.20	-3.60	0.0004
				dum5	0.13	2.27	0.02
con	16.57	0.000	0.22	urb	-0.29	-5.17	0.0000
				pop	0.17	3.02	0.002
				dum5	0.15	2.77	0.005
				dum6	0.18	3.41	0.0007
				dum8	0.42	7.44	0.0000
lab	31.71	0.000	0.40	urb	0.43	8.54	0.0000
				pop	0.11	2.19	0.02
				dum2	-0.12	-2.56	0.01
				dum6	-0.14	-2.95	0.003
				dum7	-0.36	-7.38	0.0000
				dum8	-0.48	-9.33	0.00
peri	5.70	0.004	0.08	lab	0.16	1.97	0.04
				dum5	0.21	2.65	0.008
size	24.17	0.0000	0.39	urb	0.17	2.11	0.03
				pop	0.45	3.16	0.0000
				dum8	-0.27	-3.70	0.0003
dso	9.88	0.0001	0.12	con	-0.11	-1.87	0.01
				lab	0.18	2.35	0.01
				dum3	0.26	3.36	0.001

the basis for model reduction the analysis results of data for 1994 indicate that the paths from *pop* to *fin, san, peri* and *dso*, from *geo* to *san*, from *urb* to *san, peri* and *dso*, from *fin* to *con, lab, san, peri, size* and *dso*, from *con* to *san, size* and *peri*, from *lab* to *san* and *size*, from *san* to *size, peri* and *dso*, from *size* to *dso* and from *peri* to *dso* should be deleted for the revised path model.

Fiscal independence ($R^2 = 0.06$) was affected by degree of urbanisation and geographical location (*dum5*). The path coefficients from degree of urbanisation and geographical location to fiscal independence are -0.20 and 0.13 respectively, and both are statistically significant. Hence:

Equation 1: Y(*fin*) = 2.2621 − 0.0178 x *urb* + 0.3511 x *dum5* (constant: p < 0.000)

The proportion of Conservative councillors ($R^2 = 0.22$) was determined by population size, degree of urbanisation and geographical location (*dum5, dum6 and dum8*). Three paths together explain approximately 22% of the variance in the proportion of Conservative councillors. Hence:

Equation 2: Y(*con*) = 0.2447 + 8.81803E − 07 x *pop* − 0.0057 x *urb* + 0.0897 x *dum5* + 0.1473 x *dum6* + 0.1808 x *dum8* (constant: p < 0.0000)

The effects ($R^2 = 0.40$) of population size, degree of urbanisation and geographical location (*dum2, dum6, dum7 and dum8*) on proportion of Labour councillors were fairly strong, as indicated by their explanatory power. Of these variables, degree of urbanisation (path coefficient = 0.43) was the strongest in affecting proportion of Labour councillors. Hence:

Equation 3: Y(*lab*) = 0.2693 + 6.7353E − 07 x *pop* + 0.0106 x *urb* − 0.1391 x *dum2* − 0.1456 x *dum6* − 0.2623 x *dum7* − 0.2653 x *dum8* (constant: p < 0.0000)

Of the seven paths leading to the period of contract ($R^2 = 0.08$), the two paths from proportion of Labour councillors and geographical location (*dum5*) were statistically significant. The two paths explain 8% of the variance in the period of contract. Hence:

**Equation 4:Y(*peri*) = 3.9818 + 1.3500 x *lab* + 1.1430 x *dum5*
(constant: p < 0.0000)**

Degree of urbanisation, population size and geographical location (*dum8*) affected size of contract ($R^2 = 0.39$). Of the three paths leading to size of contract, the path from population size was the strongest (path coefficient = 0.45). Hence:

**Equation 5:Y(*size*) = -152202 + 7439.51 x *urb* + 4.8083 x *pop*
− 2664415 x *dum8* (constant: p < 0.05)**

The final dependent variable, DSO output, was affected by proportion of Conservative councillors, proportion of Labour councillors and geographical location. The explanatory power of the two variables was 0.12, which is slightly lower than that for 1991.

There is a large difference between the number of observations in the two data sets (1991 and 1994). In the analysis for 1994, the total number of local authorities included is 146, while for 1991 it was 215. With a smaller number of observed cases, less significance is to be expected.

Thus, the low R-squared coefficient is not surprising. Because of the small number of observations, and the weak results, for this equation, the case study portion of this analysis will be relied on to determine how CCT in 1991 differs from that in 1994. The three paths together explain approximately 12% of the observed variance in DSO output ($R^2 = 0.12$). Hence:

**Equation 6:Y (*dso*) = 40.3898 − 22.34 x *con* + 36.1274 x *lab* +
43.9882 x *dum3* (constant: p < 0.0000)**

The revised model based on the path coefficient significance is presented in Figure 4.3.

In the data set for 1994, in terms of direct effects, DSO proportion was a function of proportion of Labour councillors, proportion of Conservative councillors and geographical location (*dum3*). Proportion of Labour councillors, proportion of Conservative councillors and geographical location (*dum3*, North-West) were directly related to DSO proportion, while degree of urbanisation, population size and geographical location (*dum2*, Yorkshire and Humberside; *dum6*, East Anglia; *dum7*, South-West; *dum8*, South-East) were indirectly related through the

Figure 4.3: Revised path model (1994)

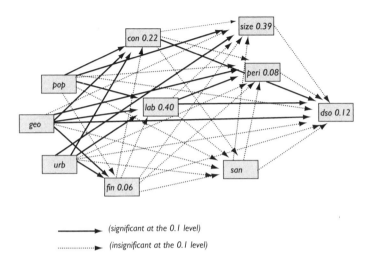

(significant at the 0.1 level)

(insignificant at the 0.1 level)

mediating effect of proportion of Conservative and proportion of Labour councillors. Table 4.7 compares the results of path analysis and research hypotheses.

In relation to the hypotheses suggested, a few of our propositions are confirmed, while most of them are rejected. Hypotheses 1a, 1b and 1c concerned the relationship between the exogenous variables and fiscal independence. Population size was expected positively to affect fiscal independence. However, there is no significant linkage between population size and fiscal independence. Therefore, hypothesis 1a was rejected. Hypothesis 1b examined whether degree of urbanisation affects fiscal independence. The effect of degree of urbanisation on fiscal independence (*fin*) was highly significant (0.0004), but in a direction opposite to that predicted. Hypothesis 1b is rejected, and the conclusion made that there is a negative relationship between degree of urbanisation and fiscal independence. Geographical location appears to affect fiscal independence. This supports hypothesis 1c. The coefficient of geographical location was significant at the level of 0.02, with a t-value of 2.27. Hence, hypothesis 1c was supported.

Table 4.7: Comparison of the results of the equations with research hypotheses (1994)

Hypothesis number	Independent variable	Dependent variable	Assumed impact	Findings in relation to hypothesis
1a	*pop*	*fin*	+	rejected
1b	*urb*	*fin*	+	rejected
1c	*geo*	*fin*	+ or −	supported
2a	*pop*	*con*	−	rejected
2b	*urb*	*con*	−	supported
2c	*fin*	*con*	+	rejected
2d	*geo*	*con*	+ or −	supported
3a	*pop*	*lab*	+	supported
3b	*urb*	*lab*	+	supported
3c	*fin*	*lab*	−	rejected
3d	*geo*	*lab*	+ or −	supported
4a	*pop*	*san*	+	rejected
4b	*urb*	*san*	+	rejected
4c	*fin*	*san*	+	rejected
4d	*lab*	*san*	+	rejected
4e	*con*	*san*	−	rejected
4f	*geo*	*san*	+ or −	rejected
5a	*pop*	*size*	+	supported
5b	*urb*	*size*	+	supported
5c	*fin*	*size*	+	rejected
5d	*lab*	*size*	+	rejected
5e	*con*	*size*	−	rejected
5f	*san*	*size*	−	rejected
5g	*geo*	*size*	+ or −	supported
6a	*pop*	*peri*	+	rejected
6b	*urb*	*peri*	+	rejected
6c	*fin*	*peri*	+	rejected
6d	*con*	*peri*	+	rejected
6e	*san*	*peri*	+	rejected
6f	*lab*	*peri*	−	rejected
6g	*geo*	*peri*	+ or −	supported
7a	*fin*	*dso*	+	rejected
7b	*lab*	*dso*	+	supported
7c	*san*	*dso*	−	rejected
7d	*pop*	*dso*	−	rejected
7e	*urb*	*dso*	−	rejected
7f	*con*	*dso*	−	supported
7g	*size*	*dso*	−	rejected
7h	*peri*	*dso*	−	rejected
7i	*geo*	*dso*	+ or −	supported
8	*lab or con*	*dso*	+ or −	rejected

Hypotheses 2a, 2b, 2c and 2d concerned the influences of demographic, economic and strategic variables on proportion of Conservative councillors. The effect of population size on proportion of Conservative councillors was expected to be negative and significant. The coefficient of population size was statistically significant at the level of 0.002; however, its slope was the opposite of that expected. Therefore, hypothesis 2a was rejected. The effect of degree of urbanisation (H2b) on proportion of Conservative councillors was significant, and its slope coefficient was the same as predicted. Hypothesis 2b, therefore, was supported. As regards the effect of fiscal independence, the analysis indicates that it is not significant in influencing proportion of Conservative councillors. The slope of the coefficient was expected to be positive; in actuality it was negative. The coefficient was not significantly different from zero (t-value of 1.433). This suggests that there is no significant relationship between fiscal independence and proportion of Conservative councillors. Hypothesis 2c, therefore, was rejected. The results of the path analysis for geographical location suggest that there is linkage between some regions (*dum5*, East Midlands; *dum6*, East Anglia; *dum8*, South-East) and proportion of Conservative councillors. Hence, hypothesis 2d was supported.

Hypotheses 3a, 3b, 3c and 3d also examined whether the demographic, economic and strategic variables affect proportion of Labour councillors. Both population size and degree of urbanisation were statistically significant in influencing proportion of Labour councillors, and in actuality the slope of the coefficients of both variables was the same as those predicted. Two hypotheses, 3a and 3b, therefore, were supported. The effect of fiscal independence on proportion of Labour councillors was expected to be negative, and in actuality it was. However, the coefficient was not significantly different from zero (t-value of -0.097). Therefore, hypothesis 3c was rejected. It was hypothesised that geographical location would be a significant factor affecting proportion of Labour councillors; in actuality it was. Four regions (*dum2*, Yorkshire and Humberside; *dum6*, East Anglia; *dum7*, South-West; *dum8*, South-East) were statistically significant in influencing proportion of Labour councillors. Therefore, hypothesis 3d was supported.

Hypotheses 4a, 4b, 4c, 4e and 4f concerned the influences of the demographic, economic, strategic and political variables on the number of sanctions issued against the local authority. None of the variables was significantly related to the number of the sanctions issued against the local authority. The findings provide no support for hypotheses 4a, 4b, 4c, 4d and 4e.

Hypotheses 5a, 5b, 5c, 5d, 5e, 5f and 5g examined whether the demographic, political, economic, strategic and organisational variables affected size of contract. Population size and degree of urbanisation were expected positively to affect size of contract, and in practice they did. Therefore, hypotheses 5a and 5b were supported. Geographical location (*dum8*, South-East) was also significant in influencing size of contract at the level of 0.000. Hypothesis 5g was also supported. Fiscal independence, proportion of Labour councillors, proportion of Conservative councillors and the number of sanctions issued against the local authority were insignificant in determining size of contract, thus providing no support for hypotheses 5c, 5d, 5e and 5f.

Hypotheses 6a, 6b, 6c, 6d, 6e, 6f and 6g concerned the influences of demographic, political, economic, strategic and organisational variables on the period of the contract. The proportion of Labour councillors was statistically significant, but in a direction opposite to that predicted, so hypothesis 6f must be rejected. Geographical location (*dum5*, East Midlands) was significant in affecting period of contract at the level of 0.008, so hypothesis 6g was supported. Population size, degree of urbanisation, fiscal independence, proportion of Conservative councillors and the number of sanctions issued against the local authority were not significant at the 95% confidence level. Hypotheses 6a, 6b, 6c, 6d, 6e and 6f were not supported by these findings.

Hypotheses 7a, 7b, 7c, 7d, 7e, 7f, 7g, 7h and 7i examined whether the final dependent variable, DSO output, is affected by population size, degree of urbanisation, fiscal independence, proportion of Labour councillors, proportion of Conservative councillors, the number of sanctions issued against the local authority and geographical location. The results of the analysis indicate that proportion of Conservative councillors and proportion of Labour councillors were significant in influencing DSO output. The slope coefficients were expected to be negative and positive respectively, which in actuality they were. The coefficients of the two variables were significantly different from zero (t-value of -1.87 and 2.35, respectively). These findings provide support for hypotheses 7b and 7f. Geographical location (*dum3*, North-West) was also significant in determining DSO output at the level of 0.001 so hypothesis 7i was supported. Other variables were statistically insignificant at the 95%

confidence level in influencing DSO output. Therefore, hypotheses 7a, 7c, 7d, 7e, 7g and 7h were not supported.

Hypothesis 8 examined whether the political variable is the strongest in influencing DSO output, the final dependent variable. Comparing the path coefficients of two significant independent variables, proportion of Labour councillors and geographical location (*dum3*), it becomes obvious that that of geographical location (0.26) is higher than that of proportion of Labour councillors (0.18). Therefore, hypothesis 8 was rejected. A summary of the decomposition of path coefficients is given in Table 4.8.

As Table 4.8 shows, the direct and indirect relationship of the variables in the data set for 1994 is simpler than that for 1991 (see Table 4.4). In sum, DSO output was directly affected by proportion of Labour councillors (*lab*, 0.18), proportion of Conservative councillors (*con*, -0.11) and geographical location (*dum3*, North West, 0.26), and indirectly by degree of urbanisation, population size and geographical location (*dum2, 6, 7, 8*) via the mediating variables of the proportion of Labour councillors and proportion of Conservative councillors. It is true that, as in the 1991 path model, political party composition, *lab* and *con*, was one of the important factors affecting DSO output. DSO output is a function of *lab, con, dum3, urb, pop, dum2, dum6, dum7* and *dum8*.

What is noticeable in the path model for 1994 is that the variable of geographical location emerged as one of the most important and direct factors in determining DSO output. This suggests that private companies interested in CCT chose particular regions as their main targets for competition in preference to other regions, believing that the latter might disadvantage the private companies or that they would not make profits in those regions.

In other words, one of the main differences between the 1991 and 1994 analyses is that while in the early stages of CCT the political factor was the strongest in affecting DSO output, over time private contractors chose specific regions as a strategic base according to previous experience and expanded this base into other regions. Goodwin (1994) explains that this reflects the growth strategy of 'base and spread' that was used by the multinationals during the 1980s, when their policy of mergers and acquisitions enabled them to gain bases nationally.

Figure 4.4 simplifies the relationships between DSO output and the other variables to make it easier to understand complicated causal

Table 4.8: Decomposition of path coefficients (1994)

Dependent variable	Independent variable	Direct effect	Indirect effect	Total effect
fin	urb	-0.20	0.00	-0.20
	dum5	0.13	0.00	0.13
con	urb	-0.29	0.00	-0.29
	pop	0.17	0.00	0.17
	dum5	0.15	0.00	0.15
	dum6	0.18	0.00	0.18
	dum8	0.42	0.00	0.42
lab	urb	0.43	0.00	0.43
	pop	0.11	0.00	0.11
	dum2	-0.12	0.00	-0.12
	dum6	-0.14	0.00	-0.14
	dum7	-0.36	0.00	-0.36
	dum8	-0.48	0.00	-0.48
peri	lab	0.16	0.00	0.16
	dum5	0.21	0.00	0.21
	urb	0.00	0.007	0.007
	pop	0.00	0.002	0.002
	dum2	0.00	-0.02	-0.02
	dum6	0.00	-0.02	-0.02
	dum7	0.00	-0.07	-0.06
	dum8	0.00	-0.08	-0.08
size	urb	0.17	0.00	0.17
	pop	0.50	0.00	0.50
	dum8	-0.27	0.00	-0.27
dso	con	0.11	0.00	0.11
	lab	0.18	0.00	0.18
	dum3	0.26	0.00	0.26
	urb	0.00	0.05	0.05
	pop	0.00	0.04	0.04
	dum2	0.00	-0.02	-0.02
	dum5	0.00	0.02	0.02
	dum6	0.00	-0.01	-0.01
	dum7	0.00	-0.06	-0.06
	dum8	0.00	-0.04	-0.04

Figure 4.4: Simple relationships (1994)

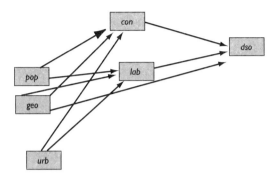

relationships. These findings can be interpreted to mean that, where the proportion of Labour councillors is high, the proportion of Conservative councillors is low, and, especially in the North–West region, there will be high levels of DSO output. Population size, degree of urbanisation and geographical location (Yorkshire and Humberside, East Anglia, the South–West and the South–East) affected DSO output indirectly (positively or negatively). It can be seen from these results that the data set for 1994 confirms that the political variables *lab* and *con* and one of the strategic variables, *geo*, were the most powerful determinants of DSO output.

Summary

The analysis for 1994 provided interesting findings in relation to private contracting. Proportion of Labour councillors, proportion of Conservative councillors and geographical location were each found to be significant factors which affect the percentage of DSO output for 1994.

The explanatory power of the hypothesised path model for 1994 is lower than that for 1991, not exceeding 12% for variations in DSO output in the data set for 1994. However, the number of local authorities which put their services out to tender for 1994, 146, is smaller than that for 1991, 215. This could account for the weak explanatory power of the equation.

However, one coefficient deserves comment. While the economic and organisational variables do not exert any direct influence on DSO output, proportion of Labour councillors (*lab*), proportion of Conservative councillors (*con*) and geographical location (*dum3*) have fairly strong positive and negative impacts on it. What is remarkable is that, for 1994, strength of geographical location is more powerful than that of the political variable in influencing DSO output. This suggests that the analysis for 1994 might have a different shape from that for 1991.

Although care should be taken not to overinterpret this finding, it indicates that local governments controlled by Labour are reluctant to introduce CCT, whereas local governments dominated by the Conservatives are more enthusiastic about it. More importantly, DSO output varies from region to region so is affected by geographical location. The North-West region, in particular, has a higher level of DSO output than other regions. The finding that DSO output varies corresponds to observations made in some other studies of CCT (Painter, 1990; 1991; 1992). However, the assumption that geographical location might affect the output of the privatisation policy has rarely been made.

Discussion

Relative strength of variables

Tables 4.3 and 4.7 show the relationships between the results of the equations for 1991 and 1994 and the hypotheses posited. These results suggest that, taken as a whole, there may not be as many contracting differences between 1991 and 1994, although some variables show an unexpected pattern. These results also show that the two analyses for 1991 and 1994 differ in terms of what dependent variables are affected by the independent variables. Tables 4.9 and 4.10 summarise the main similarities and differences between the two path analyses for the two years, particularly in terms of the direct and indirect effects of independent variables on the dependent variable, DSO output.

Summarising the results set out in Table 4.9, we may say that for 1991, the political variable does appear to have a significant effect on DSO output. However, in 1994 the strength of the political variable decreased, whereas the relative strength of the variable geographical location increased. In other words, Table 4.9 shows that in terms of the direct effect of the independent variables on the dependent variable, for 1991 the political variable, political composition of Labour councillors, was the strongest in affecting the DSO output, followed by proportion of

Table 4.9: Summary of the direct effects of variables

	pop	geo*	urb	fin	con	lab	san	size	peri
1991	-0.22	no	no	no	-0.25	0.37	no	0.13	no
1994	no	0.26	no	no	-0.11	0.18	no	no	no

Note: * the highest figure among the dummy variables (*dum2* to *dum8*) was used.

Table 4.10: Summary of the indirect effects of variables

	pop	geo*	urb	fin	con	lab	san	size	peri
1991	0.10	-0.17	0.10	0.02	no	no	no	no	no
1994	0.04	-0.06	0.05	no	no	no	no	no	no

Note: * the highest figure among the dummy variables (*dum2* to *dum8*) was used.

Conservative councillors, population size and contract size; whereas for 1994 the effect of geographical location on DSO output was the strongest, followed by political composition of Labour and Conservative councillors. It appears that many factors may account for the relative strength of the variables having changed over time. This will be discussed later in this chapter.

What is remarkable is that the effect of geographical location on DSO output was not significant at all in the analysis for 1991, while it became the strongest factor in the 1994 analysis. This reflects the fact that within the growth strategies of private firms some regions have been favoured as an initial base from which to expand before moving on to other parts of the UK. The effect of geographical location will be discussed in more detail later in the chapter.

As Table 4.10 shows, in 1991, in terms of the indirect effects of independent variables on the dependent variable, DSO output, the effect of the variable geographical location was the strongest, followed by population size and degree of urbanisation together; whereas in 1994, geographical location had the strongest effect.

What is particularly noteworthy is the apparent weakening, in the 1994 analysis, of the indirect effects of the independent variables on DSO output, compared to in 1991. In this analysis the interaction between the independent variables and the dependent variable is filtered through the mediating variables, mainly the political variable. From this it can be concluded that in 1994 geographical location rather than the political variable was the most significant factor determining DSO output, both in terms of direct and indirect effects.

Methodological discussion

This section will discuss the methodological issues connected with the results of the two path analyses for 1991 and 1994, focusing on the overall characteristics and the differences between the two path models.

On the basis of the results, it is accepted that the direct and indirect effects of the independent variables on the dependent variables for 1994 are relatively weak,[2] compared to those for 1991, suggesting an inconsistent effect which is peculiar to a particular year. According to Boyne (1996b, p 249), the impact of a local political party on policy output might be unpredictable and sporadic, and fluctuate across areas and over time. This analysis result corresponds with his argument. To account for this relative inconsistency several factors need to be considered.

One reason for this relatively inconsistent and weak pattern might be related to time-lags. Contracts were given either to private contractors or to the DSO for a fixed period of time. During that time, a change in political control could not result in a change of arrangement; the new leadership of the council would have to wait until the contracts were due for renewal. Therefore, the time-lag effect of the political variable should be taken into account (Boyne, 1996a, pp 245-6; Sharpe, 1981, p 8). To take the effect of time-lags[3] into account, data on political party composition in 1988, along with data on DSO output in 1991, was used for the 1991 path analysis – see Table 4.11. Likewise, data on the political variable for 1991, along with data on DSO output in 1994, was used for the 1994 path analysis – see Table 4.12.

When data on the political variable for 1988 was used for the 1991 path analysis, the effects of the political variable on DSO output were slightly increased and the explanatory power of the equation was also increased. As Table 4.11 shows, the explanatory power (R^2) of the equation in which the data for 1988 was used for the 1991 analysis was increased from 0.16 to 0.17. Similarly, the coefficients of the political variable (*con* and *lab*) were also increased from -0.25 and 0.37 to -0.29 and 0.39 respectively.

Table 4.11: Effects of time-lags on DSO output (1991)

Dependent variable	F	Sig	R^2	Independent variable	Beta	t-value	t-probability
dso*	10.05	0.00	0.16	size	0.13	1.87	0.06
				con	-0.25	-3.25	0.00
				lab	0.37	4.85	0.00
				pop	-0.22	-2.87	0.00
dso†	10.48	0.00	0.17	size	0.14	1.92	0.06
				con	-0.29	-4.03	0.00
				lab	0.39	4.98	0.00
				pop	-0.20	-2.67	0.008

Notes: * Data for 1991 applied; † data for 1988 applied.

Table 4.12: Effects of time-lags on DSO output (1994)

Dependent variable	F	Sig	R^2	Independent variable	Beta	t-value	t-probability
dso*	9.88	0.0001	0.12	con	-0.11	-1.87	0.01
				lab	0.18	2.35	0.01
				dum3	0.26	3.36	0.001
dso†	10.16	0.0001	0.13	con	-0.15	-2.01	0.01
				lab	0.20	2.45	0.01
				dum3	0.27	3.35	0.001

Notes: * Data for 1994 applied; † data for 1991 applied.

Similarly, Table 4.12 shows the effects of time-lags on DSO output in the 1994 path analysis by presenting data for 1991 alongside data for 1994.

A second reason for the equations being inconsistent might be because the proportion of Liberal Democratic councillors was omitted in the analysis, despite being relatively high (Table 4.13), meaning that an unstable pattern of equation might be produced.

As Table 4.13 shows, the degree of Liberal Democratic Party composition has increased and has accounted for a somewhat large proportion of political party composition. This significant political change in terms of the political composition of local councillors should be an

Table 4.13: Proportion of Liberal Democrat councillors

	1988	1991	1994
M	0.16	0.19	0.21
SD	0.14	0.17	0.18

Notes: M = mean; SD = standard deviation.

important factor affecting the difference in DSO output between 1991 and 1994. For example, in a situation where the Labour Party requests support from the Liberal Democrats and also the number of Liberal Democrat councillors is growing, it might be hypothesised that such a constellation would generate complexities of policy implementation at the local level. However, the fact that this research did not take this into account might explain the weak and unstable explanatory power of the variables.

A third reason for the inconsistent and weak pattern might be also linked to the operationalisation of the variables. In this study the political variable (*con* and *lab*) was intended to represent the proportion of local councillors from each political party among the total local councillors. However, it is important to consider that the UK has a system which is highly majority-dominated. A party needs a stake in an authority of more than 50% to be sure of influencing policy so even if Labour makes big gains in an authority, it may find it difficult to reverse a contracting out decision without an overall majority. This means that to identify the effects of an overall majority in each year the local authorities need to be classified in terms of whether Labour had overall control (more than 50% of members), the Conservatives had overall control or neither had overall control. For this purpose, 215 local authorities for 1991 and 146 for 1994 were divided into three categories: local authorities with a Labour majority; those with a Conservative majority; those with a Liberal Democratic majority and hung councils.

It appears from Table 4.14 that the percentage of local governments controlled by one political party (more than 50% of members) has noticeably changed. Generally speaking, since 1988, as the national popularity of the Conservatives has declined, their representation in local government has fallen. As it has fallen, Labour has strengthened its hold

Table 4.14: Local governments by political party majority by year
(number and %)

	1988		1991		1994	
	Number	%	Number	%	Number	%
Conservative	132	44.4	77	25.9	78	26.3
Labour	60	20.2	85	28.6	76	25.6
Others	101	34.0	131	44.1	142	47.8
Missing	4	1.3	4	1.3	1	0.3
Total	297	100	297	100	297	100

Note: Liberal Democrat councillors = (1988) 8, (1991) 21, (1994) 33.

Table 4.15: ANOVA of DSO output by political party (1991, 1994)

	1991			1994		
Group	Mean	F	Sig	Mean	F	Sig
Conservative	57.53	13.53	0.000	46.85	2.42	0.06
Labour	87.50			67.17		
Others	55.88			51.31		

in urban areas, but in many rural and suburban areas (particularly in the South) the Liberal Democrats have been the main party to gain.

As Table 4.14 and Figure 4.5 show, three groups exhibit different types of DSO output. Analysis of variance (ANOVA) was used to examine whether the means of the DSO outputs for the three groups are significantly different. Table 4.15 demonstrates that the means of the DSO outputs for the three groups were statistically significantly different at the significance level of 0.1.

Table 4.15 and Figure 4.5 show that the means of the DSO outputs for the three groups were significantly different, which supports not only the argument that DSO output was affected by the political variable but also the assumption that the analysis based on the classification of local governments using 'an overall majority' would increase the statistical significance of the variables relationship. Using that classification, the explanatory power was increased slightly in the path analysis, but not

Figure 4.5: DSO output by political party (1991, 1994)

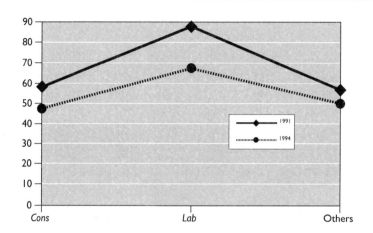

noticeably. It is assumed that where the proportion of Labour councillors is high, there will be higher levels of DSO output. More specifically, it is generally held that local governments in which Labour (or the Conservatives) have overall control (more than 50% of members) would show higher (or lower) levels of DSO output.

Theoretical discussion

Although the relationships between the dependent and independent variables are inconsistent, some of the variables which were significant in the analysis for 1991 were also significant in the analysis for 1994. For example, the political variable, political party composition, was significant in both analyses. Although for the final dependent variable, DSO output, the path coefficients of proportion of Labour councillors and proportion of Conservative councillors for 1994 (0.18 and -0.11 respectively) are lower than those for 1991 (0.37 and -0.25 respectively), only the political variable was significant in influencing DSO output in both analyses.

The finding that the political variable is one of the most important factors affecting success or failure in the privatisation policy of local government services accords with the conclusions of much existing research (Carnaghan and Bracewell-Milnes, 1993; Key, 1987; Mohan, 1986; Stoker, 1991; Yager, 1993).

The political party composition of local councillors had an important effect on how local authorities have approached the whole issue of CCT. The way in which the councillors in the districts have reacted to CCT can be considered an important feature of the success or failure of CCT in different districts (Goodwin, 1994, p 55).

It is noticeable that in the analysis for 1994 a reduction in the overall effect of the political variable appeared to have occurred. As Walsh and Davis (1993, p 24) suggest, this is due in part to the fact that the level of local councillors' involvement in the CCT process had reduced significantly over time. They point out that the involvement was highest in the early stages, when local authorities were considering how they should deal with the issue, and when a clear policy had not developed. They also indicate that the central mechanisms established for local councillors' involvement tended to persist, but with a diminishing role.

The politics of competition had changed to some degree, as was shown in the two path models. It was still a matter of basic political polarisation, with Labour against and the Conservatives in favour, but that opposition was less clear, because Labour authorities have tended to see the advantages of competition in terms of financial and service gains (Walsh and Davis, 1993, p 27). According to Walsh and Davis (1993, pp 24 and 26), the degree of political salience was a matter of priorities, and more generally the shift in priorities has been away from that of winning in the face of competition, towards a focus on the customer and on the services.

What is more noticeable in the contrast between the two path analyses for 1991 and 1994 is the role of geographical location, which affected directly and indirectly the variances in DSO output, unlike in the analysis for 1991. It is assumed that the DSO output for 1994 varied, depending on where the local authority was located. The findings suggest that while in the early stage of CCT the political variable dominated the CCT process, over time geographical location has been replacing it, coming to be the most important factor influencing DSO output. It can be assumed that there are many reasons for this situation including changes in the strategy of private firms, the reduced role of local councillors over time, and changes in the legal framework for CCT.

The fact that geographical location has become the strongest factor affecting DSO output in the 1994 analysis is surprising. However, up until now insufficient attention has been paid to the factor of geographical location in studies of CCT. As regards the direct effects of geographical location on DSO output, Table 4.16 shows more clearly that this variable emerged as an important determinant of the variances in the DSO output for 1994.

Table 4.16 and Figure 4.6 show that in some regions, Yorkshire and Humber, the North-West and East Anglia, DSO output for 1994 increased considerably while in the other regions it decreased.

As Table 4.16 shows, the analysis of variance (ANOVA), which was used to test statistical significance of DSO output by group, confirms

Table 4.16: ANOVA of DSO output by geographical location (1991, 1994)

	North	Yorks and Humber-side	North-West	West Midlands	East Midlands	East Anglia	South-West	South-East
1991	90.74	57.14	93.33	68.42	69.69	60.71	59.17	57.45
1994	66.67	80.00	98.61	56.77	42.22	61.12	41.67	45.42

Notes: For 1991, the F value was 2.503, and sig 0.017. For 1994, the F value was 3.015, and sig 0.006.

Figure 4.6: DSO output by geographical location (1991, 1994)

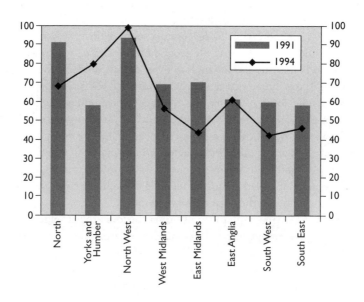

that DSO output varies significantly from region to region, at the 95% confidence level. The result of the analysis indicates that the variable geographical location is closely related to the dependent variable, DSO proportion. These findings are supported by Sharpe and Newton's conclusion, in their study of local government services (1984, p 114), that what might be termed geographical, spatial or locational variables are important determinants of local policy. These results also imply that the pattern and practices of contracting out in local authorities had altered to a certain extent owing to the effect of geographical location.

In relation to the geographical variation in DSO output, what is noteworthy is the strong relationship between the political variable (*con* and *lab*) and geographical location, shown in Table 4.2 for 1991 and Table 4.6 for 1994. The results of the analysis of variance (ANOVA) of political party composition by geographical location indicate the feature more clearly (Table 4.17).

As Table 4.17 shows, political party composition differed according to geographical location, and the analysis of variance (ANOVA) showed that the effect of geographical location on the political party composition of the local authority was statistically significant. In other words, both

Table 4.17: ANOVA of political party composition by geographical location (1991, 1994)

	Labour		Conservative	
	1991	1994	1991	1994
North	0.48	0.48	0.18	0.16
Yorkshire and Humberside	0.31	0.26	0.26	0.31
North-West	0.48	0.46	0.34	0.35
West Midlands	0.36	0.34	0.31	0.31
East Midlands	0.39	0.39	0.37	0.37
East Anglia	0.28	0.26	0.42	0.44
South-West	0.18	0.16	0.29	0.29
South-East	0.22	0.20	0.47	0.45
Average	0.30	0.28	0.37	0.36
F value	7.336	9.057	11.196	9.520
Sig	0.000	0.000	0.000	0.000

the Labour and Conservative composition of local councillors differed significantly according to geographical location.

That the spatial extent of privatisation should reflect variations in the political composition of public bodies such as local authorities or health boards was a central hypothesis put forward in Stubbs's (1990) analysis of contracting out in New Zealand. Stubbs expected that conservatively-minded officials would be more likely to initiate a trimming down of the public sector and its associated costs in favour of private provision. However, owing to the political uniformity of health boards in New Zealand he concluded that political differences in the composition of health boards management was not an important factor. In the UK, however, the politics of local administrations and their attitudes to contracting out are very important factors influencing local service provision (Goodwin, 1994, p 58). The reason for the greater divergences in political attitudes in the UK is that, unlike in New Zealand or other countries, rather than representing a response to changing needs competitive tendering was compulsorily imposed on local authorities by the British Conservative government. In other words, the local authority–central government interface has been far more difficult in the UK, making the political attitude of local authorities particularly relevant to the geography of contracting out.

What is important here is to identify the net influences of geographical location incurred by private sector choices, eliminating the effect of the political variable. These influences can then be analysed to measure their effects on DSO output.

The effect of geographical location on DSO output for 1991 was not statistically significant. Accordingly, the factor of geographical location had no net effect on DSO output in the analysis for 1991. A regression analysis was conducted to measure its net effect for 1994. The net effect on DSO output, with party effect eliminated, was 0.09, accounting for a considerable portion of the total effect (0.12: see Table 4.6) of the three significant independent variables on DSO output. This suggests that for 1994 the net effect of geographical location independent of the political effect has replaced the party effect.

There are many reasons for these private sector preferences that have fashioned the extent of contracting out for 1994. One important aspect of provider behaviour is the perception that the private sector was concentrating on 'welcoming authorities' in the short term (Walsh et al,

1997, p 110). It is clear that private firms have strategically favoured some regions as an initial base from which to expand before moving on to other regions of the UK. It is assumed that through this strategy they can save overheads and logistics. This policy of 'base and spread' may help explain the private sector's behaviour (Goodwin, 1994, p 83). This changed behaviour on the part of tendering parties, private contractors in particular, is significant in that it leads to an alternative hypothesis to the conventional one.

In the analysis for 1991 the effect of contract size was statistically significant (path coefficient, 0.13) whereas in the analysis for 1994 it was not. The period of contract had no effect in either path model. Invitations by local authorities for private companies to tender for services are by no means a guarantee that a submission will be made. The size and duration of the contract are just two of the many criteria that could influence whether a company puts in a bid. All of these factors influence the contractors' expected success rate in tendering and their expected profit should they win the contract (Goodwin, 1994, p 78).

In the analysis for 1991, contract size influenced DSO output significantly, but the contract period did not. Initially, it was hypothesised that contract period is associated with DSO output. The reason for this is that contracts which are too short can increase transaction costs on the part mainly of private contractors because they must go through the tendering procedures more often, and because start-up costs are written off over a short period. However, the hypothesis was rejected in both models. This was probably because of the low level of the standard deviation of the variable. In other words, as was reported by the Institute of Public Finance (McGuirk, 1992), the contract periods determined by local authorities were almost identical, so that there were no significant statistical relationships with DSO output.

From the 1991 analysis results it was hypothesised that contract size is negatively related to DSO output. The hypothesis is primarily based on the assumption that, as Milne (1987) suggests, small contracts discourage submissions because the contract size influences the contractor's expected return. It is not surprising that Milne found that the main contractors had limited their bids to those where there was some degree of assured return. Sherman (1985) emphasises this point when she notes how contract catering firms avoided contracts for small hospitals (those with fewer than 40 beds) which offered low profits (less than £5,000).

Low-value contracts are uncertain prospects because of the high costs of creating and submitting a tender and the financial risks of taking on small contracts with tight profit margins. The consequence of this need for large contracts has been the concentration of private sector tendering activity in and around urban districts where the volume of work is greatest (Goodwin, 1994, p 79).

However, contrary to this the relationship between contract size and DSO output found in the analysis was positive, so the hypothesis was rejected. The reason the direction was opposite to that predicted is because of the controls being *too* large. As will be found in the case study analysis in Chapter Seven, the local authorities hostile to CCT deliberately made contracts as large as possible to discourage private bidders (Walsh et al, 1997).

The practice of making contracts too big has often been regarded as anticompetitive, either in the sense of making it difficult to find private contractors able to offer an alternative to the larger DSOs, or in the sense of making much of the work suitable only for the largest private contractors (Carnaghan and Bracewell-Milnes, 1993, p 97). McGuirk (1992, pp 22-30) points out in relation to vehicle maintenance that the annual average size of contracts has risen, and that local contractors have consistently complained that the funding required to handle projects of this size tends to exclude all but the larger companies. Ground maintenance contracts are considered too large by many companies, who would like to see them broken down into manageable sizes. Many catering contractors are put off from bidding for school catering by several factors, including the very large size of contracts and the numerous sites involved. In reality it seems that the private contractors' strategy was less effective than that of local authorities.

The fact that the effect of contract size was not statistically significant in the analysis for 1994 implies that over time the legal framework for CCT became tighter. As will be discussed in the later chapters, central government defined making contracts too big as anticompetitive behaviour. It is presumed that as time has gone on that strategy has been used less by local authorities. More details will be discussed in the case study analysis.

Regarding the other variables, including the two demographic variables, although some of them affected DSO proportion directly and indirectly, their influence was not significant compared to that of the political variable and the variable of geographic location. For example, population size negatively affected DSO proportion, as was predicted in the hypothesis. However, its influence was not great in comparison to that of the political variable. This indicates that it is necessary to conduct more qualitative research work such as case studies to gain more understanding about CCT practices. For this reason Chapter Seven explores the bidding strategies and preferences of the private sector using information from interviews to examine the salience of the arguments of the private sector preferences.

Conclusions

In the way described above, I have developed the original study framework that described DSO output, and its relationships to several environmental variables surrounding local government CCT has now been tested. Through analysis of path coefficients and elimination of the weak paths the original hypothesised model has been refined to a trimmed model that should be a useful departure point for future researchers interested in pursuing how DSO output can be acquired. Five main points about these findings are worth stressing briefly.

- The results are generally not bad in statistical terms, in the sense that there are some significant beta weights even though many hypotheses are rejected. However, it should be noted that over the time period 1991 to 1994, the political variable, political party composition, and geographical location prove themselves to be among the most powerful explanatory variables so far as DSO output is concerned. In data sets for two years, organisational and economic variables have been found less useful than the political and geographical variable in explaining the variance in DSO outputs.

- Perhaps the most significant results are that in the earlier stages of CCT implementation the effect of the political variable on DSO proportion was the strongest, whereas in the later stage the effect of geographical location was the strongest. This implies that over time, member involvement in the CCT process declined and instead the private sector played an important role in the CCT process. In the field of academic and practical literature on privatisation policy, the variable geographical location has not been given much attention up until now. Although this variable was not significant in the analysis for 1991, in 1994 it was the most powerful factor affecting DSO output, leading to the assumption that contracting practices and patterns in 1994 took a different path from in 1991.

• It is generally accepted that the direct and indirect effects of independent variables on dependent variables are relatively inconsistent. The reasons for this may include the small size of samples for 1994 (146 local authorities), the effect of time-lapses, the issue of an overall majority and the problem of the Liberal Democratic Party. Several other questions[4] may also be involved. The questions to be addressed in the future study are as follows:

> • Had the previous arrangements been satisfactory from the service delivery point of view?
>
> • Had the contractor fulfilled the contract?
>
> • Had the contract been profitable for the contractor?

These questions relate to the statistical inconsistency of the equations analysed earlier. They should continue to be investigated via empirical study in the future to understand more fully the output of competitive tendering policy.

• Despite a measure of inconsistency, the findings provide the strong proposition that the political, demographic, strategic and organisation variables for two research periods were found to be significant in explaining the variances in DSO output.

• Despite the methodological efforts, causal modelling does not seem to provide any solution to the basic problem of how some environmental factors are affecting policy output, DSO output, and what role environmental factors play in this process. These results imply that another approach should be used to discuss this question.

For the reasons mentioned above, including the relatively low R-squared coefficient and the inconsistency of the equations, these results would justify the conclusion that other factors not suggested in the hypothesised path model are more important than political, demographic, economic, strategic and organisational variables. Alternatively, the results would also support the conclusion that political, demographic and other factors make a significant contribution to DSO output, because all the R-squared coefficients of the two path models for DSO output are statistically acceptable. It depends somewhat on your viewpoint what you want to emphasise, and what you are trying to prove. Politics and other factors matter, both in the political process that leads to the making of decisions and in the outputs of those decisions, although not all outputs show this clearly. At the same time, the results of this study clearly suggest that students of public policy should spend more time trying to understand the implementation process that underlies CCT output.

Given the fact that the political, demographic, economic, strategic and other variables are significantly related to DSO output, how do they affect the level of the DSO success rate, and how do they influence the way in which DSO output can be made, defeating competitors from the private sector? This is the important question associated with the CCT process. Further research, going deeper into the question of how the variables affected DSO output, produces some interesting results. To gain a deeper understanding of the determinants of DSO output, research needs to concentrate on how DSO output was achieved.

Theoretical models to explain the mechanism whereby 'environmental' or 'resource' factors affect DSO output in each local authority have not been sufficiently developed. Chapter Five deals with transaction cost theory in order to provide a coherent and theoretically meaningful framework for this.

Notes

[1] In order to prevent biases and distortions in regression analysis, three problems (multicollinearity, autocorrelation and heteroscedascity) should be solved. Multicollinearity refers to the situation in which the independent variables are highly correlated, although there is, understandably, no agreement as to what 'high' means. Some commentators speak of different degrees of multicollinearity. Autocorrelation refers to the violation of the assumption that errors associated with one observation are not correlated with errors associated with any other observation. The autocorrelation affects the validity of tests of significance. Heteroscedascity means the violation of the assumption that the variance of the residuals is constant for all levels of the independent variables (Pedhazur and Schmelkin, 1991, p 392). The foregoing assumptions are required in order to obtain the best linear

unbiased estimates of parameters. For further discussion, see Hanushek and Jackson (1977, pp 46-56).

[2] However, if the explanatory power of independent variables to dependent variable is higher than 5%, the equation is accepted as statistically significant and valid (Kerlinger and Pedhazur, 1973).

[3] For more discussion of time-lag effects, see Boyne (1996a, pp 245-6).

[4] Apart from these questions, the residuals from these path models might be explained by differences in efficiency between authorities, or incomplete or incorrect specification of the model, inevitable in all modelling of social systems and measurement error (Barnett et al, 1990, p 218).

FIVE

Politics of the transaction cost approach

Introduction

This chapter discusses the politics of transaction cost approach with a view to describing and analysing the main features of the political and bureaucratic setting within which CCT policy has been implemented and classifying the types of relationships that can exist among different actors within these settings.

As was stated in Chapter Four, proportion of Labour councillors, proportion of Conservative councillors, size of contract and population size were found to be the most crucial factors in directly determining the degree of DSO output as a policy output for 1991, whereas for 1994, proportion of Labour councillors, proportion of Conservative councillors and geographical location were the significant factors. The next step is to investigate how the DSO output has been made.

When economists and other public policy analysts think about economic policy, they often frame the basic question as a confrontation between markets and governments. On the one side are those who believe that markets are prone to failure, that governments emerge to correct the failures of markets and that on the whole they are capable of doing so. On the other side, there are those who believe that markets perform well and that governments are the problem, not the solution (Dixit, 1996, p 1). As usual, reality is much more complex and defeats any attempt to represent it by such neat dichotomies. Markets have their flaws, as do governments, and observers and analysts of the two systems have their own limitations.

This study attempts to bring a different perspective to the issues of economic policy making and their analysis. Its starting points are simple to the point of being trite: markets and governments are both imperfect systems; both are unavoidable aspects of reality; the operation of each is powerfully influenced by the existence of the other. Most importantly, it shall be argued that the political process should be viewed as a game played by many participants who try to affect the actions of the immediate policy maker (Nakamura and Smallwood, 1980).

What follows from these observations is orthogonal to, and perhaps destructive of, the whole 'markets versus governments' debate. The equilibrium or the output of the game of policy making will typically not maximise anything. Any attempts to design or even identify the desiderata for a truly optimal system are doomed to failure, and no grand or general results about the superiority of one organisational form over another can be expected (Dixit, 1996). What is possible is to understand how the whole system, consisting of markets and governments, copes with the whole set of problems of conflicting information, incentives and actions that preclude a fully ideal output. What will be offered here is a structure or framework that can help our thinking about specific issues of economic policy making and, occasionally, make it possible to identify some specific points at which intervention could usefully occur. However, it is not expected that this will lead to any settling of debates; the issues are too large and too complex, and this study was too brief to permit more than exploratory research.

This chapter will begin by briefly reviewing the two main alternatives that have dominated economic policy analysis during the last five decades, and suggest a synthesis, labelled 'the politics of transaction costs', that views policy making as a dynamic process. This idea will then be further developed, and an attempt will be made to bring some recent literature on political economy within its scope. Finally, an analytical framework for the study based on the theoretical backgrounds concerned will be constructed.

Approaches to economic policy analysis

As an applied discipline, policy analysis draws from a variety of disciplines and professions whose aims are descriptive and prescriptive, not only from the social and behavioural sciences, but also from public administration, law, philosophy, ethics, and various branches of systems analysis and applied mathematics (Dunn, 1994, p 62).

In general, the controversy about how policy decisions should be made has involved a dispute between the prescriptive–rational and the pragmatic approach (Hill, 1997b, p 99). Hill's dichotomy relates to another dichotomy between the normative and the positive approach. While these two divided approaches do not cover all the perspectives of the policy analysis carried out so far, the taxonomy offered may prove useful in confirming the broad array of observed policy analysis perspectives. The following discussion will outline the main arguments of the two approaches.

Normative approach to policy analysis

The normative approach to policy analysis is concerned with recommending future courses of action that may resolve public problems. In this case the question is one of action (what should be done?) and the type of information produced is prescriptive. For example, a policy of guaranteed minimum annual incomes may be recommended as a way to resolve problems of poverty (Dunn, 1994, pp 62-3).

Much of the theory, and almost all of the practice, of economic policy analysis views the making and implementation of the policy as a technical problem, even as a control engineering problem. You start with a model of the workings of the economy, along with some degrees of freedom, or some instruments of policy intervention. You then assume an evaluation criterion. Finally, you calculate the values of the instruments that will maximise the criterion, or directions of change that will improve the performance as judged by the criterion (Dixit, 1996, p 4). These policy choices, or reforms, are to be recommended to the government, or offered in public discussion, as the right ones. The specification of the economic models, policy instruments and evaluation criteria varies greatly in different applications. It also varies between countries. While cumulative research over time has greatly improved understanding of the issues involved in specifying models of the economy, the above description of the method of policy analysis retains its general validity.

Over time, the normative approach to policy has been greatly enriched in its treatment of the underlying model of the economy. Impressive as these achievements are, they assume a single social-welfare-maximising principle and thereby leave out a crucial aspect of economic policy making, namely, the political process. As a crude but effective caricature, it can be said that normative policy analysis began by supposing that the policy was made by an omnipotent, omniscient and benevolent dictator (Ham and Hill, 1993; Nakamura and Smallwood, 1980; Dixit, 1996). The work on the second-best removed the omnipotence. That on information removed the omniscience. However, the assumptions of benevolence and dictatorship have remained unaffected by all these improvements in the general understanding of the limits of instruments and information (Dixit, 1996).

The normative approach continues to view policy making as a purely technical problem. The implicit assumption is that once a policy that maximises or improves social welfare has been found and recommended, it will be implemented as designed, and the desired effects will follow (Hill, 1993b, pp 97-102). In reality, a policy proposal is merely the beginning of a process that is political at every stage – not merely the process of legislation, but also the implementation, including the choice or formation of an administrative agency and the subsequent operation of this agency. The standard normative approach to policy analysis views this whole process as a social-welfare-maximising black box, exactly as the neo-classical theory of production and supply viewed the firm as a profit-maximising black box (Dixit, 1996, p 9).

While some useful insights follow from this approach, it leaves important gaps in understanding and gives misleading ideas about the possibilities for beneficial policy intervention. Economists studying business and industrial organisation have long recognised the inadequacy of the neo-classical view of the firm and have developed richer paradigms and models based on the concepts of various types of transaction costs. Policy analysis also stands to benefit from such an approach, opening the black box and examining the actual workings of the mechanism inside. That is the starting point, and a recurrent theme, of this study. In brief, the normative approach to policy analysis does not emphasise the importance of the political process, whose essence is that many participants simultaneously try to influence the actions of the immediate policy maker. The equilibrium of this strategical game needs to be modelled (Chandler, 1988; Dixit, 1996; North, 1990b).

Positive approach to policy analysis

The best known alternative to normative policy analysis is the public choice or contractarian framework, long championed by Buchanan (1973, 1975, 1987, 1988), Niskanen (1971), Tullock (1965) and others. Tullock's work is generally regarded as among the earliest contributions to the public choice approach, although it does not contain much by way of economic theory. His critical observations on the self-serving nature of bureaucracy and his critique with Buchanan of party competition and its consequences (Buchanan and Tullock, 1962) may be said to have laid the basis for a debate about the dangers of the power of bureaucracy and the politicisation of the economic and public policy which other theorists – such as Niskanen – were to examine from the standpoint of economic models (Dixit, 1996, pp 13-14; Parsons, 1995, p 307).

Public choice can be defined as the economics of non-market decision making, or as simply the application of economics to political science. The subject matter of public choice is the same as that of political science: the theory of the state, voting rules, voter behaviour, party politics, bureaucracy, and so on. However, the methodology of public choice is that of economics (Mueller, 1979, p 1).

Buchanan grounds his thought upon the individual's capacity for attending to his own interests and engaging in mutually beneficial trade with others, whether in the market or the political realm. He emphasises the distinction between the constitution that governs the whole policy process and individual instances of policy making within this constitution. Constitutions are seen as a method of making commitments credible (Dixit, 1996; Self, 1993). This constitution should include more stringent safeguards than mere majority voting in order to check the incursions on individual interests of transient or tyrannical majorities (Buchanan and Tullock, 1962).

For Buchanan, the outcome of any particular policy making exercise is determined by the working of the process within the rules that were laid down. At this stage there are no degrees of freedom, so normative analysis is irrelevant. For public choice theory everyone knows that the constitution under discussion will continue to set the rules of the game for a long time to come (Dixit, 1996; Self, 1993).

Tullock (1965) has a similar theme, and makes a specific assumption about individual preferences. For Tullock the study of politics, policy making and bureaucracy should be based on the same assumption that were used to explain the behaviour of firms, business people and consumers: self-interest (Parsons, 1995, p 307). This line of economic enquiry has examined the selection and consequences of various decision-making rules in the political arena, from unanimity to majority rule to dictatorship (Twight, 1983, p 12).

Public choice theory sees political competition to win support as an activity that can be analysed like economic 'market' behaviour. It has

•

provided a set of arguments to support an attack on public bureaucracy and has stimulated thinking about how organisational outputs are analysed (Hill, 1997b, pp 74-6). The public choice approach is recognised as being important in its emphasis on the political process but, on the whole, it appears that the normative mode continues to command broader support (Dixit, 1996).

Hill (1997b, p 75) argues that "this theory has an intuitive plausibility, but comparatively little empirical evidence has been produced to support it". Dixit (1996, pp 17-18) also claims that the normative approach came ready equipped with an elegant formal apparatus, which facilitated the development of models elaborating its foundations, whereas the public choice approach initially consisted of a concept, lacking a general organising formalism, so that specific models were slow to develop.

Specifically, one important methodological problem with the public choice approach is that although policy rules and acts are useful and can be idealised conceptual categories which help to focus thought, in reality the distinction between them is more gradual, and there are some degrees of freedom for intervention at almost all points. If constitutions are contracts, they are very incomplete ones. A constitution never lays down the clear, firm, and comprehensive sets of rules that the contractrian approach depicts, so there is room for manoeuvre in individual acts. Constitutions do not spell out the rules and procedures to be followed in every conceivable instance in precise detail. They leave much to be interpreted and determined in specific future eventualities (Dixit, 1996, pp 16-31).

Previous research associated with privatisation policy conducted from the public choice perspective was based primarily on the concept of competition and emphasised the positive consequences of contracting out. However, this perspective does not recognise problems concerning the relationships between government organisations and contractors, excessive government control and restrictive regulations, and the lack of coherent public policy, all of which might have possible negative consequences. As DeHoog puts it, "Negative unanticipated consequences" may occur when "the ideal process model of contracting" is not utilised (1985, p 432).

As regards variations in DSO output influenced by political party composition and other variables, investigated in Chapter Four, it seems that a different perspective is required to understand more fully the CCT policy process. Those who anticipate potential personal or collective gain from contracting out can, politically or administratively, control the CCT process. Because of this, the test of DSO output needs to recognise the constraints imposed on the parties involved in the CCT process.

The drawbacks to the positive approach to policy analysis suggest the need for a synthesis of the normative and positive approaches. This requires the history and the institutions of the politics to be taken seriously but also permits useful economic input of various types, as will be seen in the next section.

Transaction cost perspective

Necessity for a new perspective

If the distinction between policy rules and acts is one of degree rather than of type, and if rules are subject to erosion and reinterpretation (Hill, 1997a, p 89) while acts can create durable facts and institutions, how then should the process be viewed, and what are the appropriate roles for positive and normative analysis? The required framework for analysis must be more flexible and more dynamic. It should treat policy making as a dynamic process that constantly combines some features of rule-making and some of individual acts in varying degrees. Economic policy making is a dynamic game whose conditions are uncertain and changing, and whose rules are at least partly made up by the participants as they go along (Dixit, 1996). Each participant will try to manipulate the operation of the subsequent game to try to achieve an outcome that favours his or her own interests.

The nature of these manipulations has been understood following the pioneering work of Schelling (1960): they represent various commitments, some unconditional, others specifying response rules that are contingent on others' future actions. Schelling calls such actions "strategic moves". In this view of the policy process the degrees of freedom mostly consist of opportunities to make various strategic moves.

It is assumed that the transaction cost perspective can serve as a conceptual bridge linking the large body of neo-classical economic theory, in which it is firmly rooted, to much of the non-economic literature on public organisations that shares its view of institutions as governance structures. According to Bryson (1984, p 460), it holds considerable promise in terms of allowing both public organisations and public policy to be understood. Moe (1984, p 740) sees it as destined to provide one of the major competing perspectives in the analysis of public organisations.

This perspective can enable a synthesis between the normative and the contractarian approaches to policy mentioned earlier. Each policy act can be viewed, not as a choice to be made to maximise a social welfare function, but as an episode or play of the game within the set of existing rules and institutions, while at the same time admitting some leeway to make strategic moves that are capable of affecting or altering future rules and institutions (Alvesson, 1993; Dixit, 1996; North, 1990b; Pettigrew and Whipp, 1991). Constitutions and rules should also be viewed not as sacred texts written under ideal *ex ante* conditions of lack of conflict, leading to unanimity and providing a complete set of rules for the making of future policy acts, but as incomplete contracts which cope with a complex and changing world and contain some provisions for procedures to deal with unforeseen contingencies, yet which are subject to explicit amendments as well as changes implicitly inflicted by policy acts (Dixit, 1996).

Transaction cost perspective

This review of the normative and positive alternatives in economic policy analysis engenders a perspective that combines some elements of each approach, yet differs from both in essential ways. Economic policy making should be seen as an ongoing, imperfect and incomplete process, with powerful but slow dynamics.

This viewpoint has many similarities with the account of economic institutions that has been developed by Williamson (1975; 1989; 1991), North (1990a; 1990b), Twight (1988; 1994) and others. The organising concept of their analysis is transaction costs. In the present study, much attention is paid to Williamson's theory of transaction cost. Before giving an outline of his work, it will facilitate later discussion to first acknowledge the economic antecedents on which his work is built.

Antecedents of transaction cost economics

Perhaps the obvious place to start is Arrow, the first author to use the term 'transaction costs'. Arrow (1969, p 48) claims that "market failure is not absolute; it is better to consider a broad category, that of transaction cost, which in general impedes and in particular cases blocks the formation of markets"; such costs are the "costs of running the economic system".

The second building block for Williamsonian economics is, allegedly, Herbert Simon's (1972) "bounded rationality". This concept is based on two principles:

- Individuals, or groups of individuals, are subject to inevitable limits on their ability to process or use information that is available. This limited computational capacity exists because of difficulties in understanding and manipulating the sense data involved in any but trivial situations. In short, *informational complexity* exists.

- It is equally implausible to suggest that all possible states of the world and all relevant cause-effect relationships can be identified, following which probabilities can be calculated, presumably on the basis of previous occurrence. This implies that economic actors are inevitably faced with incomplete information: that is, *informational uncertainty* exists. According to Simon, economic actors are "intendedly rational, but only limitedly so".

One further building block in the transaction cost structure is the economics of information. For some time the problems of asymmetrically distributed information have been recognised. It is usual to distinguish between *ex ante* and *ex post* asymmetries (Dietrich, 1994, p 21). *Ex ante* problems occur when one party to a transaction has less information about a potential purchase or sale than the other, but this information disadvantage is eliminated after the transaction is completed. Such a situation is frequently called one of adverse selection, after the seminal work of Akerlof (1970). *Ex post* information asymmetries occur when one party to a transaction has less information than another even after the transaction has occurred. This was first recognised by Arrow (1962) in the context of insurance: an insurance company has no obvious way of knowing that a holder of an insurance policy is revealing all relevant information that is pertinent to a claim. In this context, *ex post* information problems have been dubbed 'moral hazard'. Clearly the problem extends beyond insurance. Williamson (1975) conflates *ex ante* and *ex post* information asymmetries into a more general category of information impactedness, on which his centrally important assumption of opportunism is based.

Transaction cost economics

The core concepts of the transaction cost approach cut across public and private organisational dimensions that define policy arenas (Calista, 1987). This means that a transaction cost approach can display how private markets replace public organisations (Wolf, 1988). A transaction costs view seeks to determine how organisational decision making creates an institutional basis for capitalism (Williamson, 1985). In political science, similar issues are raised about institutional contexts at every juncture of policy intervention – not only for implementation. At the very least, transaction cost theory will be able to provide insights into the organisational and interorganisational dimensions of implementation that political science has been able to do for itself (Moe, 1990).

The genesis of transaction cost theory can be ascribed to the earlier works of institutional economists, including Commons (1934), Coase[1] and Hayek (Dietrich, 1994, pp 2-3). The 'institutionalists' differ from those advancing a neo-classical understanding of economic relations in a number of fundamental ways. The prime objection of the institutionalists to the neo-classical tradition has been the over-rational qualities which it ascribes to economic agents and the static nature of its analysis (Pettigrew and Whipp, 1991, pp 19-20). Institutionalists do not assume that such agents are rational in the sense of maximising their resources within a framework of known alternatives. Instead, economic relations are in large measure the result of experience and learning over time.

One of the sharpest differences between the institutionalists and the neo-classicists arises over the issue of competition. The former see competition as a process; the latter regard it as a state. The institutionalists point out that economic explanation should be a dynamic exercise and be concerned with a sequence of events taking place in real time. As a result, they place great emphasis on the dynamics of the competitive process in the explanation of economic relations (Dietrich, 1994, pp 2-5; Pettigrew and Whipp, 1991, p 20).

Recent work, based on the institutional perspective, by Williamson (1971; 1975) has given transaction cost theory strong conceptual backing as an explanatory tool for strategies involving comparative economic organisation. This exposition and discussion will be based largely on Williamson's two works *Market and hierarchies* (1975) and *The economic institution of capitalism* (1985). While these two works exhibit minor differences,[2] the later work should be seen as a development of the earlier analysis.

Williamson (1975; 1985) argues that the basic principle underlying transaction cost economics is that economic institutions will develop ways to economise on transaction costs. Such institutions are usually dichotomised as atomistic markets, which involve anonymous, short-run relationships, and intra-firm hierarchies. In between, quasi-integration exists where long-term relationships between identifiable (rather than anonymous) economic actors are important.

Williamson (1985) follows Arrow's definition of transaction costs as the costs of running the economic system, and as such they are equivalent to 'friction' in the physical sciences. More specifically, *ex ante* transaction costs are the costs of drafting, negotiating and safeguarding an agreement. *Ex post* transaction costs include:

- maladaptation costs incurred when transactions drift out of alignment with requirements;

- haggling costs incurred if bilateral efforts are made to correct *ex post* misalignments;

- setup and running costs associated with the governance structures (often not the courts) to which the disputes are referred;

- bonding costs of effecting secure commitments.

At the heart of transaction cost theory is the relative efficiency of alternative forms of organisation (governance). This view of efficiency extends that of the neo-classical model, which looked exclusively at cost minimisation of the firm's production function. A definition of organisational efficiency must necessarily incorporate an analysis of the comparative costs of different forms of governance. Simply put, governance costs are the costs associated with seeking efficient exchange of goods and services (transactions). Efficiency demands that the costs associated with engaging in transactions (transaction costs) outside the organisation are equal to the transaction costs incurred by the governance of transactions within the hierarchy (Williamson, 1991).

During its early conceptual development, transaction cost theory illustrated these cost considerations in a firm's decision to contract out for supplies or to integrate vertically (Williamson, 1971; 1975). Assuming that all other costs have been considered and are equal, the firm would integrate vertically if the transaction costs of internal governance were less than the transaction costs of contracting with an outside supplier.

Metaphorically, transaction costs represent the economic counterpart of friction in a physical system (Williamson, 1989).

According to Walsh (1995, p 35), Williamson's argument is that markets will fail not only for the reasons that have led to the development of state provision of services, but also because of the costs of transactions. Markets will not instantaneously and perfectly reach equilibrium. The structure of information and the nature of assets will determine whether or not the market is an effective medium for conducting transactions. Walsh also points out that the basis of Williamson's argument is that the most advantageous institutional form will depend on the level of transaction costs.

Williamson (1985; 1991) also argues that transaction costs may well be high when the process of exchange is difficult or complicated, for example if detailed contracts must be prepared and managed or if it is difficult to evaluate the quality of products. In these circumstances hierarchical organisation may be more efficient than market processes. Williamson (1979) points out that the existence of transaction costs depends on the factors of uncertainty, bounded rationality and asset specificity, and also that whether markets or hierarchies are the more efficient will depend on these factors. Taken together, these variables help to illustrate the depth of this model and the differences in types of contracting.

Uncertainty: Level of uncertainty refers to the extent to which it is possible accurately to predict future circumstances (Walsh, 1995, p 34). Uncertainty is widely conceded to be a critical attribute. Uncertainty makes monitoring difficult and allows scope for opportunism to take effect (Williamson, 1979, p 239). Uncertainty arises, for example, when contracts are incomplete, in the sense that not all contingencies are covered by the contract's terms and specifications (Milne, 1993, p 305). Asymmetric distribution of information can raise the level of uncertainty, thereby increasing transaction costs.

Hill's discussion (1993a, p 18), which argues that data is not necessarily neutral but may advantage particular interests, backs up the argument. Hammersley (1995, pp 100-2) also claims that even social research has always been political even though it has pretended to be otherwise. He argues (1995, p 113) that Weber also recognised that social research is almost inevitably influenced by the various other value commitments that researchers have as individuals and as members of the social categories and groups to which they belong. His promotion of the principle of value neutrality as an ideal to be striven for is precisely motivated by a recognition of the influence on social research of values other than truth, and of the threat that this posed to the validity of his findings. In this sense, too, he recognised that research is not free of the influence of values. However, while he believed that this sort of influence was almost inevitable, he regarded it as something which could and should be minimised.

For these reasons, contracts are most incomplete when they are first put out to tender. Experience reduces uncertainty, but it cannot be entirely eliminated. It is assumed that the greater the uncertainty, the more difficult it will be to carry out transactions in the market. In such circumstances, where uncertainty is great, hierarchy will have advantages over markets because adaptation by hierarchy will be more rapid and less expensive since it can be carried out without formal negotiation and can be more far-reaching (Walsh, 1995, p 34).

Bounded rationality: Transaction cost economics assumes that rationality is bounded, owing to the fact that principals do not have perfect information on agents, or on agents' work performance (Williamson, 1985, pp 15-17). Where there is a high level of bounded rationality,[3] it will be difficult to write contracts, and there are likely to be continual variations and renegotiations. It is assumed that, in such circumstances, hierarchy will have advantages over markets because those in power in organisations will be able to react to unforeseen events by changing the pattern of organisational action. Williamson (1975, p 23) also claims that "as long as either uncertainty or complexity is present in requisite degree, the bounded rationality problem arises".

Bounded rationality refers to the limits on the computational and analytical abilities of individuals (Walsh, 1995, p 34). In his influential work on organisations and individuals, Simon suggests that bounded rationality is the limited human capacity for rational actions. He suggests that humans are not perfectly rational beings, but rather 'satisfice' or make decisions based on rules of thumb. In any given organisation a pure economic human will strive rationally to maximise the "attainment of certain ends with the use of scarce means" (Simon, 1987, pp 176-7). Simon contends that because man is human, he is subject to limits in the quantity and quality of his output (Simon, 1987). His ability to perform and make correct decisions is affected by the information he collects on the world around him. Because this information provides only a partial view of the real world, 'administrative' man is forced to work with narrow information, conflicting values and loyalties, and his own limited skills (Simon, 1987).

Bounded rationality replaces pure rationality under such assumptions of imperfect information and limited capabilities and skills (Simon, 1987). It suggests that the individuals who work within an organisation, for the good of the organisation, will be attempting to behave rationally, but will only achieve this on a limited basis (Simon, 1987).

Asset specificity: One of the main tenets of transaction cost theory is that of asset-specificity-related problems. Asset specificity arises when principals seek agents to complete those jobs which they cannot, will not or do not want to complete themselves, owing to various circumstantial factors (Williamson, 1985, p 17). The motivational factors behind a principal's actions may include:

- the desire to open up competition (and thus attempt to foster cost efficiency);

- the need to complete a job for which the principal does not have adequate expertise, equipment, or manpower;

- an attempt to restructure programme initiatives and manpower on other tasks.

In the presence of specific assets, and by virtue of the idiosyncratic knowledge available to one of the transacting parties, the party may conceal this information in a deceitful manner (Akerlof, 1970).

The significance of asset specificity is the 'sunk cost' associated with it, and this needs more explanation. It includes not only financial assets and physical assets such as buildings and machinery, but human assets such as staff experience. Reve (1990) identifies four ways in which investment might be 'specific': expertise, temporary workers, specific assets and urgent needs.[4]

Walsh (1995) argues that asset specificity leads to a situation of bilateral monopoly. Once the investment has been made it is difficult for the buyer to go to alternative providers and the person who has made the investment gains quasi-monopoly advantages. The market may not be contestable because of the existing supplier's control of the necessary resources. *Ex ante*, many potential buyers and sellers may exist, but *ex post* this need not be the case if idiosyncratic investments are required (Walsh, 1995, p 35).

Transaction costs and governance structures

According to Williamson (1985) if uncertainty, bounded rationality and asset specificity are not all present, transaction costs will not exist. Given the existence of contracting problems (the above factors), transaction cost economics claims to be able to specify the governance structures that can efficiently manage economic activity in any situation.

Most research to date has examined the question of whether to conduct transactions within organisational hierarchies or with outside contractors. This is evident in recalling the prevalence of studies concerning vertical integration strategies. Two types of transaction costs would enter into these strategic decisions. In the case of service contracting, managers would be concerned with the costs of negotiating, monitoring and enforcing a contract (Williamson, 1975). Providing a good or service within organisational boundaries requires consideration of bureaucratic costs. These transaction costs are associated with obtaining information about managerial inefficiencies, opportunistic behaviour and the pursuit of sub-goals among organisational actors. To counteract bureaucratic costs, organisations incur governance costs associated with production or bureaucratic controls such as procedures, rules and budgets (Williamson, 1975).

In the following sections, this idea will be illustrated and developed into a conceptual framework for studying the political process of CCT. A natural way to begin is to examine the integral aspects of transaction cost theory as factors which affect contracting decisions.

Political market and economic efficiency

Transaction costs can be manipulated in the political arena.

Political markets are characterised by imperfect information, subjective models and high transaction costs (North, 1990b). In the political markets the affected parties are ill-informed, and not all the affected parties have equal access to the decision-making process. The political market has been, and continues to be, one in which the actors have an imperfect understanding of the issues affecting them and, equally, in which the high costs of transacting prevent the achievement of efficient solutions (North, 1990b).

The transaction technology and the limitations it imposes on economic possibilities are just as real as the production technology and its limitations. Stiglitz (1994) has repeatedly emphasised this with regard to information asymmetries, and Williamson's (1989) analysis of other types of transaction costs reinforces the point. Williamson and others have pointed out that in all interactions subject to transaction costs, it is in the interests of the participants to devise methods, market or non-market, official or private, by which such costs can be reduced. The success of such devices will depend on such factors as related institutions, and the history and the likely future duration of the interactions (Dixit, 1996).

There are several other sources of transaction costs in a political context, and they all introduce departures from the Coasean[5] benchmark of efficient outcomes that maximise total economic benefits and then negotiate to divide them up. The efficiency of these policies can be examined and alternative hypotheses and theories within this overarching framework of transaction costs compared. When doing this, the whole broad categories of these costs must be recognised, or the whole class of frictions that pervade the political process. As in economics the participants in the policy process must also be recognised, whether they are in the public or the private sector, and whether they have natural and endogenous incentives to manipulate transaction costs (North, 1990b). This framework, which has been labelled 'the politics of transaction costs', is developed in more detail in the following section.

Politics of the transaction cost framework

Overview

Transaction cost theory is one general model of exchange and hierarchy that can be applied to both public and private sector transactions to aid understanding of organisational exchange behaviours. It is increasingly being applied in relation to public policy issues. As regards the scope of the transaction cost approach, Williamson (1975, p 17) claims:

> **The proposed approach adopts a contracting orientation and maintains that any issue that can be formulated as a contracting problem can be investigated to advantage in transaction cost economising terms. Every exchange relation qualifies. Many other issues which at the outset appear to**

> **lack a contracting aspect turn out, upon scrutiny, to have an implicit contracting quality.**

As Williamson states, the transaction cost approach, originally an explanation for the scale and scope of the firm, is now used to study a variety of economic policy issues, ranging from vertical and lateral integration to transfer pricing, corporate finance, marketing, the organisation of work, long-term commercial contracting, franchising, regulation, the multinational corporation, company towns, and many other contractual relationships (Twight, 1990).

The main insights and predictions of the transaction cost approach – in particular, the importance of governing transactions – are becoming increasingly accepted. However, the empirical support for these claims is much less well-known. For instance, Ferris and Graddy (1991) utilise a transaction cost approach in their analysis of US local authorities' experience of contracting out services. Within a UK context, Milne (1987) has noted the potential applicability of Williamson's analytical framework in examining competitive tendering in the health services. Walsh and Davis (1993) found that the costs of preparation for CCT in local government were 7.7% of the annual contract value. They also noted that these costs were largely associated with the preparation of specifications, for example the measurement of sites on which work is to be done, and the costs of letting contracts.

Experience of contracting in the US also shows that there are considerable preparation costs. These costs are partly one-off, but managers suggest that about two thirds of the initial costs will be incurred every time a contract is let (Walsh, 1995, p 237).

In general, transaction cost theory has been used almost exclusively in the private sector. However, Williamson and others have suggested that this theory could be a useful tool in understanding the economic factors associated with public sector systems (Williamson, 1985, pp 15-17). In particular, since North's (1990b) call for the development of a 'transaction-cost theory of politics' this framework has been used to uncover linkages between political contexts and transaction costs. The pioneering work of Coase, Williamson, North and others has led to the recognition that various transaction costs are the primary reason why impersonal competitive markets do not function as effectively as might be suggested by the neo-classical benchmark. This in turn explains the emergence of different mechanisms and institutions as devices that enable the participants to mitigate or to cope with transaction costs. This mode of analysis has been developed and tested most fully in industrial economics and in economic history (see, respectively, Williamson, 1989 and North, 1990a).

The idea of viewing the process of economic policy through a transaction cost lens is not new. The idea of studying the political process in the transaction cost mode originates with North (1990b). His main focus is on a particular facet of transaction costs, namely, a failure of 'instrumental rationality' for participants in the process. However, there are other aspects of transaction costs that are also prominent in industrial economics. They are concerned with game-theoretical issues of asymmetric information and time-consistency of action, and they persist and affect outcomes even if there is full instrumental rationality, that is, even when every participant knows the correct theory of the world and can perfectly calculate his own optimal strategy. The problems arise in the strategic interaction between such individuals and the equilibrium of their game. Therefore the scope of transaction cost analysis is much broader than is suggested by North (Dixit, 1996).

Some previous articles treat specific transaction costs which arise in the making of economic policy, and some surveys make this connection more explicit, but the connection does not appear to have been explicitly recognised or exploited (Twight, 1988). Two classes of example will make the point. Analyses of time-consistency and commitment in fiscal and monetary policy, derived from Kydland and Prescott's (1977) and Baldwin's (1997) work on rules versus discretion, show that difficulties with the credibility of commitments constitute an important class of transaction costs. Problems of agency in politics and administration have been studied by several researchers (such as Banks, 1991; Grossman and Helpman, 1994). Agency problems involving moral hazard and opportunism, dynamics, incentive constraints, politics, and the costs of controlling these informational asymmetries are some of the major transaction costs that Williamson and others have emphasised in industrial economics. Many models of macroeconomic policies have analysed specific issues of this type. However, these do not make any connection with Williamson's work. Most of these macroeconomic models are theoretical, and suffer accordingly from a lack of empirical grounding, but similar issues are recognised in practical policy discussions too.

North's (1990b) analysis of transaction cost politics leads him to the conclusion that we should expect political markets to be even more beset by transaction costs, and therefore to operate even less efficiently, than economic markets. His emphasis is on the effect of information costs on individual decision making. This study develops a broader theme, involving a larger class of problems that have been studied in transaction cost economics. The classification used mostly derives from Williamson. It is believed that the presentation of the politics of transaction costs used in this study will help to improve understanding of the operation of policy processes and public and private institutions. The following section looks at the implications for economic policy of the politics of transaction costs.

Transaction costs and the political process

Contributions of transaction cost economics to the analysis of the continuous trade-off among decisions of using the price mechanism are now widely recognised. Alternative 'governance structures' (Williamson, 1985; 1991; 1997) or 'institutional arrangements' (Davis and North, 1971) have been identified, and attributes of transactions have been explored to explain how and why shifts from one form to another occur. Numerous empirical tests have shown the robustness of these hypotheses (Menard, 1997, p 30). However, one dimension of the transaction cost approach, the politics of transaction cost, is much less developed. A politics of transaction cost framework will now be developed to analyse how DSO output has been made.

The emphasis on the politics of transaction costs does not imply that other considerations are unimportant or insignificant. The success or failure of the implementation of policies is dependent on economic factors such as the availability of money and other resources, on geographic considerations such as territorial jurisdiction, and on sociological factors such as interpersonal work relationships (Nakamura and Smallwood, 1980).

However, the major concern in this study is with the pressures and constraints which influence the CCT policy process. The terms 'politics' or 'political' are used in diverse senses. There are broad and narrow interpretations. At one extreme, their use may be restricted to issues subject to dispute between contending national political parties or pressure groups or to the interests of nation states. At the other extreme there is the argument that micropolitical processes are to be found in all realms; or that all human relations and contracts are political, as implied by the slogan 'the personal is political' (Hammersley, 1995, pp 102-3).

This study focuses on politics in the broadest sense of the term. It is not limited to partisan politics – how one or the other political party attempts to influence the policy process. Instead, it is concerned with the conflicts over values which permeate many, if not all, aspects of public life, and with the making of value judgements and the performing of actions on the basis of them.

Defining transaction costs

The fundamental logic of the transaction cost approach – involving different cost-comparing ways of regulating given transactions – should not (or cannot) be interpreted too literally. To determine empirically and measure the costs and thereby the value of alternative (existing and potential) organisational solutions would probably entail formidable difficulties. Above all, there is considerable divergence of views about the content of the transaction concept.

Transaction costs are notoriously difficult to define, and a number of commentators have exploited the vagueness of the term. Too broad a definition may render the concept vacuous, incapable of generating useful economic implications. Too narrow a definition may destroy its capacity to yield generalised insights into economic processes and choices. Nevertheless, as with many definitional questions, the definition chosen depends on the purpose at hand. For example, for this study transaction costs could be defined as "the costs of effecting a transfer of rights" (Posner, 1972), or all the costs involved in human interaction over time (North, 1997, p 149). In particular, the latter definition is made in the larger context of societal evolution and is closely akin to the notion of social capital advanced by Coleman (1990) and applied imaginatively to studying the differential patterns of Italian regional development by Putnam in *Making democracy work* (1993).

These broad definitions are useful and productive when the aim is to highlight the multiplicity and magnitude of real-world costs that exist as a result of living in a society consisting of many people.

Although such definitions capture the essence of transaction costs, they create some hazards for the economic practitioner. One danger is that if observed behaviour does not match the predictions of the economic theory, an incautious practitioner can gloss over the discrepancy by facile reference to transaction costs. If these definitions are applied too loosely, almost any cost in real-world societies is susceptible to being labelled a 'transaction cost', and the productivity of transaction cost analysis may be curtailed correspondingly. A troubling question lingering in the wake of expansive definitions is: what is not, in some dimension, a 'transaction cost' according to these formulations? (DeHoog, 1983, pp 6-9.)

Alternatively, the definition could focus on the cost categories most indisputably subsumed under the concept of transaction costs. Among these categories most economists would include group decision-making costs (that is, costs uniquely associated with making multiparty decisions), such as communication/negotiation expenses incurred only because multiple individuals conjoin to decide on a particular course of action. Arrow's definition of transaction costs (1969), accepted by Williamson, is a good example. In effect, these costs in the category are distinguished by their timing – whether they occur before or after the awarding of the contract. The costs of negotiating and enforcing contracts clearly fall under this heading of the transaction cost.

Another important factor is information costs incurred by individuals in order to make a multiparty decision. Although this category might be subsumed under the preceding one, it is distinct in that it focuses on costs incurred by individuals separately for the purpose of engaging in a multiparty exchange (Dixit, 1996). Agency costs comprise another identifiable subcategory of transaction costs, since they too arise exclusively as a result of multiparty exchange. The further the list is extended, the more likely it is that the addition will provoke economic controversy. Beyond this inevitable controversy on the periphery, the chief danger of this approach is that in enumerating specific categories[6] of transaction costs, it is possible to lose sight of the common thread that unites them.

With these difficulties in mind, the definition of transaction costs used for this study will include three main classes: information costs, negotiation costs and monitoring (or enforcement) costs. Information costs arise when we drop the neo-classical assumption of perfect information and recognise that economic agents face costs in the search for information about products, prices, inputs, and buyers or sellers. Negotiation costs arise from the physical act of the transaction, whether it be negotiating and writing contracts (costs in terms of managerial expertise, perhaps the hiring of lawyers), or paying for the services of an intermediary to the transaction (such as an auctioneer or a broker). Monitoring or enforcement costs arise after transaction. This may involve monitoring the quality of goods from a supplier or monitoring the behaviour of a supplier or buyer to ensure that all pre-agreed terms of the transaction are met. Also included are the costs of seeking restitution when a contract is broken.

This definition does not avoid all of the hazards alluded to above, but it does focus attention on the costs of multiparty agreement, which is by all accounts at the core of the transaction cost concept and which is the aspect most important for this study. According to this definition, the previously described communication, negotiation, information, and agency costs will be labelled as transaction costs, while other costs incurred for the purpose of market exchange but not partaking of such 'agreement-and-enforcement' attributes will be excluded. By making transaction costs a bounded set, this definition avoids emasculating the concept. However, it is still necessary to be precise when identifying any transaction cost constraints alleged to explain observed behaviour.

Transaction costs in the political process

Transaction costs often determine political outcome (Twight, 1994, p 190). As Dixit (1996, pp 37-8) states, the true value of the Coase theorem is not as a description of reality, but as an idealisation or benchmark that serves to focus attention on the specific ways in which the reality differs from the ideal, and the consequences of these departures. The real task is to recognise, categorise and study the multitude of these causes and their effects.

In private markets, transaction costs denote costs attributable to the multiparty character of economic exchange, encompassing information costs, negotiation and enforcement costs. All forms of these costs exist, in many cases with greater strength, in political processes. Accordingly, in a political context transaction costs denote most of the costs of multiperson political exchange – more precisely, the costs of reaching and enforcing political agreements. Those transaction costs exist because individuals strive to act collectively (Heckathorn and Maser, 1987; McMaster, 1992; Twight, 1988).

In this study, the politics of transaction cost, based on the definition of transaction costs in a political context, can be defined as the volitional use, shift or manipulation of transaction costs by the main parties to a contract constraining the other party's choices. It is seen as a strategically manipulable concept in that such manipulation leads the political process to be distorted and to suffer a lack of efficiency and rationality.

The definition of the politics of transaction cost offered above is based on the following assumptions. First, in the political process the policy output is a result of the 'game' of the politics of transaction cost caused during the process of policy implementation by the main parties to a contract. The policy participants of the policy process attempt to put what Bardach (1977, p 56) calls the 'implementation machine' together to exercise 'control' through bargaining, persuasion and manoeuvring under conditions of uncertainty. The idea of the 'game' will serve as a metaphor that directs attention and stimulates insights. It directs us to look at the players, what they regard as the stakes, their strategies and tactics, their resources, the rules of play which stipulate the conditions for winning, the rules of 'fair' play which stipulate the boundaries beyond which lie fraud or illegitimacy, the nature of the communications among the players, and the degree of uncertainty surrounding the possible outputs. The metaphor also directs attention to who is not willing to play and for what reasons, and to who insists on change in some of the game's parameters as a condition for playing (Nakamura and Smallwood, 1980, pp 15-16).

A further assumption is that many different actors, operating in diverse arenas, can attempt to exercise various leverages within the implementation environment. As regards who can be the main parties, the parties to a contract should be those which have a direct interest in the contract: the local authority and private contractor in the CCT process, for example.

Traditional contract approaches imply that the identities of the client and contractor are clear, and that the world is one of principals and agents. However, in reality it may be difficult to identify precisely who the parties to the contract are, mainly because contract relationships may be difficult to define. In complex contracts there are likely to be more than two partners to the exchange, which leads to the assumption that there should be many participants and interested parties in the contract process (Walsh et al, 1997, p 38). Accordingly, it is expected that in practice these actors can include the policy maker, policy implementor, interest groups, policy recipients or 'consumers', the mass media and other interested parties (Nakamura and Smallwood, 1980, pp 46-53).

In the CCT policy process, central government as policy maker can attempt to influence the local authority as policy implementor by monitoring, intervening and/or credit claiming (Nakamura and Smallwood, 1980, p 47). The signals central government transmits through its activities can have a significant political impact on the implementation process.

Central government, in the case of contractual arrangements, uses a compliance mechanism, or legal framework, as a device in the pursuit of a public policy objective. According to Marston (1990, p 1), central government influences the competitive tendering process via inserting clauses into a legal framework, with which prospective or actual contractors with public bodies must comply. By using its contractual powers to achieve a public goal, central government may be one of the main parties to a contract. In this study it is assumed that central government is involved in the CCT process as an interested party which can manipulate the transaction costs.

For example, in the case of CCT, whether or not central government takes a neutral stance towards the interested parties, fostering a 'level playing field', is crucial in influencing the increase or decrease of transaction costs for the local authority and private contractors. If central government sets the rules so that there is a slope in favour of the private sector, this means transaction costs are being decreased for private bidders and increased for local government, and vice versa. Politically, whether central government takes a neutral or prejudiced stance to a particular policy, CCT, for example, depends on policy targets, national objectives and the power relationship between central and local government.

The local authority is an actor who is expressly granted the legal authority, responsibility, and public resources to carry out policy directives. Such an implementor can include administrators within its organisation, agencies, bureau and regulatory commissions.

Interest groups can also constitute a powerful set of actors in the implementation environment. In the CCT process a trade union can be an interest group. The interest groups can pressure the implementor to administer policies in ways which advance their perceived self-interest.

Although many governmental policies are intended to benefit different groups of beneficiaries, some observers would argue that the policy 'consumers' are to be included in the implementation process. This may well have been true historically, but as new policies have placed increased emphasis on a growing range of social concerns there has been a parallel movement to involve recipients more directly in the implementation of those policies (Nakamura and Smallwood, 1980). However, up until now most research on transaction cost conducted from the political point of view has tended to focus on the political transaction costs incurred by the government officeholders only. This ignores the importance of the role which the recipients (or consumers in the CCT process) can play in the political process.

In the UK, there has been in the 1980s and 1990s a 'rediscovery' of the public in local government, in the form of a consumer perspective, a 'closeness' to the public, or a responsiveness to the 'customer'. The relationship between the local authority and the public is changing. In particular, there has been a rapid growth of interest in the public as consumers or customers. Local authorities are being asked to identify the 'customers' for the services which they provide and communicate with those customers in order to provide services which are of value to them (Fenwick, 1995, pp 45-50).

In view of this, it is expected that consumers' determination not to be misled operates as a significant constraint on the policy originators' ability to effect contrived transaction costs. Despite the largely external and indirect nature of potential benefits derivable from the political market, in political markets the incentive of private individuals to acquire and act on transaction costs relating to the acts and performances of the interested parties is likely to be significant.[7]

The press and other mass media can also shape the perceptions of the public, policy makers and policy implementors. Today, in particular, because the media can influence these different groups, it has the capacity to exercise tremendous leverage on the implementation process (Nakamura and Smallwood, 1980).

It is hypothesised that all these many actors possess the means to influence the other party in the political process through manipulating transaction costs. However, for simplicity of analysis this study limits the main parties in the CCT policy process to central government, the local authority and private companies.

The definition of the politics of transaction cost put forward in this study differs from that of previous research in the following ways. First, it focuses on the politics of the economic transaction costs *per se*, whereas most previous studies primarily address the political transaction cost. Political transaction cost is a very broad concept and comprises all the costs of perceiving and of acting on the assessment of the net costs of particular governmental actions and authority (Twight, 1994, pp 190-1). Twight (1988; 1992) refers to 'constitutional-level' transaction costs, to emphasise their influence on the nature and extent of government authority over private decision making tolerated by the public.

In this respect, the politics of transaction cost are narrower in scope and more specific than political transaction costs: the latter can include the former. The framework of political transaction costs can provide a more integrated understanding of the dynamics of government, and can be a prerequisite for institutional improvement. It also makes it possible to investigate the external influences that motivate individual government actors to support transaction cost-increasing measures.

However, the framework of political transaction cost has some limitations. It is both too universal and too narrow. On the one hand, it is seen as a universal theory because it can be used to describe almost any tangible and intangible cost-based contracting situation. It has been argued that because this framework can rationalise almost anything, it is useless as a tool for clear conceptual study (Korosec, 1994). In short, because there are 'too many degrees of freedom', there is no definitional clarity. It is argued in this study that the political transaction costs associated with any given transaction may be so numerous that it is not possible to consider adequately the true political transaction costs.

On the other hand, the framework is narrow because it only focuses on the political transaction costs manipulated by government officeholders, underestimating the importance of the role which the other parties can play in the political process. Prior analyses of transaction costs using this framework have focused exclusively on the actions of government officeholders that alter the actions of the other party or parties (such as private companies, citizens) (Twight, 1988; 1994). Consequently, the political transaction cost literature does not recognise that the actions of the other party can change the transaction costs facing the government officeholders and as a result also fails to analyse these actions.

Main issues associated with the politics of transaction costs

If the politics of transaction costs are defined in this way, then theoretically the following five questions[8] are raised:

- What makes government and private companies attempt to manipulate the transaction costs? Why are they interested in the politics of transaction cost?

- How is it possible for them to engage in the politics of transaction costs?

- What types of strategy can be applied to reflect their interests in the political process?

- What will happen in the policy output if the politics of transaction costs dominates the political process?

- What measures would be needed to cope with the politics of transaction costs?

These questions pave the way for the construction of the analytical framework for this study. Before these questions can be answered it will be necessary to consider why the politics of transaction costs is used, how it can occur, and what the related strategies are.

Why the politics of transaction cost?

In general, government officeholders tend to manipulate transaction costs in order to protect their interests in the political process (Dixit, 1996; Twight, 1988, 1992). In this respect it does not matter whether government officeholders are elected or appointed, and so both are called government officeholders in this study. In a political process, transaction costs are assumed to be actively manipulated in the public sector by those who anticipate potential personal gain from such action. Over time, changes in transaction costs created by government decision-makers may fundamentally influence the success or failure of the other party, private company, citizen, voluntary organisation or such like.

Supposing that the politics of transaction costs exists, the question must be asked, why? Issues relating to the incentives of government officials and private companies to engage in such behaviour will be considered below. Although scholars in diverse fields (Nordlinger, 1981; Twight, 1994; Weaver, 1988) have described examples of what is conceptualised here as transaction cost-manipulating behaviour, less attention has been devoted to the predictive task of identifying what conditions – what independent variables – influence the degree to which such intentional manipulation of transaction costs occurs.

If you were a local government official (councillor or bureaucrat) with issue-specific personal policy preferences at odds with those of the relevant public or private companies, clearly it would help you to prevail politically on this issue if you could manipulate transaction costs in ways favourable to your preferred policy output. This ideology will work for the occurrence of transaction-cost-manipulating measures. For example, if ideologically you as the local government official favour the privatisation of local government services in particular areas such as refuse collection, you are more likely to endorse measures that raise the transaction costs of resisting such privatisation measures. On the other hand, if ideologically you oppose such privatisation policy, you are more likely to oppose provisions that increase the transaction costs of resisting it. Whether the politics of transaction costs happens or not depends on whether or not a particular policy matches a government official's political ideology (Twight, 1988; 1992).

Party demand and support may also positively influence my decision to manipulate transaction costs in the political process, although undoubtedly less so in situations in which party influence has declined (such as the US Congress) than in situations in which party control is more dominant (such as the British Parliament). As a policy maker, you would be more likely to endorse a transaction-cost-manipulating measure if it is favoured – implicitly or explicitly – by the party to which you belong, *ceteris paribus* (Dearlove, 1973; Hampton, 1991).

Perquisites of office associated with your support as a policy maker for a transaction-cost-manipulating measure will be likely to influence your decision. Here you may think not only of material perquisites, but also the sometimes even more attractive perquisites of power and esteem (Twight, 1994).

The perceived importance to constituents of the transaction-cost-manipulating measure will positively influence your choice. Even if you are otherwise predisposed to oppose a particular policy – for example CCT – as a representative of a local authority in which many small private companies are operating and showing eagerness for CCT, or in which most constituents want efficient and effective provision of services by privatised companies, you are more likely to favour its transaction-cost-manipulating measures in the hope that it will be able to meet the requirement of the constituents whom you are supposed to serve (Twight, 1994).

Expected or actual pay-off by third parties may also influence your willingness to support a transaction-cost-manipulating measure. Such returns as campaign contributions and future job opportunities clearly matter (Twight, 1988). Supposing that trade unions or government officials promise local councillors that the unions will campaign for the councillors on condition that they do not introduce, for example, CCT, then local councillors are likely to manipulate transaction costs in the interests of the trade union. A DSO or DLO is part of the council; its staff are council employees. Given these factors, it is unsurprising that councils will be biased in favour of their own service organisations. For these reasons it can be assumed that the government officeholders are likely to engage in the politics of transaction cost.

The manipulation of transaction costs also applies to the private sector, and similar incentives operate. The real issue is what makes the private sector engage in the politics of transaction costs. Simply put, the answer is economic profit, whether in the form of short- or long-term returns. Although private firms operating in a textbook-style perfectly competitive market have no incentive or leeway to manipulate transaction costs, firms in imperfectly competitive markets by definition experience looser constraints on their transaction cost functions (Dixit, 1996).

In connection with this, it would be interesting to examine, for example, the actions of private companies which engage in seemingly irrational behaviour (for example, loss-leading[9] or going through the process of being accepted on to a select list and then not submitting a bid). Do these private companies have every intention of bidding for the contract but find themselves deterred by the actual documentation, or is their behaviour part of a long-term rational strategy? Loss-leaders, for example, could be viewed as an investment in information, buying a foothold, learning by doing (Walsh et al, 1997, p 112).

In this manner, private sector providers operate in a transaction-cost-ridden environment, and their 'market power' is in part defined by the politics of transaction costs. If a private company's continued prosperity (economic profits) depends on such a transaction cost configuration, its owners would be willing to spend any amount up to the threatened loss of economic profits (Twight, 1994).

In some cases central government as policy maker intentionally influences the 'slope' of the 'playing field' by setting rules or guidelines which are actually favourable to a particular group or party. If in this case the rules are advantageous to private sector providers, it is assumed that private companies are willing to employ various strategies able to use, shift or manipulate transaction costs to their advantage with increasing speed.

This does not deny that such transaction-cost-sustaining efforts may be doomed economically in the long run, for the firm is incurring additional unproductive costs which a more effective enterprise could avoid. It merely recognises that the real-world emergence of that doom is subject to lags that may be distended by a firm's volitional efforts to manipulate the transaction costs encountered by its rivals (Twight, 1988).

How can the politics of transaction cost occur?

Unattainability of perfect implementation: Although a particular policy is centrally imposed, at the local level its perfect implementation is unattainable (Hogwood and Gunn, 1984, pp 198-9). Simon (1978) indicated that many constraints (or 'bounds' in Simon's language) impede rational policy making in practice. In other words, the descriptive model of policy making was developed in terms of observed deviations from the ideal-type model of rationality.

This study will proceed in the same way, borrowing Hood's (1976) useful analytical concept of 'perfect administration'. In an article entitled 'Why is implementation so difficult?', Gunn (1978) drew on Hood's analysis, and those of Pressman and Wildavsky (1973), Etzioni (1976) and Bardach (1977), to provide a short explanation for civil servants of some of the reasons why any state of 'perfect implementation' is likely to be virtually unattainable in practice. Hood emphasised that 'perfection' in this context is an analytical concept or 'idea' and not, in the colloquial sense of the term, an 'ideal' to be achieved.

No prescriptive model was offered and several of the logical preconditions for perfect implementation were identified as being morally and politically unacceptable, as well as unattainable in a pluralist democracy. Hill (1997b, p 129) exemplifies this phenomenon, pointing out that it is wrong to take it for granted that the implementation process will be smooth and straightforward. These discussions emphasise that:

- the perfect implementation of policy is unattainable;

- while being implemented policy *per se* can be influenced by the parties concerned, including policy actors and policy recipients;

- during the policy implementation the politics of transaction cost can take place.

Contract is incomplete: The contractual element usually relates to a specific written document, which illustrates the terms and conditions of the interrelation. Contract, in its traditional, neoclassical form, is a relatively impersonal process in which the parties to an agreement state their formal commitments to each other. Most often, the principal and the agent will communicate the actual 'build' or 'deliver' process through the contract, so that both parties have a written document stipulating what is expected of each other (Korosec, 1994; Walsh et al, 1997).

However, in the real world, in the public sector in particular contracts do not spell out in detail terms and procedures to be followed in every conceivable instance. It is common for contracts to be vague about risks and responsibilities, to ignore sanctions that are available for failure to perform, and to be imprecise about time. In many cases, contracts are deliberately left incomplete. They leave much to be interpreted and determined in specific future eventualities. The reasons for this are basically the same as the reasons for most business contracts being incomplete:

- the inability to foresee all the possible contingencies;

- the complexity of specifying rules, even for the numerous contingencies that can be foreseen;

- the difficulty of objectively observing and verifying contingencies so that the specified procedures may be put into action (Williamson, 1985).

All these problems are even more important in the public sector than they are in the private sector (Dixit, 1996; Twight, 1994; Walsh et al, 1997; Williamson, 1985).

Conflicts and disagreements about contingencies are much more common in the political arena than in business. A constitution of economic policy has to be couched in sufficiently general terms that it can be interpreted and applied as the economy itself changes in dramatic and unpredictable ways. In this process of interpretation and application, there can be very large variations in the way a given rule operates. These variations naturally occur in response to the political realities of the time. In other words, an incomplete contract can be easily manipulated by the participants to serve their own aims (North, 1990b).

Discretion: According to the power-dependence model briefly discussed in Chapter Three, both central departments and local authorities have resources which each can use against the other and against other organisations (Wilson and Game, 1994, p 110). Even though there are likely to be inequalities in the distribution of resources local authorities as well as central government have resources to influence the other party and discretion as to whether to implement even centrally imposed policy. Once discretionary power is vested in the government, its officials have both the capacity and the incentive to restructure the transaction costs constraining the activity of the other party, the private company (North, 1990b; Dixit, 1996).

In relation to the discretion of local authority as policy implementor, Rein and Rabinovitz (1978) have identified three patterns of implementation relations. The *legal imperative* describes the relations in which the implementor is responsive to legal mandates. The *rational-bureaucratic imperative* describes the relations in which implementors pay more attention to the bureaucratic process, and the maintenance of self-interest and organisation. The *consensual imperative* describes the situations in which implementors are primarily concerned with the welfare of their clientele. These three imperatives imply the existence and significance of relations in implementation – relations between the implementors and other players in the process who directly or indirectly influence the implementation.

It has been argued that in the UK since 1979, as some powers have been taken away from local government, those remaining have been increasingly limited and subject to greater national direction and control. Switchback changes in local government finance have been accompanied by the imposition of steadily tighter conditions, with government ministers and civil servants becoming more directly involved in declaring what they calculate each local council ought to be spending on different services (Elcock, 1994; Kerley, 1994).

The outcome has been a perceptible reduction in local discretion, in the ability of local councils either to decide for themselves or to finance effectively the services that they would wish to provide for their local communities (Wilson and Game, 1994, p 14). However, to date, at least, there is no suggestion that all local discretion has been eliminated. Local councils still have some opportunity to determine their own political priorities and to embark on their own policy initiatives in response to the needs and wishes of the residents of their local communities.

As Lipsky (1980) shows, informal discretion is still extensive in the field of central and local policy making, although formal discretionary decision making was reduced to a minimum through extensive use of rules and procedures.

Private interest: Grossman and Hart (1986) pointed out that in a contractor–contractee relationship (or a principal–agent relationship), the contractee (or the agent) usually has more discretion and has residual rights of control over actions that are not specified in the contract. These residual rights of control over non-specified actions are critical to a contractee's responsive allocation of resources according to its local conditions. In public service contracting out, to what extent a government contractor's actions are specified is a critical component of the government's contractual policies.

In other words, private contractors have some freedom in service provision, that is, in managerial discretion, as a result of central government's policies. This applies to CCT policy in Britain. This freedom and flexibility is said to be essential to the contractor's capacity to allocate its resources wisely in order to be more efficient and effective (DeHoog, 1984a; 1984b), which is one of the major arguments that support contracting out with the private sector. It is also said that excessive government control may create private sector dependence on government contracts, which may reduce the benefits gained from a self-supporting organisation (NAPA, 1989). The degree of contractor independence may be observed by examining the contract-related Acts and regulations. However, the role of the private sector (ordinary citizen, private company or voluntary organisation) as a policy object group in affecting the political process has been greatly underestimated, and yet this has had a fundamental impact on both the process of policy implementation and policy output.

Some studies of policy implementation (Hill, 1997a; Hood, 1976; Pressman and Wildavsky, 1973) emphasise that 'perfect implementation' is unattainable for many reasons. However, a problem with these studies is that they do not emphasise the role of the private sector as a policy object group affecting the process of policy implementation. For example, Pressman and Wildavsky (1973) deal with 'bad execution', 'bad policy' and 'bad luck' as three causes for implementation failure. Hogwood and Gunn (1984) instance 10 preconditions necessary to achieve perfect implementation. These studies focus not so much on the role of the policy object group as on internal factors relating to policy implementation.

Most debates on policy implementation up until now have examined as main issues the nature of policy, and the implementation structure or control over implementing actors, while private sector groups (private companies, citizen groups and so on) are left subservient to the policy implementation process and regarded as passive beneficiaries of government policy rather than as active participants influencing the policy process. However, this study argues that the private sector is fundamental to policy implementation, thereby assuming that the private sector engages in the politics of transaction costs for its benefit.

If the specification of the relevant independent variables made in this study is substantially correct, this should make it possible to predict when a society will experience more transaction cost manipulation incurred by political actors and the private sector and when it should experience less. Corrective institutional changes, if feasible, presuppose such an understanding of the underlying politico-economic processes.

***What are the strategies for the politics of transaction costs?*:** The strategies which the government and the private sector can adopt may vary both in theory and in practice. The scope and forms of the strategies selected can also vary, depending on the definitions both of transaction costs and of the politics of transaction costs.

If the definitions of transaction costs and the politics of transaction costs put forward in this study are accepted, many forms of the strategy associated with the politics of transaction costs can be discovered. They include, for example, the overt distortion of information about the contract, the restriction of access to information about the contract, and so on. This study will put forward six strategies which the parties will possibly use in the contracting process: information asymmetry, incumbency, use of a compliance mechanism, transfer of transaction cost to the other party, asset specificity and opportunism.

Information asymmetry: The term 'information asymmetry' was emphasised by Williamson in order to capture all the aspects of limited and asymmetric information (Williamson, 1985). This category includes all the mechanisms used by one party to alter information costs facing the other party (Twight, 1994, p 207).

Imperfect information has long been recognised as an obstacle to rational human decision making (Simon, 1978). Information systems allow the production of relevant information at a reasonable cost (Bouttes and Hamamdjian, 1997, p 81). Uncertainty arises whenever complete information is not available. As a result of uncertainty, optimal decision making cannot be achieved. Principal-agent theorists further suggest that there is an information asymmetry between a principal and an agent. The agent always knows more about the true ability of the service provider to meet its commitments, which, to the principal, involve hidden characteristics and efforts (Austin-Smith and William, 1987; Korosec, 1994).

An agent is hired by a principal to act on its behalf, and the principal expects benefits as a result of the agent's action. Therefore, an agent's action should be expected to add to the welfare of the principal. Problems arise when an agent has its own preference and utility functions, which may not be the same as those of its principal. Combining information asymmetry and different preferences, the agent has a tendency to evade transaction costs, that is, to maximise its own benefits, instead of those of the principal. As a result, so-called 'misrepresentation' (Weisbrod and Schelesinger, 1986, p 134), such as promising to deliver a specific level of quality and quantity but actually delivering a lower level, is prone to occur. To remedy the agent's tendency to evade transaction costs, information asymmetries must be minimised (Dixit, 1996).

Information asymmetries are present in government contracting out. Contracted providers always know more about who they are, and what they are doing, than the sponsoring government does. Compared to the contractors themselves, the government is always less knowledgeable about the contractors' characteristics and efforts. In this situation, the contractor has an informational advantage over the government (Rehfuss, 1990).

On the other hand, contrary to the view of many principal-agent theorists mentioned earlier, a principal sometimes has informational advantages over its agent. As Perrow (1986) suggests, an agent sometimes has less information than its principal about the true state of the production environment, although both are essential for efficient and effective production.

Twight (1994) puts forward the argument that information asymmetry arises for a number of reasons. One of these is overt distortion of information about the contract on the part of the parties involved. The other is the restriction of access to information about the contract by the parties. The parties engaged in the CCT process are able to influence both the other party and, eventually, the CCT policy implementation process by employing the strategy of information asymmetry.

Incumbency: This is one of the practical and specific strategies by which the politics of transaction costs can occur. Institutional patterns, according to Williamson (1985), tend to evolve in a way that will minimise the costs of transactions. Briefly, firms and hierarchies act to minimise the transactions cost involved in making exchanges. However, in contrast, when they work as incumbent for a contract either hierarchies or firms also tend to act in such a way as to maximise transaction costs to prevent the other party from entering the market they operate.

Incumbent contractors have an informational, political and demonstrational advantage over non-incumbent contractors (Denes, 1996; Dixit, 1996). These three attributes can restrict competition for government contracts, leading to an increase in transaction costs for non-incumbent contractors.

The incumbent firm enjoys an informational advantage over other bidders (Vickers and Yarrow, 1988). This information may include knowledge about costs that outside competitors may not be able to obtain (Starr, 1991) as well as information about the project site and the client (Rothkoph, 1983). This information may be available to the non-incumbent, but only at a cost. Stigler (1966) found that although most economic information is available to all, it may take 'time and effort' to uncover such information in the marketplace. For example, an incumbent refuse collection contractor has considerable information about the types of problems encountered by the client and knowledge of the approaches to problems that best please the client. Some scholars (Engelbrecht-Wiggans et al, 1983; Hendricks and Porter, 1988) found that incumbent firms were more likely to win the following contracts and more likely to generate profits than firms that relied only on publicly available data.

An incumbent contractor may also have information on the number of competing bidders on follow-up contracts. If the incumbent anticipates a large number of competitors, it may lower its bid. Conversely, if few competitors are identified, the incumbent can raise its bid (Denes, 1996).

An incumbent contractor also has the opportunity to garner the political goodwill associated with successful performance of the contract as well as to establish the interpersonal connections necessary for a successful rebid. To continue using the services of the incumbent contractor, programme managers may tailor their procurement specifications to favour the incumbent contractor or may delay the procurement procedures until the last minute to preclude the contracting officer from fully advertising the procurement (Cohen, 1983). The high performing incumbent also has an opportunity to demonstrate to the government its superior performance (Denes, 1996).

It could be argued that incumbents will have lower winning bids because they will use their informational advantage to beat the competition and that the incumbent may have the information to bid just low enough to beat the competition. Aside from fairness, the incumbent may be bidding well above its marginal cost, gaining a substantial windfall (Denes, 1996).

Use of compliance mechanisms: Since the policy implementation environment consists of so many actors and institutions, it is assumed that these different actors may attempt to resist or circumvent policy directives for a variety of reasons (Nakamura and Smallwood, 1980, pp 59-60).

In his paper 'Legal analysis of economic policy', Daintith (1982) has indicated that a government has two means at its disposal to pursue policy objectives: it may change the behaviour of those with whom it deals by reducing the costs of behaviour which complies with a given policy; or it may increase the costs of behaviour which fails to comply. To adopt either means, the government must deploy certain compliance mechanisms to provoke various actors to carry out certain policy instructions. This raises a central issue of the politics of transaction cost: How can one set of actors influence another set of actors to carry out a policy directive, particularly if there is disagreement over those directives?

In *Modern political analysis*, Dahl (1976, p 29) points out that "the notion of politics and a political system presupposes that words like control, power, authority and influence have a definite meaning". However, the fact is that these words are ambiguous; their meaning is elusive and complex. In an effort to clarify these "influence terms", Dahl discusses power relationships between two individual actors. While his analysis indicates that relationships of influence between two individuals are diverse and complicated, these relationships become even more complex when efforts are made to secure compliance within, or between, bureaucratic institutions or organisations that consist of many different actors.

Etzioni (1964, pp 59-60) has observed that "the means of control applied by an organisation can be classified into three analytical categories":

1. **Physical (coercive) power** – the application, or the threat of application, of punitive sanctions.

2. **Material (utilitarian) power** – the allocation of material resources such as goods and services (eg salaries, fringe benefits).

3. **Symbolic (normative) power** – the allocation and manipulation of symbolic rewards and deprivations (eg prestige, esteem).

Hence, Etzioni's classification indicates that different types of negative sanctions and positive rewards can be employed in an effort to secure compliance.

'Compliance mechanism'[10] is one method whereby government can secure policy goals. For example, central government can use it to pursue social objectives by inserting onerous clauses into its legal framework, with which local authorities or private contractors must comply. Given that government has such diverse means at its disposal, it may use one or all, or a combination of, methods to secure compliance with its policy goals.

Accordingly, what matters is the policy objectives of central government. Depending on the policy objectives government wants to realise through the policy, it can use existing legislative powers or create new legislation which can be advantageous to either one or the other party, whereby government intentionally ends up destroying the level playing field. In this case, if central government is biased towards private providers in the CCT legal framework this implies that it intends to decrease transaction costs for private bidders and increase them for local government (and vice versa if its bias is against the private sector).

Transfer of transaction costs to the other party: Another example of strategies which are to be mobilised by the parties concerned is the transfer of transaction costs to the other party. Hill (1997b, p 76) argues that where market considerations apply, organisations are likely to try to externalise costs. Twight (1994) also implies that contract parties tend to transfer to the other party the transaction cost burden entailed in effecting the change. In an empirical analysis, Walsh et al (1997) argue that there have been a number of cases of attempts to shift costs and risks between purchaser and provider, emphasising that various patterns of CCT process can be identified as being a result of transaction cost issues such as shifts of risk from one party to the other.

During the CCT process, it is likely that attempts can be made to shift the costs, risk or default to the other party, for example by making the private contractors responsible for coping with variations in the quantity of work or the impact of external factors (Walsh et al, 1997).

Asset specificity: Asset specificity relates to skills or equipment which cannot commonly be used in other endeavours. Under such conditions, the acquisition of specific assets indicates that a type of dependency exists between two parties (Williamson, 1985, pp 52-4). Asset specificity leads to a situation of bilateral monopoly. Once the investment has been made it is difficult for the buyer to go to alternative providers and the person who has made the investment gains quasi-monopoly advantages (Coulson, 1997, p 109; Walsh, 1995, p 35). Accordingly, it appears that the main parties involved in the CCT process seek to make the other party dependent on asset specificity for their benefits.

Opportunism: Opportunism is "self-related interest undertaken with guile" (Williamson, 1985, p 30). This is what Knight called 'moral hazard'; others have called it deviousness, or deceitfulness (Coulson, 1997, p 109). It means that people take advantage of situations where they can benefit by so doing. It includes "blatant" forms such as "lying, stealing, and cheating", and more subtle forms such as "the incomplete or distorted disclosure of information ... calculated efforts to mislead, distort, disguise, obfuscate, or otherwise confuse" (Coulson, 1997). It can happen before or after a contract is awarded or a decision made.

This concept suggests that the doing of whatever is necessary to achieve your desired goal is an action which may take place (in either latent or manifest form) within and among organisations (Williamson, 1985, p 30). Because of this, transaction cost theory is subject to opportunistic functions such as adverse selection, moral hazard and other problems of information asymmetry (Williamson, 1985). When the parties to a contract have differential access to information, or one is stronger than another, for example in terms of wealth, then it is possible that the party with the advantage will be able to exploit the other, for example by breaching the terms of the contract, safe in the knowledge that the powerless partner can do little about it (Walsh, 1995, p 34).

The dangers of opportunism are enhanced where there are small numbers bargaining, that is, when there is imperfect competition in markets, because it will be difficult to jettison those who have behaved opportunistically in the past at the time when agreements are renewed. Even if you know you are likely to be exploited you may have little choice but to contract with the potentially exploitative party (Korosec, 1994; Walsh, 1995).

Opportunism has been a part of interactions since Niccolò Machiavelli noted that a prince should trust no one other than himself and should make efforts to keep citizens under his control, owing to the fact that he can never fully anticipate how they will act in any given situation (Korosec, 1994, pp 80-1). Efforts to control an organisation or group and have it act in the desired way result in obedience. Obedience can often be obtained by creating incentives and other regulations (through monitoring) so that the agent will act in a way which is acceptable to the principal (Korosec, 1994).

The existence of opportunistic behaviour within an organisation may run counter to the efficiency-based motive, since self-interested actions may not be the most cost-effective means to an end. When a local authority is able to observe a contractor's opportunistic behaviour (such as shirking and moral hazard), it may work to erode the local authority's confidence in the contractor's behaviour, or in contracting in general. These conditions signal the need for monitoring (Denes, 1996; Walsh et al, 1997).

What will happen as a result of the politics of transaction cost?

It is hypothesised that in the local authority, genuinely competitive contracting environments do not exist. The number of qualified and bidding service providers may be limited. Procedures and processes which promote competition may not be used. Excessively comprehensive specifications may eliminate many smaller private companies from competing, leaving only larger, more experienced private companies or DSOs qualified to bid. Awards may even be predetermined because of certain criteria or limitations. This can easily lead to abuse, poor programme evaluation, and so on (Goodwin, 1994; Twight, 1988; 1994).

It is also hypothesised that decision-making processes are far from perfectly rational. Decisions regarding whether contracts will be awarded and to whom will be based on limited or erroneous data. It may be difficult to compare public and private costs because of accounting differences. This difference may be increased by a reliance on providers for data concerning the costs of contracted service alternatives. It is also conjectured that these governmental units have not framed clear policy objectives, nor established clear lines of accountability (Denes, 1996).

It is expensive to draw up enforceable contracts. There is a conflict of interest between business interests and government interests, profit versus the obligation to represent and perform services for all citizens. The monitoring and assessment of contractor performance is not only expensive, but, because of ineffective techniques and incapable personnel, may often be ineffective. When the politics of transaction cost are involved in the CCT process, it may be, as DeHoog asserts, that "negative unanticipated consequences" occur (DeHoog, 1985, p 432; Rehfuss, 1990).

Mechanisms for coping with the politics of transaction cost

Many apparent inefficiencies in the policy process are the consequences of constraints imposed by various transaction costs. A policy should not be condemned as inefficient unless a superior alternative that respects all these constraints can be demonstrated; this is Williamson's criterion of remediability.

From the point of view of service recipients (ordinary citizens) the mechanisms by which the politics of transaction costs can be removed or relaxed in the policy process should be developed for the ordinary citizen to benefit from the policy.

The politics of transaction cost framework recognises that all parties to a transaction can benefit if they can develop ways to prevent the politics of transaction cost, just as they can reap mutual gains by economising on resource costs of production, for example by specialising according to comparative advantage (Dixit, 1996, p 61).

Each of the participants diverges in some way from the others, and has some informational advantage and some freedom of action. Therefore, the institutions or processes must evolve to ameliorate problems such as opportunism, either with feasible external enforcement mechanisms or with credible internal ones. The success or failure of economic ventures and transactions may depend on the ability of the participants to devise such institutions and enforcement mechanisms (Dixit, 1996).

There is benefit to be gained from economising on transaction costs. Rules and institutions should, and do, evolve to serve this purpose. The precise nature of the institution depends on the nature of the problem to be addressed. The mechanisms for coping with the politics of transaction costs will be briefly examined in Chapters Seven and Eight.

Methodological assumptions behind the politics of transaction cost framework

Conditions or assumptions about the politics of transaction costs need to be stated before constructing the analytical framework. These assumptions are described below.

Contract as the unit of analysis

In the transaction cost approach, the basic unit of analysis is a 'contract', or single transaction between two parties in an economic relationship. Such contracts are generally promises whereby one party agrees to take an action of economic value to the other, in return for some reciprocal action or else a payment. These actions are generally taken with different degrees of observability, at different points in time, and with different degrees of sunkenness or reversibility (Dixit, 1996, p 48).

In the politics of transaction cost, the parties to a contract are citizens (individuals, the general public, interest group[11] organisations or private companies) on the one hand, and politicians (individuals or parties) or administrators (such as regulatory agencies) on the other. However, contracts in the public sector differ from those in the private sector in several ways, all of which make them more complex and more difficult to enforce.

Contracts in the public sector are rarely between two clearly identifiable contractors; there are multiple parties on at least one side of the relationship (Dixit, 1996). For example, in the CCT process there are at least three main parties concerned: central government, the local authority, and private companies or other local authorities as external providers. The general public can also become an important party. However, the general public as a party to a contract is not always clear and specific. Hence, in this study the number of the main parties to a contract is limited to three: central government, the local authority and private contractors.

CCT policy is central government-imposed privatisation policy, which means that the politics of transaction costs can take place between central and local governments. Government officeholders, whether they are central or local, elected or appointed, have the incentive and ability to manipulate the transaction costs facing each party, operating as they do in an environment highly conducive to intergovernment manipulation of transaction costs.

The terms of such contracts are generally more vague than those of economic contracts. They leave a great deal of room for interpretation, many loopholes for escape and many opportunities to blame third parties. Theoretically, the politics of transaction costs can occur in every relationship. Rather than attempt to analyse all the possible relationships between them, the more limited purpose of this study is to focus on characteristic phenomena relating to transaction costs.

Difficulties with measurement

Empirical work drawing on transaction cost analysis uses a variety of econometric and historical methods. In general, these studies fall into one of three categories: qualitative case studies, quantitative case studies, and cross-national econometric analyses. Williamson's (1976) study of cable TV franchising in Oakland, California is an example of the first category, while Walsh and Davis' (1993) investigation of contracting practices is an example of the second, and Levy's (1985) study of vertical integration across industries an example of the third.

The bulk of the empirical literature in transaction cost economics consists of case analyses of various types. This is primarily because the main variables of interest to transaction cost economists – asset specificity, uncertainty, frequency – are difficult to measure consistently across firms and industries. Typically, these characteristics are estimated, based on surveys or interview. For example, a manager might be asked to rate on a Likert-type scale of 1 to 7 the degree to which an investment has value in outside uses (Klein and Shelanski, 1995, p 337). Such data is subject to the general limits of survey data: namely, that it is based on the respondents' stated belief, rather than on their beliefs or valuations as revealed through choice.

Since these measurements are based on ordinal rankings, it is difficult to compare them from industry to industry. What is ranked as a relatively specialised asset in one firm may be rated differently in another firm or industry. Similarly, what one firm considers a comparatively uncertain production process may be the standard operating environment in another. Multi-industry studies may contain variables that are labelled the same thing but are really incommensurable or, conversely, may contain variables that are identical but labelled differently (Klein and Shelanski, 1995).

Williamson is somewhat indirect in his measurement of transaction costs. While he notes that transaction cost theory looks at the differences between various contracting options, he believes that it is the "differences between rather than the absolute magnitude of transaction costs that matters" (Williamson, 1985, p 22). He cites and agrees with Simon's notion that comparing costs need not be a function of elaborate mathematical systems. He contends that "much cruder and simpler arguments will suffice to demonstrate an inequality between two quantities". He also states:

> **Empirical research on transaction cost matters almost never attempts to measure such costs directly. Instead, the question is whether organisational relations (contracting practices, governance structures) line up with the attributes of transactions as predicted by transaction cost reasoning or not ... transaction costs are always stressed in a comparative institutional way, in which one mode of contracting is compared with another. (Williamson, 1985, p 22)**

As with transaction cost economics, in the politics of transaction costs the problem of how to measure the costs associated with the manipulation of transaction costs still remains unresolved. In terms of the politics of transaction costs it is likely to be much more difficult to resolve.

Governance structures

Transaction cost economics suggests a strong relationship between the characteristics of the transactions at stake and the governance structure adopted (Menard, 1997, p 36). It views firms as governance structures, replacing the neo-classical view of them as a production function. According to the neo-classical view, once the quantities of inputs used in a production process are specified, exogenous technological considerations will fix the quantity of output (Dixit, 1996). Williamson (1985, p 15) noted that over time, governance structures tend towards efficiency and against monopoly. He also maintains that lower costs (such as those associated with contractors) are the main impetus behind economic institutions changing their focus from hierarchies (internally produced goods) to markets (externally produced goods).

In the transaction cost economics view, the differing degrees of sunkenness of different inputs will affect the behaviour of their owners, unobservability of quality or effort will influence the effectiveness of other inputs, managerial quality and effort will determine how well the inputs are combined, and so on. The mechanisms that are in place to counter these transaction cost problems, for example incentive schemes, will also influence the behaviour of the various parties (Dixit, 1996). The organisational and governance structures of firms will have an important impact on what they do. Political institutions and private organisations are governance structures and are well recognised as such.

Governance structures are characterised by various relationships. In a firm, for example, the managers act as agents of the equity owners, who are the principals. The hierarchy of a firm often involves other agency relations, for example between managers and line supervisors, or purchasers and outside suppliers (Dietrich, 1994; Dixit, 1996).

The general idea of the transaction cost framework is that the interests of the parties to a transaction are at least partially in conflict. Agency relationships are often more complex in the political than in the economic context. Wilson (1989) has emphasised the multiplicity and complexity of agency relationships in politics and public administration. Most importantly, it is not always clear who is whose agent. Different models have taken different views on this. In many models of macroeconomic politics, the government or the treasury is the principal and the central bank the agent. Similarly, in CCT policy, central government can be the principal and the local authority the agent, or alternatively the local authority can be the principal and the private sector the agent.

Weaknesses of the politics of transaction cost framework

The politics of the transaction cost approach offers the promise both of a better analytical understanding of the policy process at a given moment in time and of an explanation for the differential performance of politics and economies over time. It does so because the level of transaction costs is a function of the institutions (and technology) employed. Not only do institutions define the incentive structure at a moment in time; their evolution shapes the long-run path of political/economic change (North, 1990b, p 367).

Nevertheless, the politics of transaction cost approach is open to some criticisms, which derive from the assumptions and implications of the transaction cost economics theory. Williamson (1985) notes that this model is still somewhat "primitive and in need of refinement". He suggests that the theory should be used with other methods of examining the same situation. He correctly states that others who make systematic headway by using this alternative will help restore even sceptics' perspectives. For their part, sceptics have been very vocal in condemning the utility of transaction cost theory.

Fisher (1977) has noted that the bad name this theory has is warranted. He argues that because almost anything can be rationalised by this theory, it is useless as a tool for clear conceptual study. He suggests that the costs associated with any given transaction may be so numerous that it is not possible adequately to consider the true (transaction) costs.

Schneider (Bamberg and Spremann, 1987, pp 487-9) contends that transaction costs are a 'flop', and lists many reasons for this belief. They include the idea that many costs are ignored or unable to be measured through this model, the claim that 'cost' is used as a vague conception in transaction cost theory and the allegation that the theory does not go far enough in comparing the sum or costs and residual claims.

Walsh (1995, p 238) also argues that, to date, no comprehensive evaluation of transaction costs has been undertaken, although some figures have been published relating to transaction costs, such as consultancy fees and redundancy pay in the CCT process. He adds that new techniques such as the use of computer packages for monitoring contracts, or for managing the internal market, may reduce costs in the long term, but will have high short-term costs.

The majority of the criticism of transaction cost theory seems to focus on the idea that the theory is both too universal and too narrow. It is seen as a universal theory because it can be used to describe almost any cost-based contracting situation. In the same way, it is narrow because some contracting systems may contain costs for which no monetary number can be determined.

The debate so far has established the theoretical background to the conceptual framework for the politics of transaction cost. Chapter Six presents the analytical framework and the research methodology used in the case studies.

Notes

[1] Coase (1937, p 390) is generally acknowledged as the 'founder' of transaction cost economics (although he does not use this term in his 1937 paper), and for this reason his work is important in its own right (Dietrich, 1994, p 15). Coase opens his paper with the simple, but startling (for his times), observation that if the price mechanism can effectively allocate resources, there is no obvious reason why resource allocation

should be planned/directed within firms. To solve this apparent problem he suggests that "the main reason why it is profitable to establish a firm would seem to be that there is a cost of using the price mechanism". This cost can be reduced to a number of factors: (a) the cost of discovering prices and (b) the cost of negotiating and concluding contracts. Rather than construct an individual contract for each person employed specifying detailed responsibilities, obvious economies are available by using employment contracts that specify limits to the power of an employer – detailed direction is undertaken within a firm. In addition, with long-term contracts there is a further cost in terms of the price mechanism because forecasting, and consequently contract specification, problems inevitably exist.

Dietrich (1994) describes Coase's later (1960) definition of transaction costs:

> **In order to carry out a market transaction it is necessary to discover who it is that one deals with, to inform people that one wishes to deal and on what terms, to conduct negotiations leading up to a bargain, to draw up a contract, to undertake the inspection needed to make sure that the terms of the contract are being observed, and so on. The above constitutes the central features of Coase's analysis. (Dietrich, 1994, pp 15-16)**

[2] Williamson has changed his view concerning the relative importance of different governance structures. In his 1975 work he was of the opinion that economic institutions clustered at either end of the governance spectrum: hence the title *Market and hierarchies*. Intermediate structures were viewed as unstable. In his 1985 work he was persuaded that "transactions in the middle range (between market and hierarchy) are much more common". However, what is not clear is whether he believes his earlier work to be mistaken or obsolete (Dietrich, 1994, p 22).

[3] Williamson (1985) recognises his debt to Simon, who was the first scholar systematically to develop the idea of bounded rationality.

[4] The four types of asset specificity put forward by Reve (1990) are characterised as follows. First, certain service areas may require a specified type of skill that the government otherwise may not have or cannot afford. Experts may include licensed professionals or others with advanced expertise in certain areas. Contracting out these services may serve as a

means to provide needed expertise at costs which are lower than the fees government would otherwise have to pay these permanent professionals (*expertise*). Second, a government often finds that it needs a particular asset, but only on a limited or seasonal basis. Examples may include tasks associated with different seasons or special events, such as concerts or civic events (*temporary workers*). Third, certain tools or assets may be too expensive, too rarely used, too new, or too cumbersome for certain governments to maintain. Under such circumstances, governments may be likely to contract with private agents to provide the needed assets (*specific assets*). Fourth, there may be instances which may warrant governments to contract out with private firms to provide services, even when governments have the tools and expertise to do the job themselves. Examples of this may include weather-related emergencies or disasters which disrupt basic public services (*urgent needs*).

[5] If all participants in the economy could be brought together, if initial ownership rights to all economically valuable entities were assigned among these participants, and if they could costlessly make fully specified and fully binding agreements, then the outcome should be an efficient economic plan, leaving only the division of the spoils to be determined by the bargaining strengths of the participants. Here there would be no role for politics (Dixit, 1996, p 37). For detailed discussions see Demsetz (1964) and Buchanan (1973).

[6] Whatever the categories of transaction costs, it appears that in practical terms there are many areas involved in the CCT process. The list below represents the main areas in which transaction costs would be incurred by local authorities. These costs include the following (Foster, 1991; Walsh, 1995; Walsh et al, 1997):

- preparing tender documents and inviting tenders through advertising;

- drawing up stringent specifications in contracts and consequently monitoring the tender to ensure that specifications are being met;

- organising tendering arrangements, including costs from investigating contractors, evaluating tenders, and meeting with contractors;

- preparing an inhouse tender;

- the cost of training staff to deal with statutory tendering;

- the cost of keeping separate tendering accounts for each activity and annual financial accounts for publication as required by legislation;

- possible redundancy costs incurred from disbanding a DSO if a tender is lost to the private sector;

- the costs of consultants' reports, etc.

[7] There is an opposite view to this argument. Twight (1988, p 143) points out that in the political market, unlike in the private market, the incentive of private individuals to acquire and act upon information relating to governmental officeholders' performance is very small, due to the external and indirect nature of the benefits they can receive.

[8] The sources of these questions are also addressed by Williamson (1997, p 5).

[9] Loss-leading refers to the practice of diversified firms offering some portion of their product range at prices below cost, in the belief that this will encourage sales of other higher-profit-margin products. This is common among retailers, who use 'loss-leaders' to attract customers who then may buy high-profit-margin goods as a matter of convenience or impulse (Pearce, 1981, p 261).

[10] Analogous with compliance mechanism is 'contract compliance'. This was first introduced in the United States in 1941, when discrimination against black workers in connection with all federal government war contracts was prohibited (Marston, 1990, p 1). Put at its simplest, it means that in obtaining goods and services through contract, a public body may at the same time pursue social objectives by inserting clauses into its contracts with which its contractors must comply (Marston, 1990). Public sector purchasing power is used as a means to achieve various policy objectives, through the medium of clauses inserted into contracts, with which prospective or actual contractors with public bodies must comply (Daintith, 1982; Martson, 1990).

In Britain, contract compliance has been the subject of much controversy in recent years, both between Government and Opposition and between central and local government. Central government and local authorities have historically used their contractual powers in pursuit of a host of policy objectives. Government employment of contractual clauses has provided a tool whereby policy objectives could be pursued and enforced on the private sector via the law of contract (Marston, 1990, pp 13-14).

[11] For further discussion of local interest groups see Cross and Mallen (1987, pp 142-4), Dearlove (1973, pp 155-62) and Stoker (1991, pp 114-37).

SIX

Analytical framework and research methodology: case studies

Introduction

The previous chapter laid the groundwork for understanding the CCT process from the politics of transaction costs perspective. This chapter explains the analytical framework for the case studies, and the methods used to apply the politics of transaction cost perspective to the CCT process empirically. At this stage it would be too ambitious to attempt to generalise the various forms of the politics of transaction cost incurred by the main parties in the CCT process.

The political dynamic associated with the CCT process was found to be inextricably linked with sequential events happening during the policy process. It will be imperative to include the time dimension within the study's design. Consequently, an exploratory-longitudinal design was selected to uncover more of the nature and meaning of the politics underlying the CCT process.

Overview of the analytical framework

Perhaps one of the best ways to begin to understand the debate on privatisation is to restructure it into a model which makes it possible to categorise privatisation as a type of bureaucratic behaviour within a system of rational actions. In this way the focus can be on the function of interactions between individuals belonging to differing groups. Goals, incentives, institutions and actors all differ under such assumptions. Yet the symbiotic nature of the relationship suggests the need for cooperation and communication between the parties concerned (Dixit, 1996).

Adopting the transaction costs framework broadens the base of policy choices. Its search for organisational optimality avoids adherence to a top-down view of implementation (Sabatier, 1986). The top-down view tacitly assumes there is one organisational best way that inhibits implementation from refining policy instruments or from correcting hierarchies. Movement away from the top-down view will also reduce lingering normative attachment to the dichotomy between politics and administration (Nagel, 1994).

Main components of the analytical framework

Figures 6.1 and 6.2 set out the main constituents of the analytical framework. Figure 6.1 shows that this research framework pays due regard to the way such a CCT process is structured by a trinity of forces

Figure 6.1: Three essential dimensions of the politics of transaction costs

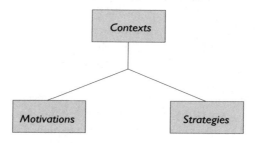

Figure 6.2: Understanding the dynamics of the CCT process

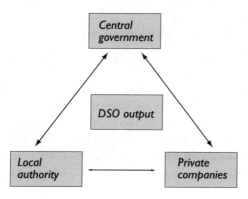

– contexts, motivations, and strategies – while Figure 6.2 assumes that the output of CCT policy, DSO output, is influenced by the politics of transaction costs incurred by various parties, limited in this study to central government, local authority and private companies, who try to shift, manipulate or use them for their political and economic ends.

As was discussed earlier, the normative approach to policy analysis assumes that once a policy that maximises social welfare has been found, it will be implemented as designed, and the desired effects will follow. The positive view of policy analysis views the policy output as being determined by the working of the process within the rules that were laid down. However, in the politics of transaction cost framework it is assumed that the strength of the motives each party has for manipulating transaction costs, the contexts surrounding each party and the strategies by which each party can mobilise will affect the output of CCT policy, DSO output. Regarding the politics of transaction costs, DSO output is a function of the motivations, contexts and strategies of the three parties. This logic can be illustrated by the equation Y (DSO output) = f (M + C + S), where M is motivations, C contexts, and S strategies.

Each of these three areas contains a collection of research themes and issues. Complete answers to these issues are clearly beyond the scope of a single research project. This study will focus on what it perceives to be the key issues.

Contexts

In this study, *context* refers to the 'what' surrounding the main parties in relation to the politics of transaction costs (Pettigrew and Whipp, 1991, p 26): the conditions or circumstances under which the main parties were able to activate and to manipulate the transaction costs in their own interests. The contexts in which the main parties operate are not inert or objective entities. Just as the main parties perceive and construct their own versions of those contexts, so they subjectively select their own versions of the competitive environment together with their personal versions of how to reorder their strategies to meet those perceived challenges. Three groups of issues which arise in relation to the context in which CCT policy has been implemented will be emphasised: legal framework, local organisational culture, industrial relations.

The study will examine whether the legal framework grants discretion to the main parties in relation to use of transaction costs or not. In so doing, a documentary analysis will be made of the 1988, 1992 and 1994

Acts and EU regulation. The views of a solicitor interviewed for the study will also be examined.

As regards local organisational culture,[1] what the councillors and officials thought of CCT in general is investigated via interview, and documentary analysis[2] of unpublished materials such as minutes, reports to councillors, tender documents of tender evaluation, and inter-office memoranda.

Finally, regarding context, whether the trade unions were able to participate in the process of CCT at the local level or not, whether industrial action took place in protest to CCT implementation, and what role councillors and officials perceived trade unions played in the CCT process were analysed via documentary analysis and interviews with local government officials.

Legal framework and local organisational culture have been addressed in the analysis of institutional changes regarding CCT and commonly appear in academic and popular discourse. However, by contrast, rather less attention has been paid to the responses of trade unions themselves to CCT developments, on the basis that union membership, economic power and political influence have all been eroded since 1979 when Margaret Thatcher came to power. This argument is unfortunate for three reasons. First, it understates the degree to which economic and political change is actively contested (or supported) by the groups affected by it. Secondly, it gives the impression that organisations such as trade unions are simply at the mercy of a wider process of structural social change over which they have no control. Thirdly, it can lead to an inadequate understanding of the ways in which institutions actually operate by, for example, underpinning a functionalist interpretation of social phenomena in which changes in institutions are the result of the 'needs' of some wider system.

In actuality, many empirical analyses have shown that trade unions played a major role in opposing both competitive tendering and contracting out. This has been observed by, among others, Asher (1987, p 1) in Britain, Savas (1987, p 257) in the United States and Shann (1990) in Australia. Itani in Japan refers to a considerable number of conflicts between local authorities and unions (1989, p 52). Savas notes that contracting is seen as a profound threat by government-employee unions, although he adds that, ironically, the contractor's private employees are themselves often unionised. This framework will include an examination of the ways in which trade unions and their members actively respond to, and intervene in, some of the processes of CCT which affect them.

Motivations

The second main area of the research framework relates to the motives for using the politics of transaction costs which each party has had during the CCT process. *Motivations* refers to the 'why' of the politics of transaction costs: the particular reasons for the politics of transaction costs. Central government, local authority and private companies can have motives for using transaction costs in relation to CCT. Whether these motives are strong or not will influence the output of CCT policy, DSO output, since in theory, motivation determines behaviour (Plunkett and Attner, 1994, p 388).

Motivation is the result of the interaction between a person's internalised needs and the external influences that determine behaviour (Plunkett and Attner, 1994, p 388). People make conscious decisions for their own welfare. In this case the question is why do some use transaction costs whereas others do not? The study of motivations concerns what prompts people to act, what influences their choices of action, and why they persist in acting in a certain way.

A person's needs provide the basis for a motivation model. Needs are deficiencies that a person experiences at a particular time. They can be physiological or psychological. Unsatisfied needs stimulate wants and behaviours. In choosing a behaviour to satisfy a need, a person must evaluate several factors (Plunkett and Attner, 1994, pp 388-9), as follows:

- *Past experiences:* All the person's previous experiences of the situation in hand enter into the motivation model. These include the satisfaction derived from acting in a certain way, any frustration felt, the amount of effort required, and the relationship of performance to rewards.

- *Environmental influences:* The choice of behaviours is affected by the environment, which in a business setting comprises the organisation's values as well as the expectations and actions of management.

- *Perceptions:* The individual is influenced by perceptions of the expected effort required to achieve performance, and the value of the reward both absolutely and in relation to what peers have received for the same effort. These variables can determine whether a person performs a particular task.

According to Vroom's motivation theory (Vroom et al, 1992), the organisation's performance depends on whether its motivation to achieve a particular goal is strong or not. Some scholars (Nakamura and Smallwood, 1980; Van Meter and Van Horn, 1975) point out that policy output or administrative performance can be influenced by the psychological motivations of the interested parties. In discussing psychological motivations Van Meter and Van Horn (1975, p 473) note that "implementors may screen out a clear message when the decision seems to contradict deeply cherished beliefs".

This study argues that this logic applies to all parties involved in the policy process, such as policy makers, policy implementors, policy recipients and interest groups. In view of this argument it can be hypothesised that the intensity of the interested parties' dispositions towards the use of transaction costs affects their performance. For example, holding intense negative preferences may lead to outright and open defiance of the programme's objectives. Similarly, less intense attitudes may cause implementors to attempt surreptitious diversion and evasion. Likewise, whether the motivation towards the manipulation of transaction costs is strong or not is important in determining the policy output. For these reasons, the study investigates and analyses whether central government, local authority and private companies were motivated to use the politics of transaction costs or not, and whether their possible motivations were strong or not.

To analyse the motivations of central government it is necessary to examine the differences between the 1988, 1992 and 1994 Acts, focusing on clauses[3] inserted into the Acts by central government with which local authorities and prospective or actual contractors must comply. This will shed light on the attitudes of the DoE towards CCT, which are examined via document analysis and discussion with a solicitor.

To analyse the motivations of local government, the general view of local authorities towards transaction costs and their attitudes to the relationship between transaction costs and the chances of private contractors winning the contract are investigated via document analysis and interview.

As regards measuring the motivations of private contractors towards the politics of transaction costs, the anecdotal evidence available is not sufficient to allow a verdict. Analyses of the motivations of private contractors towards it did not reveal information which could directly determine the effect of it on the CCT process. To evaluate the motivations of the private companies operating in each local authority it is necessary to use a proxy variable. For this purpose, in this analysis the number of private companies tendering for the contracts is utilised to measure qualitatively the motivation of private companies. It is hypothesised that the greater the number of the private companies that tendered for the contract, the stronger the motivation of the private sector to use the politics of transaction costs.

Strategies

The third and perhaps most critical – yet elusive – area of the research framework concerns the strategies used by the main parties. These are concerned with the processual dimension of CCT policy implementation. *Strategy* refers to the 'how' of the politics of transaction costs and considers the actions, reactions and interactions of the main parties as they seek to fulfil their goals. This relates to the strategies they use to manipulate transaction costs. Both in theory and in practice, the scope of the strategies they could adopt in the CCT process depends on the motivations of the main parties and the underlying contexts.

These strategies, as stated earlier in the previous chapter, can include compliance mechanism, information asymmetry, incumbency, transfer of transaction costs to the other party, asset specificity and opportunism. The use of a compliance mechanism can be referred to as a strategy for achieving various policy objectives, through the medium of clauses inserted into the legal framework for CCT, with which the other parties (a local authority or prospective contractors) must comply.

Information asymmetry captures all aspects of limited and asymmetric information. It has a close parallel in the work of Stiglitz and others in information economics, where the corresponding concept is split into three different aspects (Dixit, 1996, p 54):

- a pre-contract informational advantage for one of the parties (adverse selection, leading to signalling and screening costs);

- non-observability of the agent's action (moral hazard, leading to costs of monitoring or incentive schemes);

- non-verifiability of information to outsiders (leading to auditing costs or costs owing to misrepresentation when an audit is too costly); this category includes self-interested volitional manipulation of information.

Incumbency is a strategy by which incumbent contractors can win the subsequent contracts by having informational, political and demonstrational advantages over non-incumbent contractors. Asset specificity can be also a strategy through which the party to a contract is able to win the subsequent contracts by making the service provision dependent on it, leading to a situation of bilateral monopoly. Opportunism involves an 'interest-seeking with guile' strategy employed by the parties to a contract. The transfer of transaction costs to the other party is a strategy by which the parties to a contract attempt to shift risks or burdens to the other party in the policy process.

The politics of transaction costs comprises all types of action by which the parties to a contract can influence the other party during the competitive tendering process, constraining and impeding the other party's choices in the different stages of competitive tendering, such as negotiation, and monitoring. Interview and documentary analysis are used to analyse the strategies employed by the three parties in the CCT process.

Connections with DSO output

As much of the foregoing implies, the analytical challenge is to connect context, motivation and strategy with the output of CCT policy, DSO output. A range of possible linkages has already been implied. Perhaps the most critical connection for the research is the way in which the three main parties mobilise the strategies and in so doing provide legitimacy for their purpose. Specifically, it is hypothesised that the connection between the party which can manipulate, or change, the transaction costs in the CCT process and the other party is controlled by these transaction costs. The politics of transaction costs should not be regarded as some static backcloth to the DSO output but should be seen as a legacy of resources, constraints and opportunities that are bequeathed to the main parties.

In essence, the research uses a synthesis of a contextualist and processual orientation to the CCT policy process to discover how DSO output relates to the dynamics of CCT policy implementation. This research framework is contextualist, in that it not only focuses on the actions of individuals and groups in implementing or retarding the development of contracting out during the process of competitive tendering, but also takes into account the constraints imposed on those actions by social, cultural and historical contexts (Pettigrew et al, 1992). The approach links both individual action and structure, in contrast to that of previous studies which have largely separated these levels. The approach is processual in that it explores the continuous process of CCT in selected local authorities as they seek to implement the CCT policy. The CCT process consists of many stages. One of the first stages in the process is tender specification. Tenders are written by client departments of the authorities. The council then seeks financial quotes. This involves advertising contracts in local, national and relevant trade journals. Interested contractors can apply for details and submit a tender. After contractors submit bids, the local authority establishes a short-list with a view to selecting a final candidate from that list. The main factors taken into account in drawing up the short-list are normally such things as the contractor's past experience, past work record and financial standing. The final decision is usually dictated by price. Tenders are assessed by a panel comprising representatives from the authority's legal and financial management services and client departments. They make recommendations – based on their assessment of the resources and financial stability of the firm offering the lowest price – to the client committee, which awards the contract (Barker, 1993).

Assuming that the CCT policy process is not separate and discrete but continuous, this research will try to describe and analyse the CCT process as the local authorities selected operate at the local level but within their appropriate contexts, both inside and outside the organisation. Via contextual and processual examination of the CCT process, the analytical framework distinguishes between the contexts, the motivations and the strategies of the main parties, and offers a theory of the interplay between the three.

Characteristics of the analytical framework

The starting point for the analysis of CCT process is the notion that theoretically sound and practically useful research on CCT policy output should involve the continuous interplay between ideas about context, motivation and strategy. Each of these three areas and their interconnections suggests a series of research themes and issues.

The simplified analytical framework for this study differs from that of other commentators in the following ways:

- it emphasises action as well as structure, encompasses competitive versions of events, is sympathetic to the effect of different local contexts that may affect outputs, and is historically sensitive to the evolution of policy and to the stimuli for change over time;

- it sets out a model for the manipulation of transaction costs in a political context to facilitate a more comprehensive specification of the determinants of such political behaviour and a more accurate assessment of the likelihood and consequences of institutional change;

- it allows investigation of the external influences that motivate individual government actors and the private sector to support transaction–cost–increasing measures;

- the politics of transaction cost model also makes it possible to understand and predict policy implementation strategies; the model explains changes in the nature and degree of transaction cost manipulation over time in response to diverse political and economic circumstances;

- this analysis requires the indepth examination of case studies, which necessarily means that the number of case studies that may be undertaken is small; this approach also means that the studies must be processual, pluralist and comparative.

Case study methodology

Need for a case study approach

The analysis of the CCT database in Chapter Four indicated that although the main variables affecting DSO output could be identified, the way in which these variables affected it was left unexplained. The fact that local authorities can achieve different outputs via the CCT process means that the process is complex and needs to be examined in greater detail. A case study approach should be capable of identifying those characteristics and complex processes of CCT in local authorities which result in differing outputs.

The complexity of CCT issues requires the intensive analysis of a few cases rather than a superficial analysis of a larger number. This should ensure that the key components of the CCT process are not overlooked. Case studies offer an insight into the influence the attitudes and behaviours of the main interested parties involved in the CCT process have had on recent tendering exercises.

Characteristics of the case studies

The analytical framework developed in Chapter Six posed the analytical challenge of connecting up context, motivation, and strategy surrounding CCT policy. The methodology developed for the analysis examines the evolution of the tendering process in both its national and local context and draws knowledge from various levels of analysis to examine how context, motivation, and strategy interact to produce DSO output.

The analytical framework highlights the importance of the evolution of the policies in each district and the political and economic histories that impact on subsequent events. The case study approach was necessarily retrospective in its interpretation of the current levels of DSO output and involved detailed analysis of the history of CCT in each case so as not to miss any key components.

Case study methods

Three major methods were used to study the four selected local authorities:

- a preliminary interview with a local government official (contract expert);

- a study of pertinent elementary local governmental documents, such as DSO output, socioeconomic background, political composition (documentary analysis);

- a series of indepth interviews and documentary analysis.

Appendix B lists the sources of information used.

The first wave of interviewing established the extent and character of contracting out, laws and regulations governing the process, major problem areas, and so on. To obtain this information, a local government official was interviewed as a pilot study. This official also assisted in the second phase of research by providing a number of documents pertaining to CCT.

Published materials, such as statistics regarding political party composition, DSO proportion and socioeconomic background, were collected for the second phase. This facilitated a background knowledge of the context in which CCT was occurring and provided evidence which would acclimatise the researcher to the key developments in each district and supply a chronology of change.

The third phase involved documentary analysis and indepth interviews. The documentary analyses were made on the basis of investigating the unpublished materials, including tender documents of tender evaluation, reports to councillors, minutes, inter-office memoranda and published material such as *The municipal yearbook*, *The contract handbook* and *Direct service organisation statistics*.

The interviews were with the four chief officers and one lawyer with considerable experience of CCT-related legal matters. The choice of a standardised interview questionnaire as the major method of gathering data was largely determined by the theoretical and substantive goals of the study and the lack of relevant information available by other means.

The interview approach produces a rich supply of information that not only meets the research requirements of the theoretical perspectives, but also suggests hypotheses that could be tested elsewhere. In this study, the interview schedule also offers distinct advantages over the survey questionnaire. A seasoned political researcher, Lewis Dexter, argues that the interview method is especially appropriate when trying to obtain complete information from élite or specialised individuals, particularly where the researcher is not certain of all the dimensions of the subject (Dexter, 1970).

Gorden (1969, pp 52-4) points out that the interview format allows the interviewer the opportunity to control the administration setting, to interpret complex questions correctly for the interviewee, to probe for further clarification or examples, to evaluate the validity of the information, and to ensure that the interviewee considers the questions seriously. The result is more relevant, accurate and complete information than may be obtained via a questionnaire.

The major weakness of this data-gathering method is the interviewer. Hyman (1975, pp 150-92) points out several potential sources of bias:

- the interviewer's political orientation, and his/her beliefs about the true opinions of the population;

- the respondent's beliefs about the interviewer's 'real' intentions;

- differential effects owing to personal interaction;

- systematic effects of group membership disparities between the interviewer and the respondent (such as race, sex, age);

- situational determinants of interviewer effect (such as sponsorship, anonymity).

In addition, the interviewer can make many mistakes in asking, probing and recording.

Because the results of the interviews in most cases are only as good as the interviewer and the interview schedule, particular attention was paid to developing a standardised schedule and a standardised interview style to reduce interviewer variations. The interviews were conducted by means of a pre-tested interview schedule that used terminology with which all the respondents were familiar (Appendix A).

Other biases listed by Hyman were also minimised. In setting up the interview appointment and beginning the interview it was always stressed that the researcher was working on an independent academic study of compulsory competitive tendering for local government services. The researcher referred to his lack of relevant professional experience at least once during each interview, in order to dispel any notions about ulterior motives or affiliations. Interviewees were promised that neither their identities nor their positions or the name of their organisations would be disclosed to other officials or revealed in the research.

The researcher believes he was successful in achieving good, trusting relationships with interviewees. All the respondents were very friendly, open and helpful. The researcher's customary approach to building rapport was to show an interest in the individual's own position (or agency), to avoid expressing disapproval of the interviewee's statements, and generally to be sympathetic to the respondents' views and problems. In addition, the researcher does not believe that interpersonal barriers were erected because of his race, gender or age. In fact, his gender and status as a foreign student probably aided in dispelling distrust or suspicion. To prevent creating bias in the results, the researcher did not communicate anything about the theoretical perspectives and their bearing on CCT, even though he was often asked what his personal orientation regarding the subject was.

The content of the interview schedule was also important in establishing credibility and rapport with interviewees. The format and questions were based on the initial interview and pre-test with a local government official, as well as the researcher's own background knowledge. As a result, the respondents generally experienced little difficulty in understanding and answering the questions.

The interview schedule was designed to examine the CCT procedure and the viewpoints of those involved in the process – senior district officials and a lawyer. All the district officers were chief officers, who have all been working in their local authorities for more than 14 years, so that they have experienced the CCT activities of their local authority from the introduction of CCT to the present. It follows that they have been responsible for all CCT activities, and have also given advice to contractors. The lawyer has acted for about 250 local authorities up until now and has gained fairly broad experience – not just in England but in Scotland and Northern Ireland – in consultancy work for them.

This information is crucial in evaluating the theoretical perspectives. The schedule itself had three parts:

- personal background questions (period of service in a position, previous positions, and so on);

- questions about the CCT process;

- opinion and attitude questions.

Many of the questions were open-ended or included probes that allowed the interviewee to explain or restate an answer. While it was important for the researcher to establish credibility and interest in the subject, it was just as necessary to make clear to the respondents that he was open to being 'taught' how CCT really has operated. These interviews lasted for about one hour, depending on the respondent's talkativeness. Where possible, the same questions were incorporated or slightly reworded to provide points of comparison between the interviewees.

To supplement information obtained from the interview and to verify some unclear points, the interviewees were asked to send additional data such as tender documents. All the respondents were very cooperative.

Case selection

Since the respondents were from just four local authorities, caution must be used when interpreting the results. The sample is hardly large enough to generalise for all similar schemes. There are considerable regional variations in relation to the level of competition and the impact of CCT on the local authority. The four local authorities were selected to represent different political mixes and different DSO output in order to show any variations in the implementation of CCT. They consisted of two Conservative local authorities, one Labour and one hung council (Table 6.1).

Although the four local authorities were not a statistically representative sample of all 296 non-metropolitan districts in England, they were selected to ensure that the results of path analysis in Chapter Four were reflected, notably:

- political control;

- DSO output.

The pattern of distribution of the sample in relation to the variables in the sampling frame is shown in Table 6.1.

Five interviews, with one lawyer and the four chief officers, were conducted between May and June 1997. The choice of interviewees was based on their lead positions in the organisation and their direct involvement in the CCT process.

Interviews with private bidders and civil servants were initially considered. However, the private sector representatives and civil servants associated with CCT who work in central government were omitted from the interview due to constraints of access and time. Analysis for the two parties is based on second-hand data. One reason for this is that it was difficult to identify the names of the persons who worked as contract experts for the private companies in 1991 and 1994.

Table 6.1: Characteristics of the four local authorities selected

	Number of authorities
Political control	
Conservative controlled	2
Labour controlled	1
Hung council	1
Geographical distrbution	
North	1
East Midlands	2
South-East	1
DSO proportion	
High	2
Low	2

Note: This table is based on the data for 1994.

Secondly, it is assumed that the politics of transaction costs engaged in by the private companies and central government can also be discovered via indirect methods such as documentary analysis and interviews with the chief officers. This is because the chief officers and the lawyer selected for the interview have experienced the whole process from the viewpoint of, respectively, senior local government officers in charge of CCT and the legal consultant, and therefore have been conversant with the reaction of central government and the private sector to the CCT process. Crano and Brewer (1986) and Hakim (1982) indicate that even a third party's behavioural intentions can be investigated by judicious interviews with outsiders.

This is not to say that the data obtained in such research circumstances is perfectly trustworthy. It implies that although there is some danger that such interviews could bias subjects' responses, if used judiciously such a tactic appears capable of stimulating more complete answers without unduly influencing their content. With this problem in mind, an interview with a lawyer was conducted to minimise possible misinterpretation and to make the chief officers' answers more complete.

Chapter Seven provides closely relevant and essential points linked to the analysis of the politics of transaction cost; it is not intended to supply an exhaustive description of the CCT process relating to the four local authorities. For this reason, not all the empirical findings derived from the case study will be reviewed. Instead, the discussion will be limited to the most notable actions of the main parties regarding the politics of transaction costs.

Notes

[1] An organisation is a collection of human beings. As such, it exhibits the characteristics of a society. Like a society, each organisation embraces a system of shared beliefs, values, and norms unique to it. The organisational culture defines what is important to the organisation, how people should behave, how they should interact with one another, and what they should be striving for. Employees who share these beliefs, values, and norms tend to develop a sense of group identity and pride, important elements of organisational effectiveness (Plunkett and Attner, 1994, pp 264-70).

This study deals with the perceptions and attitude of the councillors and the officials towards CCT as the main factors associated with the local organisational culture. This is because an organisation's culture is greatly affected by the objectives, strategies, personal characteristics and inter-relationships of its managers, who form the dominant coalition (Plunkett and Attner, 1994).

The notion of local organisational culture is intimately bound up with the management of change associated with competitive tendering. Here, local organisational culture refers to the ideas, meanings and values that the local authority management (councillors and local government officials) hold in common and to which they subscribe collectively.

[2] In qualitative research, documentary analysis seeks to analyse small numbers of texts and documents in order to understand the participants' activities (Silverman, 1993, pp 8-10).

[3] As was mentioned earlier, the term 'contract compliance' has been used in relation to the clauses inserted into contracts or legal acts. It refers to the use of public sector purchasing power as a means of achieving various policy objectives. In recent years, contract compliance has been the subject of much controversy between central and local government. Its use by both central and local government has been criticised as an illegitimate interference with local government and the private sector. However, the principles which lie behind contract compliance are not novel, but well-established in central government practice (Marston, 1990, pp 1-3).

SEVEN

Case study analysis

Introduction

In the previous chapter it was assumed that the overriding characteristic of the CCT process has been its variability, with the politics of transaction costs playing a significant role in the determination of the output of CCT policy, DSO output. It was also argued that a case study approach was essential in understanding the different levels of DSO output that exist between authorities. To analyse the different levels of DSO output in some detail it was argued that a politics of transaction cost approach was required which addressed the actions of the main interested parties during the CCT process along with the constraints imposed on these actions by each party. The case study analysis attempts to identify how the politics of transaction costs have been influential in shaping districts which face similar policy pressures 'from above' and yet have behaved differently and achieved different outputs through local mediation.

This chapter uses the case study results to detail how the politics of transaction costs influenced the CCT process, addressing the contexts, motivations and strategies in which the politics of transaction costs has determined the DSO output.

The main aim is to highlight the transaction cost aspect of the situations, in the hope of proving that these costs are significant to policy issues of major importance, and that the politics of transaction cost approach is likely to be useful in more detailed studies of these issues.

The format of the case studies combines a narrative of developments with some informal conceptual discussion of the role played by transaction costs in the story and of how the actors in the drama attempted to influence the other party, and finally the policy process.

The legal framework of CCT as a component of contexts, and the motivations and the strategies of central government regarding the transaction costs, will be addressed, since all these apply to all local authorities. This is followed by an analysis of the four local authority districts.

Legal framework for CCT and the motivations and strategies of central government

Legal framework

The legal framework for CCT is one of the important components of the context in which CCT operates. Analysis of the legal framework gives understanding of whether it grants central government, local authority and private companies discretion or room for manipulating transaction costs during the CCT process. The more it gives discretion to the interested parties involved in the CCT process, the more likely it is that the transaction costs can be manipulated.

The legal framework for CCT applies not to a particular local authority, but to all local authorities in the UK, including the four local authorities selected for this research.

One of the parties in the CCT process, the local authority, is subject to two sets of controls over the contracting process in order to ensure competition. The first comes from domestic policies and the second from the European Union. The relationship between the two is that they are separate but overlapping systems with different purposes and principles. Each is given separate treatment in this section.

The 1988 Act

The first stage in the introduction of CCT was the 1980 Local Government, Planning and Land Act, which introduced controls in relation to DLOs. The Act imposed a regime of regulation of all functional and works contracts relating to construction and maintenance to ensure that they were entered into and undertaken only under conditions which required a measure of competition with other non-public contractors. This Act was limited not only in its coverage, but also with regard to the rigour of the competition requirements (Carnaghan and Bracewell-Milnes, 1993, pp 27-9).

After the 1980 Act, the 1988 Local Government Act introduced four important changes:

- it expanded the scope of the functions covered by the tendering rules;

- it tightened the rules to ensure a higher degree of compulsory competition and privatisation of service provision;

- it outlawed the use of 'non-commercial matters'[1] in the course of tendering procedures;

- it gave the Secretary of State the power to prescribe exemptions from the application of CCT (Bailey, 1997, pp 178-82).

CCT was extended to:

- the collection of household and trade waste;

- cleaning of buildings;

- other cleaning, such as of streets, litter;

- catering for schools and welfare establishments such as old people's homes;

- other catering;

- management of sports and leisure facilities;

- maintenance of grounds, parks and so on;

- repair and maintenance of vehicles.

This list can be amended or expanded by means of an order of the Secretary of State (Bailey, 1997, p 179).

More detailed tendering procedures were introduced for both external and internal contracts. For an 'external' works contract, not only must the service in question be opened up to tender from the private sector, but the other contracting party has also not to act "in a manner having the effect or intended or likely to have the effect of restricting, distorting, or preventing competition". For internal functional work a number of conditions were introduced, and the bid from the council's own direct labour or direct service organisation needs to have been prepared on the same basis as that for the private sector. In determining the terms of the contract or in choosing the tenders or successful bid, the council must not act in a manner that restricts competition and must not vary the terms of the specification if it awards the work to its own labour force (Bailey, 1997).

The Secretary of State has the power to modify and otherwise regulate the terms and conditions of the contract. For both external and internal contracts, there are also more detailed and stringent regimes for accounting, annual reporting and access to information. Policing of these requirements is given, not to the authority itself or an independent auditor or other person, but to the Secretary of State. They may issue notices requiring further information to be supplied to them if it appears that there has been a breach of these conditions. If, in the light of that information, they decide that there has been a breach, they may issue a direction either requiring compliance with their decision or removing the power of the authority to carry out the work. There is no appeal against the decision of the Secretary of State and actions by councils under judicial review have met with little success because of the widely expressed powers in the legislation (McShane, 1995).

The third aspect expanded by the 1988 Act is the concept of anticompetitive behaviour or 'non-commercial' matters. The duty for authorities to avoid anticompetitive behaviour and non-commercial matters extends beyond the matters covered by CCT. A long list of non-commercial matters is listed in the Act but can be supplemented by regulations made by the Secretary of State. These rules are designed to prohibit the use of 'contract compliance' as a device for enforcing other policies of the authority. Aggrieved contractors may sue for damages on the basis that these restrictions have not been followed (Bailey, 1997; McShane, 1995).

The fourth aspect is that the Secretary of State has power to prescribe exemptions for matters which are otherwise included in the competitive regime. This power has been exercised in respect of the following:

- an activity whose gross cost in the immediately preceding financial year does not exceed £100,000;

- work carried out through employees who are required as a condition of employment to live in particular accommodation for the better performance of their duties where the work forms part of these duties;

- the repair or maintenance of fire service vehicles;

- work carried out pursuant to an agreement with the Training Commission (McShane, 1995, pp 121-2).

Apart from this general *de minimis* exception, there are numerous other more specific exemption orders which are used for different purposes. Some are used to phase in new activities generally, specify contract lengths or impose higher *de minimis* limits for a specific function, while others are used to exempt specific projects in single authorities (McShane, 1995).

The prohibition of anticompetitive practices contained in the 1988 Act is perhaps the single most important aspect of the tendering regimes established by that statute, in view of the fact that the prohibition relates to the conduct of authorities at every stage of the tendering process. That the prohibition is limited to local authorities and that the statutes do not outlaw such conduct on the part of other participants in the tendering process is burdensome to local authorities (McShane, 1995). This is highly important in assessing the politics of transaction costs instigated by central government.

The 1992 Act

All the rules relating to CCT covered by the 1988 Act were further tightened in the third stage by the 1992 Local Government Act. CCT has been extended to other areas, including other manual services, theatre, library and arts management, and also professional services, such as legal, architectural, financial and engineering services. While the authority is not obliged to accept the lowest tender, cost can be seen as the most important consideration since many other matters are excluded as being 'non-commercial'. The 1992 Act created a new power for the Secretary of State to make further regulations specifying and enforcing what is deemed to be 'anticompetitive', which goes beyond the provisions relating to 'non-commercial' matters in the 1988 Act (Bailey, 1997, p 180; McShane, 1995, pp 173-5; Wilson and Game, 1994, pp 334-9).

In the 1988 Act there was no regulation associating power with the condition of anticompetitive behaviour. As a result the Secretary of State relied on circular advice to disseminate his opinion about what has the effect of restricting, distorting or preventing competition. The 1992 Local Government Act provided for such regulation, giving the power to define conduct as 'competitive' or 'anticompetitive' and to structure the tendering process (Section 9) (Wilson and Game, 1994, p 335).

Given the central importance of the prohibition of anticompetitive practices contained in the 1988 Act, it is curious that no attempt has been made to attempt a legal definition of what would constitute anticompetitive conduct: consequently, between the passage of the 1988

Act and the issue of the Competition Regulations in 1993, the most effective means of ascertaining what would constitute such conduct was to observe the circumstances in which the Secretary of State used his powers to issue directions under Section 14 of the 1988 Act (McShane, 1995).

Pursuant to Section 9 of the 1992 Local Government Act and Regulation 15 of the Local Government (Direct Services Organisations) (Competition) Regulations 1993, the Guidance on anticompetitive conduct[2] makes clear at an early stage that:

> **Neither is this guidance, nor the Regulations, intended to be exhaustive. Authorities should consider all aspect of conduct, whether covered by the Regulations and this guidance or not, from the point of view of avoiding anticompetitive conduct. (Para 4)**

As the Regulations and Guidance do not purport to be exhaustive, there is still a considerable degree of uncertainty regarding what conduct will violate the prohibition contained in Section 7 (7) of the 1988 Act. Consequently, the Secretary of State's exercise of their powers under Section 14 of the 1988 Act will still be of considerable importance to those wishing to ascertain what may constitute anticompetitive conduct.

The 1992 Local Government Act extends the compulsory competitive tendering regime into technical and professional work. From the point of view of the politics of transaction costs, it also tightens the grip of competitive tendering in the services covered by the 1980 and 1988 Acts by seeking to outlaw what the government defines as various anticompetitive practices on the part of local authorities.

The 1994 Act

The fourth stage is provided by Part II of the 1994 Deregulation and Contracting Out Act, which makes provision for the contracting out of the functions of ministers and officeholders and, in Section 70, local authorities. This is aimed at removing the remaining statutory obstacles to the use of private contractors, and at overcoming the general presumption against delegation inasmuch as it has not been overcome by Section 101 of the 1992 Local Government Act (Bailey, 1997, pp 10-11).

As with the 1992 Act, the 1994 Act was altered to the advantage of the private sector, not to the local authority. One interviewee, a solicitor (Mrs S), commented as follows on the 1994 Act:

> **"DSO felt considerably disadvantaged compared to its private sector competitors, since the latter were able to access financial information which could assist them in preparing bids (such as the information relating to the specification that has to be provided for a TUPE[3] bid and DSO accounts). DSO, on the other hand, did not have access to similar information about its competitors."**

As was stated above, the legal framework for CCT has been changing and has been supplemented in various ways since the introduction of CCT.

Initially, competitive tendering was voluntary. However, requirements for compulsory competitive tendering have been introduced through consecutive key legislative stages and through the delegated legislation and informal 'advice' issued by the government. The main purpose of this legislation has been to turn local authorities from direct providers of services to 'enablers' of service provision and to have services subjected to market 'discipline'. The changes in the law have also been accompanied by increased financial and management controls through audit. The strategy of increasing private sector involvement in the activities of local authorities also involves financial controls and the Private Finance Initiative (Carnaghan and Bracewell-Milnes, 1993; Wilson and Game, 1994).

European public procurement controls

The organs of the European Economic Community have not failed to provide their own regulations about public procurement. The Works Directives[4] have for some years applied to the biggest 1980 Act. As a result of the EEC's Compliance Directive, the Government issued new regulations for 'Public Supply Contracts' and 'Public Works Contracts' (PSCR and PWCS), which took effect on 21 December 1991 (Bailey, 1997).

In June 1992, the European Economic Community (EEC) issued a directive on 'Public Service Contracts' (EC 92) with an implementation date of 1 July 1993, which applied to several types of 1988 Act work. The Chartered Institute of Public Finance and Accountancy (1991) has observed that although the purposes of the UK legislation and the EEC's directives are different, there are market similarities between them. The two regimes conflict inasmuch as observing both sets of rules simultaneously will for most authorities be more than twice as hard as following either set on its own (Carnaghan and Bracewell-Milnes, 1993).

In his detailed analysis, Digings (1991, pp 20-1) states:

> **... practically every local authority contract of any magnitude for works, supplies or services will be subject to complex public procurement rules and procedures emanating from Brussels .... The extent of regulation is already great and the situation ... will be awesome.**

The directives come into effect only when the total value of a contract is above the relevant threshold, such as 200,000 European currency units (ECUs) or about £165,000, but this is not a large amount for an authority in the UK.[5] Although the regulations are formally impartial, contracting authorities in the UK are expected to bear a heavier administrative burden than those elsewhere because of their large size. For example, in England more than 99% of municipalities have a population of 10,000, whereas in France about 2.5% are that large, and in Germany about 14%. The likely consequence of these added regulations is more bureaucracy, particularly for the UK, without any tangible benefits (Carnaghan and Bracewell-Milnes, 1993).

The AMA stated, in response to the EC Services Directive at its proposal stage, that a DSO, having won a contract under both the 1988 Act and the EC Directive, could then be subject again to the requirements of this or other requirement directives, for example to obtain supplies. Such requirements would not apply to a private contractor, and would mean DSOs being subjected to unfair additional costs (AMA, 1991, p 1).

The public procurement controls over the European Union (EU) are designed to ensure that there is no discrimination against nationals of other member states, or products from these states, in the award of public contracts for works, information, technical specification, and selection of tenders. There must be advertising across the Community for contracts above a specified monetary threshold, there must not be use of discriminatory technical standards, and there must be objective and open criteria for the evaluation and selection of tenders (Bailey, 1997, p 181).

There must be compliance with the EU Treaties and any relevant Directives. The public procurement controls of the EU prohibit qualitative restrictions on imports between member states and measures having equivalent effect to such restrictions. The relevant directives require the abolition of any restrictions or discriminatory practices which might prevent contractors from other member states from participating in public contracts on equal terms with national contractors. Not all public contracts are so included, only those as defined and above the appropriate monetary threshold. For those purposes, not only the local authority itself, but also bodies financed or controlled by the local authority, will be subject to these controls. Where there is government subsidy of more than 50% for certain construction projects the rules also apply (Bailey, 1997, p 181; McShane, 1995, pp 219-20).

The controls are of three main types (McShane, 1995):

- there must be advertising across the Community, through prior notice to the *Official Journal of the European Communities* (*OLJEC*), for contracts above a specified threshold;

- in investigating particular technical standards and specifications, the authority must not discriminate against other European states;

- there must be objective and open criteria for the evaluation and selection of tenders, following the appropriate procedure.

Experience with the 1988 Local Government Act is still limited. There are many areas of uncertainty and differences in interpretation. Although the 1992 Act, the 1994 Act and other regulations[6] supplemented the 1988 Local Government Act to a certain extent, the legal framework for CCT still has some limitations. It gives the main parties some discretion in dealing with CCT. For example, the meaning of 'anticompetitive' behaviour is not yet fully clear, and this provides much room for debate, for example about what are acceptable methods of packaging the contract. The meaning of 'non-commercial matters' is also open to interpretation. There are difficulties over matters relating specifically to contract law, notably what are acceptable forms of default clauses. The role of lawyers in interpreting the legislation has been important because of the difficulties involved (Walsh, 1991).

European legislation is becoming increasingly important. The Acquired Directive of 1987, which protects the rights of workers who move from one employer to another, was incorporated into British law by the Transfer of Undertakings (Protection of Employment) regulations in 1991, although the circumstances under which TUPE applies are still contested (Walsh et al, 1997, p 104).

European public procurement law is also not perfect. This is partly because the law, by definition, cannot cover everything and partly because each country has its own legal system on which the detailed legal framework of each local authority has been based. Paddon (1994, p 182) points out that in the practical application of the EC directives, and hence in their real impact for public bodies such as local authorities, public procurement is one of the policy areas in which there appears to be a tension between two of the major dimensions of the Single European Act: the Single European Market and the 'social dimension'. He adds that the application of the EC directives in practice is less clear-cut, and much will depend on how they are interpreted.

Contractors who believe that procurement processes have been manipulated to their disadvantage or conducted outside EC rules can bring actions either through the national court or through the EC courts (McShane, 1995). This suggests that the EC directives also make room available for the politics of transaction costs.

The various stages in the process of CCT, although laid down in the relevant Acts and regulations, are still vague (Walsh et al, 1997). In some respects this state of affairs is inevitable as it allows people to use their discretion when going through the processes involved. However, it can also be used to give an advantage to one party and therefore disadvantage another. What is missing are clear concise guidelines for local authorities to follow.

Motivations

Central government's motivation towards the use of transaction cost is difficult to evaluate in real terms so some indirect means of ascertaining it must be used.

It appears that the motivations of central government to use transaction costs have been strong. There are basically two reasons for this. First, CCT is the result of a carefully crafted government policy; without government interference, it is unlikely that CCT would have witnessed any significant growth in tendering activity (Walsh et al, 1997). Even though evaluating the Government's motivation regarding the transaction costs is difficult, when we examine it in relation to its political objectives of reducing the size of the state and neutralising trade unions, it appears to be very strong.

CCT has been viewed as a highly political Conservative crusade by all participants in the process (including private contractors). The highly political nature of the initiative was reinforced during the early stages of its implementation, when the government publicly demanded timetables from reluctant authorities and attacked the behaviour of those which adopted unfair wages and other 'restrictive' clauses in their tendering document (Walsh et al, 1997).

What central government has done is to set the wheels in motion for the removal of a great many services from local authorities to the private sector. In so doing, local authorities were prevented from deciding themselves who should carry out work on their behalf. Power is being wrested from local authorities by central government, a process which, as more and more services are forced out to tender, will ultimately result in council structures of a relatively small number of technical and professional staff, essentially contracts managers, running service provision through private firms (Walsh et al, 1997).

Central government's attitude towards CCT has been clear: it is keen to change the pattern of local government service provision. The Acts involved and the related circulars imply that central government applied itself to implementing CCT via a top-down approach (Kerley, 1994, p 107).

The second reason for central government's motivations being strong is that in its view, CCT policy has saved much money in the provision of local services. Central government has argued that many organisations which conducted surveys on CCT have revealed that local authorities made great savings as a result of competition. In reality, many research results, including those of the INLOGOV Study, Audit Commission Findings, the Local Government Chronicle Survey, and the PULSE Assessment (Public and Local Service Efficiency Campaign), show that the CCT policy has brought about financial savings, and that increased efficiency has very often been found to result from competitive tendering (Carnaghan and Bracewell-Milnes, 1993, pp 81-4).

For example, the two detailed surveys carried out by INLOGOV in 1991 (Walsh) and 1993 (Walsh and Davis, 1993), of 40 panel authorities, show that on average the estimated annual costs for defined services after competition were 5.7 and 6.5% lower, respectively, than the costs before competition, although the variations in results were considerable. They also make it clear that changes in estimated costs varied according to the type of service. As a result of these research findings, central government planned to extend CCT from the manual services to white collar services.

The Thatcher government emerged with a strong commitment to the notion of an enterprise culture, which was to have important implications for local government. As Cochrane (1991, p 294) argues, the language of welfare has been replaced by a language of growth, regeneration and public/private partnership. If the approach of the postwar period was, to some extent at least, based on the needs of people, the New Right replaced the social democratic consensus with an approach which starts from the needs of business. In so doing it actively espoused aspects of business organisation which it saw as positive in other social contexts. The approach has two important elements: the active modelling of local government on what are taken to be elements of best practice from the private sector; and the active and increasing involvement of business itself in the activities of local government.

On this evidence, the attitudes and perceptions of central government towards CCT have been positive and optimistic, leading to the assumption that the motivations of central government to use the politics of transaction costs in the CCT process have been very strong.

Strategies

It has long been recognised that incentives and rewards of various types have a role in reinforcing and sustaining change processes (Goodman and Dean, 1982; Kanter, 1985). As was shown in the analysis of the legal framework for CCT, central government has used a compliance mechanism strategy, incorporating a legal framework in the pursuit of CCT objectives.

Strictly speaking, it might be debatable to include the strategies or measures used by central government in the category of the politics of transaction costs. This is mainly because the relationship between central government and the local authority is not the same as that between the local authority and the private sector. Logically, the concept of transaction cost should be applied to the relationship between the local authority and the private sector only. However, broadly speaking, the constraints imposed by central government on the local authority or the private sector can be included in the broad sense of transaction costs, because the rules set by central government can directly or indirectly impose costs on the activities of private contractors and the local authority. The politics of transaction costs engaged in by the activities of central government will be discussed.

Meeting with steadfast resistance to its initial attempts to control local authorities, the Government embarked on a series of legislative moves to hit the authorities where it hurt most. Accordingly, the Local Government Acts were not about 'freedom of the individual'; they were about the increasing marginalisation of local authorities, the removal of democratic choice, and an increase in transaction costs for local authorities.

The underlying purpose of the legislation was made clear by Michael Heseltine, the then Secretary of State, when he stated that:

> **There is no doubt that these disciplines will result in a contraction of direct labour activities as local authorities come to appreciate the relative costs of direct labour and the relative advantages of private companies. (Marston, 1990)**

In considering the 1988, 1992 and 1994 Act's regulation of CCT from the point of view of the politics of transaction costs some conclusions can be drawn. One of the objectives of the legislation is to constrain the discretion of local authorities to make certain decisions regarding the delivery of services, by virtue of a regime which is closely prescribed by central government. In this respect, it is suggested that central government used the compliance mechanism by inserting onerous contractual clauses into the legal framework in order to pursue its own CCT objectives. These clauses concerned such areas as the prevention of anticompetitive behaviour, and non-commercial matters, which means that central government has tightened its compliance mechanism by means of changes to the legal framework. As a result of the changes to the legal framework, it is more difficult for a local authority to know what costs it is competing with, or what the terms and conditions of employment of external contractors are, leading the local authority to bear the transaction costs in order to obtain the relevant information.

Another example clearly reveals that the legal framework for CCT is predisposed towards the private sector. In 1993, the Secretary of State issued 20 notices for alleged anticompetitive behaviour, and gave 12 directions, normally requiring retender. However, there have been no parallel sanctions against providers, despite the fact that the evidence suggests that providers behave tactically, targeting strategic locations or using the strategy of loss-leaders. This impacts on what has been called the 'level playing field' (Walsh et al, 1997, p 105), given the shifting fortunes of internal and external providers in relation to competitive advantage. It follows that transaction costs are decreased for private providers and increased for local authorities.

The second conclusion that can be drawn is that it appears that local authorities perceived the compliance mechanism as a threat. The mechanism could prove to be a strategic weapon to fight local governments with an anti-privatisation culture on the issue of privatisation of council services.

The manner in which the compliance mechanism has been used suggests that the prevention of anticompetitive behaviour became uppermost as the policy progressed. By inserting contractual clauses in the legal framework for CCT, the government was able to pursue CCT policy objectives and enforce them on the local authorities.

Local authority CCT studies

Four case studies are presented[7] and analysed in this section, based on interviews and on the tender documents, reports, minutes and unpublished internal documents of each local authority. Each case study represents a longitudinal description of a local authority's CCT process, with particular emphasis upon the politics of transaction costs. Each case study begins with a brief explanation of the background of the local authority. The events of the tendering process in each local authority are described, using the previously described data sources to gain a deeper understanding of developments.

Since this study is exploratory in nature, the chief concern is to identify the dynamic interplay of context, motivation and strategy behind the CCT process rather than to test preconceived hypotheses. However, the generation of testable hypotheses may be an outcome of this study, which may be used in subsequent research on CCT.

Attention is paid to power relationships within the authority, and between the authority and central government and private companies, with a view to making the politics of transaction costs more explicit and understandable. The development of private contractors in each local authority and their attitudes to the contracts tendered are also addressed. The interplay between context, motivation and strategy is examined and the case is interpreted from the politics of transaction cost perspective.

The description of the CCT process is not intended to be exhaustive in its explanation of what has happened to each local authority, but does set out to provide a total framework for understanding the processes involved, focusing on the characteristics of the dynamic relationships that have occurred in relation to CCT.

Local authority A

Background

The first local authority for case study, which will be termed 'Local Authority A' to preserve anonymity, is an urban one neighbouring a metropolitan area. Like most of its neighbouring areas, Local Authority A has a long history of control by the Labour Party and a high proportion of DSO output. The area suffered considerably through the closure of the coal-mines, and the loss of shipbuilding and ship-repair yards.

Local Authority A had manufacturing bases that experienced a substantial decline in the 20th century, leaving a legacy of deprivation. Its economic prosperity had been based on the worsted industry that flourished in the 18th and 19th centuries. However, by the 20th century the growing weakness of the worsted trade and the increasingly poor position of the industry in Local Authority A mirrored the decline of the area. Throughout the early 1980s, of all the districts in the area, Local Authority A had the worst overcrowding, the most families in shared accommodation, the highest percentage of one-parent families and the highest unemployment.

As expected given this socioeconomic background, this district is noted for the presence of strong trade unions. The north-east of England is dominated politically by a paternalist, right-wing labour movement (Painter, 1991, p 220). The region is characterised by public sector employment and provision, as a result both of the collapse of its manufacturing industry and of its corporatist and labourist traditions. Both these characteristics were influential in the development of CCT.

The history of local politics in this district reveals an element of support for the Communist movement, particularly in the 1950s. As befits this chiefly working-class town, it has returned Labour MPs and Labour councils since the War. In the 1990s there have been some incursions into local politics by Liberal Democrats. However, overall control remains with Labour. As a further consequence of this socioeconomic background, there has been evidence of frequent opposition to CCT.

Review of CCT in Local Authority A

In Local Authority A, those services that have been affected by privatisation nationally were kept inhouse until 1994. Like other local authorities, Local Authority A did not begin extensive preparation for competition until the 1988 Local Government Act was actually enacted. Statuary Instrument No 1,371 laid down the timetable for implementation of the legislation in July 1988. All shire counties and shire districts were allocated to groups, each with a different timetable for putting services out to tender (Walsh, 1991, pp 23-4). Local Authority A was also required to put defined activities to tender, starting in August 1989. The initial reaction in Local Authority A to CCT in 1988 was to establish a Competition Working Group to oversee all aspects of CCT, which was attended by the chief or deputy chief officer for each client service and the legal, personnel and financial services. This group was appointed by the Chief Officers Group and still continues with its role at the present time.

In March 1989 Local Authority A established the Direct Service Board, made up of 12 elected members together with the DSO managers, the chief executive/borough treasurer, the borough personnel and management services officer and the borough secretary. Workforce representation consisted of three employees nominated by the workforce. However, only elected members were elegible to vote on the Direct Service Board.

When a CCT policy was eventually initiated, the lack of enthusiasm for the policy in Local Authority A was quite evident among the local councillors and officials. The councillors and officials would not have introduced tendering voluntarily. As was the norm with districts reluctant to test the market by tendering, it used many forms of strategy to deter the private sector from winning contracts.

The contract for refuse services and street cleaning was tendered in 1989. However, the district combined two different services into a single large contract in order to make the package unattractive for specialised businesses and hence to prevent all but the largest contractors from being able to participate. In effect, only very large enterprises could bid. Local Authority A stated that contracts were packaged to reflect the way that services were run, or the need for economies of scale, and not to deter competition. However, Mr A, its chief officer, admitted that the contract for refuse services and street cleaning was written defensively, to cover "every possible contingency against the private sector". Eventually, there was no private bidder for the contract and it went to the DSO.

The second contract, in 1991, was for ground maintenance. This was attractive to the private sector, which had extensive experience of it in other areas. Four tenders were received. All three firms quoted cheaper bids than the inhouse tender.

At a meeting to award the contract, trade union representatives lobbied officials and councillors in an attempt to get them to agree that the bids the private firms tendered for the contract were loss-leaders. In the meantime, the private firms stated that they would pay sufficient wages to ensure that a workforce of the calibre required would be attracted and retained in order to perform the service to a satisfactory standard. Eventually, both the councillors and officials felt that the private bids were 'loss-leaders' and that the prices quoted were too low to run the contract without significant loss in the quality of service. In a DSB meeting to award the contract, the majority vote was in favour of returning the ground maintenance service inhouse.

Contractors' dissatisfaction manifested itself in a continuing stream of complaints to the government about both real and perceived biases in the tendering processes of Local Authority A. In the meantime, during this period, the local trade unions came to realise from the experience of other local authorities that competitive tendering would not go away and that the best solution to prevent further contracting out was to negotiate with the councillors and compete with the private sector on their own terms.

Trade unions came to accept that it is difficult to compete on cost with the private sector and that the alternative is to compete on quality by the use of contract specification. To this end, they began to pay attention to exerting influence on the drawing up of specifications, to ensure that these are stringent regarding the level and quality of service required. The unions believed that this principle would give them a competitive advantage over private candidates, since private contractors aim to compete largely on cost. Councillors still remained sympathetic to their workforce and helped them to develop inhouse bids which would win the contracts.

Eight months after the contract for ground maintenance was awarded inhouse, vehicle maintenance was being prepared for tender in Local Authority A. Private contractors were attracted to this large contract, which offered scope for considerable profits. Five were invited to tender. However, as in many other districts, the officials disallowed the release of some information about the potential costs, the terms and conditions of employment of the authority workforce. According to the tender document for the contract, Local Authority A refused private contractors the use of depots and vehicles, thus increasing the transaction costs on the part of the private contractors and ensuring that the DSO would have a very good chance of winning the contract. Finally, it went to the DSO.

In 1992, another contract for ground maintenance was tendered and four tenders were received. For the contract the performance bonds were for 15% of the value of the contract, despite the fact that such bonds were normally for 10% of it. The tenderers were required to supply information concerning their technical competence, details of quality assurance procedure and financial issues. In this process, the trade unions provided the DSO with extra information about the private companies. One of the companies was rejected without further evaluation because of its excessively high bid. The other company was also rejected, on the grounds that the information supplied did nothing to suggest that the authority could have confidence in its capacity to perform the contract for the price. The third company was also rejected as a result of financial analysis which confirmed grave doubts as to its technical competence. Only the inhouse tender bid had no 'unsatisfactory' mark throughout the evaluation process. Eventually, the award went to the inhouse tender.

The contract for leisure management, tendered in 1992, underwent a similar process to that for ground maintenance. Four tenders were received. Two of the private bidders were rejected through the tender evaluation process. The reasons were the absence of a detailed marketing plan, insufficient customer care policy, no details of staff members, and no draft rotas. Finally, the inhouse tender, the lower of the two valid bids, was awarded the contract.

Cleaning of buildings was put out to tender in 1994, but received no private competition because of the detailed and excessive specifications of the tender documents, the strict tender evaluation and low expectations on the part of private companies. Before this tender, in Local Authority A there were at least three private contractors bidding on public works. However, for this tender there was no private contractor candidate. Consequently, the inhouse tender was awarded the contract for six years.

It is clear that officials and councillors still did not want to put this service up for tender, but were forced to do so.

According to Mr A, the private sector's interest in tendering in the district seemed to have decreased, since it believed that it did not have many chances of winning contracts because of the various constraints imposed on it.

Analysing contexts, motivations and strategies

Contexts: In Local Authority A, both councillors and officials were actively hostile to privatisation and they believed that the private sector would behave opportunistically. The 1988 Act was seen by Local Authority A councillors as a clear political attack on the role of local government. These councillors were also critical of CCT since using private sector companies to deliver services challenged their belief in the local, public and democratic provision of services. Such concerns were translated in Local Authority A into a strong desire to maintain its own inhouse workforce by winning the contracts.

According to Mr A, there was no disagreement or conflict between the councillors and the officials concerning their view of CCT. Both groups were keen to discourage and avoid competitive tendering. When asked to characterise their attitudes towards CCT, Mr A depicted it as one of 'avoidance':

> **"Primarily it's too restrictive, although it does bring a certain amount of discipline to all the services, so that you are constantly reviewing how the services are provided and then making sure that you are doing that in the best way and giving value for money. But CCT – because it is compulsory, you have to do everything within the government's guidelines, regardless of how the authority wants to do it itself."**

While in 1988 the government noted that CCT had highlighted past inefficiencies in the previous internal service that needed to be addressed, the councillors and officials of Local Authority A felt that this could have been resolved without recourse to competitive tendering. There was widespread agreement that the service should be provided by the DSO.

Turning to industrial relations, in Local Authority A the power of the trade unions has traditionally been very strong and the trade unions were able to mount long-term industrial action against privatisation. They were also able to draw on the close relationship they enjoyed with the local authority, to exert influence on the drawing up of the specifications of the contract to ensure they were stringent regarding the quality of service required. In discussing unions, Mr A characterised the local union's power as very strong. He noted, for example, that within the realm of vehicle maintenance in 1991, the union was newly formed, but appeared to be fairly strong in its ability to get things done its way.

The unions (and the workforce) played a 'proactive' role, participating fully in council decision making about all aspects of CCT, for example, as members of the Joint Competition Working Group, which consisted of officers, members and trade union representatives, trade union representatives. The group had met to deal with consultation on competitive contracts being let and it was found to be the most useful vehicle for general discussion of the issues surrounding competition.

According to Mr A, the trade union activities in Local Authority A were far ahead of those in other local authorities. The council unions were particularly well organised and well prepared, and highly informed: private contractors could be defeated without having to worsen the employment conditions of the council's workforce. While Mr A believed local unions very strongly resisted privatisation, he did not agree that the less influence they had, the more likely contracting out would be, because only elected members were eligible to vote on the issues.

Using the terms of the industrial relations model, the approach of the trade unions in Local Authority A could be classified as 'militant'. Although the councillors and officials were strongly in favour of service provision via DSO, it was found that the trade union lobbied the councillors and officials. Throughout the period 1989 to 1994 the trade unions in Local Authority A had generally been hostile towards CCT.

Motivations: In relation to transaction costs involved, Mr A stated that they are very high throughout the CCT process. He also emphasised that there are costs for contractors when they try to win the tender because they have to look at the documentation and look at the service. He claimed:

> **"If the authority, like ourselves, wants to win the contract inhouse, it has to go through that process and make sure that everything is documented properly so it takes a lot of officer time and the costs of that can be very high."**

When asked to explain the relationship between transaction costs and the opportunities for private companies to win the contract, Mr A noted that there had been a strong relationship between the two, implying that transaction costs can be shifted from one party to the other party. However, he added that although transaction costs could be shifted from the local authority to the private companies at the early stage of CCT, over time it had been difficult to do that since the government has prescribed too many things in order to ensure that external companies can win the tenders. Judging from these comments it can be inferred that at the early stage of CCT the motivations of Local Authority A to use transaction costs in its interest were strong, whereas over time they might have weakened due to the legal framework reinforced by central government.

One of the most important prerequisites for CCT is, naturally, interest on the part of private firms in the contracts put out to tender. In Local Authority A, the region could be said to have possessed an anti-privatisation culture, manifest in the widespread disputes over tendering that took place throughout the late 1980s and the early 1990s. Nevertheless, four or more private contractors took part in the tendering for vehicle maintenance and ground maintenance in 1991. However, as the local authority became known as an anti-privatisation region over time, private companies who had experiences of tender in this district were looking to tender in new market areas, regarding this area as a region where there was no chance of getting an award. This implies that the motivations of the private sector in Local Authority A grew weaker over time.

Strategies: With regard to the strategies employed during the CCT process, Local Authority A in general imposed onerous or irrelevant conditions on private business, within the limit of the law. It sought to make the most of the provisions of the Act, which allow contractors who have submitted tenders to be vetted for financial integrity, track record and so on. The practices of Local Authority A sometimes involved a 'tacit threat' to private companies and sometimes attacked the freedom of the private companies to sell their labour wherever they chose.

Three key strategies were used. Local Authority A adopted the information asymmetry strategy. It reduced the chances of private companies gaining information regarding the costs, terms and conditions of employment on the part of the local authority. Information asymmetry was seen as the medium whereby some measure of control could be exercised over the private sector and accountability maintained. It was felt that, in Mr A's words, information protection could be an "essential part of the authority's strategy to defend direct labour from the Government's plans to contract out".

An antiprivatisation culture among management was manifest in the tendering of unattractive contracts with onerous performance bonds and over-detailed specifications attached. Using this strategy, Local Authority A made the private contractors bear the transaction costs needed to fulfil those requirements.

Local Authority A's implementation of the tender evaluation process was to the advantage of the inhouse. The authority requested the private bidders to submit information regarding the operating of the contract, such as their technical competence and their ability to perform the contract. In interpreting information from the private bidders, Local Authority A was very rigorous and had an inclination for the inhouse. To this end the trade unions provided some extra intelligence on companies.

The strategy employed by private contractors who tendered in Local Authority A does not seem to be obvious. According to Mr A, private contractors were dedicated to keeping secret their information about their financial situation and the potential costs of contracts. However, mainly because no contractors had been awarded contracts in Local Authority A, it is difficult to examine the strategy of the private sector. Nevertheless, it would be interesting to investigate the seemingly irrational behaviour of going through the process of being accepted on to a select list and then not submitting a bid.

Interplay of contexts, motivations and strategies

An essential ingredient of the politics of transaction cost framework is the ability of context, motivation and strategy to interact with each other and eventually to influence the CCT policy output, DSO output. In this sense, the three components are not some static backcloth, but are constantly being re-formed by the actions of groups and individuals. For example, while context can be seen to have a major influence on motivation and strategy, so motivation and strategy themselves can impact back on the context within which CCT operates.

One of the major characteristics of the contexts of Local Authority A is that the local organisational culture was radically antiprivatisation-oriented. Local Authority A has been Labour-dominated, with little enthusiasm for government reforms, which it regarded as unwelcome and unnecessary. Local councillors' and officials' sympathy towards the inhouse providers continued and antiprivatisation culture persisted, which clearly favoured the retention of contracts inhouse.

The legal framework for CCT gave some discretion and room for the local authority to manipulate the transaction costs. Although, as time went on, the legal framework had been corrected to reflect private contractors' interests and prevent local authority malpractices (anticompetitive behaviour), Local Authority A's strategy and strong predisposition towards the politics of transaction costs overcame the constraints imposed by the regulations issued by central government.

On the whole, it can be said that in Local Authority A, DSO output was affected by a combination of the local organisational antiprivatisation culture and the local authority's strong predisposition towards the politics of transaction costs. In other words, central government and private contractors had no significant power in affecting the DSO output.

Interpretation via the politics of transaction cost framework

The starting point for this analysis of the case study was the assumption that the different levels of DSO output in the local authorities could be explained by the interplay between the context, motivation and strategy behind the CCT process. The following conclusions are derived from the politics of transaction cost perspective.

Analysis of Local Authority A supports the assumption of the politics of transaction cost perspective. Throughout the period of the analysis, the CCT process in Local Authority A was seen as a complex strategical game with many players. The imposition of new constraints on the activities of the one party led the other party to adopt a new strategy.

Local Authority A was hostile to privatisation. One of the main reasons for this was that local organisational culture was definitely antiprivatisation-oriented, which influenced the process in many ways. Accordingly, the local organisational culture of Local Authority A played an important role in defining a local context which controlled the actions of the actors involved. While the councillors and officials recognised the need for efficient service provision, they did not favour privatisation and, as a consequence, tendering exercises were always regarded as alien to service provision.

In Local Authority A, among various strategies employed for the politics of transaction cost information asymmetry was influential and prevalent, and it gained ground in the sense that the local authority itself and the private contractors involved in the CCT process made great efforts to manipulate the information costs incurred. Information resources are possessed by the main interested parties, central government, the local authority and the private sector, and each party may volunteer information to the others or else withhold it as a sanction. More specifically, the strategies used in Local Authority A can be characterised as offering a pre-contract informational advantage for one of the parties. This can be the result of direct manipulation of the information network to promote personal goals.

Private interest has also played a crucial role in contracting out in the district. Whether a private bid for contracts has been received has been very much influenced by the perception of the private contractors of the context within which they may have to operate. In Local Authority A, the antiprivatisation management culture, unattractive contracts and poor industrial relations put off private contractors.

Local authority B

Background

With a hung council, a low DSO output and a population of approximately 77,700, Local Authority B is predominantly rural in character, with an emphasis on agriculture, agri-business and small light industry. In 1994, out of 37 council seats, 13 were held by the Liberal Democrats, 10 by others, nine by the Conservatives and five by Labour. The population density of Local Authority B, which is in the East Midlands, is much lower than the average of the county to which it belongs and the national median figure. Population change during the past 10 years has also been lower, implying that this district is rural and economically less developed.

Politically, Local Authority B has been a hung council for more than 15 years. While there was no one party in overall control, it was mainly Liberal Democrat and Independent.

As a consequence of this background, trade union action has not been militant. While there is evidence of opposition to tendering in Local Authority B during the 1990s, there has been no record of organised trade union activity.

Review of CCT in Local Authority B

In contrast with Local Authority A, Local Authority B, as is usual in rural district, exhibited a less strong labour movement and a less militant trade union presence. Industrial relations were generally good, with the council taking care to keep the trade unions happy.

Prior to the 1988 Act the local authority had experience of letting the building maintenance contract in 1985 under the 1980 Act. By 1994, refuse collection, street cleaning, five ground maintenance tenders, and leisure management and facilities management had come under scrutiny. Three of these nine services, refuse collection, street cleaning and leisure management, had been kept inhouse and the others were privatised.

Competitive tendering in Local Authority B began in 1990 when the refuse collection contract went to the DSO, which then made the third lowest tender out of five bids. At that time the district could take into account redundancy costs,[8] and so following the post–tender evaluation, the contract was awarded inhouse because this was seen as being financially the most beneficial course.

In 1990, the contract for ground maintenance went to a private contractor. At the time of the tender, Local Authority B lacked the needed tools, resources and equipment to complete the job, which meant that the DSO was not in a good position to compete with the private sector. The private contractor winning the tender was in a good position to possess the relevant information on the client needs and other bidders. Since then, four more contracts for ground maintenance have gone to the same private contractor.

In 1992 and 1993, contracts for leisure management and facilities management went to the DSO and a private company respectively. In the former case there was no competition; in the latter case, the private company which had repeatedly won contracts for ground maintenance also won it for facilities management in 1993.

Since the introduction of CCT, there had been very few complaints about the way Local Authority B let the contract or the specification. Everything was seen as fair and above board. However, in relation to the contract for ground maintenance in 1994, the inhouse provider complained that the private company put in loss–leaders, taking advantage of its status as the existing holder of the contract. The private contractor which had provided the service of ground maintenance since 1990 was in the powerful position of being the incumbent. The allegation was compounded by the fact that despite the contract for ground maintenance for 1994 being initially a contract for five years, it was later extended to seven years. Although it was not a massive contract financially (£ 26,093 pa), it was seen by the inhouse provider as financially beneficial.

In 1994 when the contract for leisure management was tendered, there was also a complaint from inhouse that the external contractors put in loss-leaders to establish a base in the area. The officers thought that this was true to some extent and a fair criticism, but there was no reason why the local authority should not benefit from a loss-leader. Finally, the inhouse provider lost the contract to a private company.

The reaction of trade unions to competitive tendering in Local Authority B was somewhat militant at first, but later not strong. No record of industrial action against the privatisation of the service exists in the local press and the interviewee could not remember any being taken.

Analysing contexts, motivations and strategies

Contexts: In Local Authority B, initially the councillors and officials were not in favour of competition and were rather supportive towards the inhouse contractor. The DSO was closely involved in contract specification in some instances.

The authority's chief officer, Mr B, noted that the authority recognised that "over time CCT had been a good thing and inhouse services could be changed without the threat of action from the workforce". He added:

> "At the beginning [CCT] was seen as a threat to the authority.
> However, as time went on there was a change in regard to
> competition. From a client point of view and a public point
> of view, it's been a good thing because we've been getting a
> better quality service than we did, say, 10 years ago. We've
> got to price a specification and everybody is more clear
> about what exactly you require. I think we're getting a better
> output from the contractor and at a better cost. However,
> we hope the inhouse will maintain the services."

In Local Authority B, the local organisational culture was somewhat negative towards CCT; however, over time it changed from being negative to being more neutral. One factor affecting the change in attitude was that the contract for ground maintenance for 1990 saved money by 25%. Mr B stated:

> **"The contract for ground maintenance then, in money terms, wasn't a big contract – it was costing us £40,000 prior to CCT. That contract was then £30,000 for the same amount of work. They were very competitive but they have become competitive by changing their whole method of working. Since the financial savings from the contract for ground maintenance in 1990, greater emphasis was placed on the creation of savings."**

There has been somewhat less commitment to the approach of total support for the DSO, since commitment to service and the importance of the client grew. This can be seen as not so much a change in respect of CCT as a reflection of the increased priority of other aims and objectives and a reluctant acceptance of the inevitable. Even where there was commitment to the DSO, the authority was happy to make savings.

In Local Authority B, the local organisational culture has developed around the need to promote savings and develop new ideas about the structure of services to improve efficiency. In the manual services sector, this philosophy appears to be a driving force throughout the organisation, from senior officials to the lower grades of functional official. The councillors and senior officials of Local Authority B emphasised the need for rationalisation and the importance of creating savings. A council minute explains the general attitude of Local Authority B towards CCT:

> **The council would not approach any service area with a dogmatic 'privatisation only' attitude. It will approach each service area pragmatically and will look to provide its services in the best way possible – encouraging fair and reasonable competition. In particular every effort will be made to define and redefine the inhouse delivery group so that they can deal even-handedly with the private sector.**

Over time Local Authority B became interested in saving money and in the efficient provision of services, whether the provider was inhouse or private sector.

The power of trade unions in Local Authority B has traditionally not been great. Above all, because the entire organisational hierarchy had accepted the principles of competitive tendering and the need to make its services more cost-efficient, all officials were under pressure to achieve savings, so there was all the more incentive to accept the senior officials' philosophy. The highly top-down approach also seriously weakened the trade unions' role and the reduction in their power was seen as a positive spin-off of competitive tendering.

The trade unions in Local Authority B were fully involved in the preparation of service specifications. In this district, the officials and councillors involved the union representatives in discussions about the level and quality of local services. However, according to the minutes of Local Authority B, the trade unions' participation in the decision-making process was not great.

Motivations: The attitude of councillors and officials in Local Authority B to transaction costs was that they were high and could be an imposition both on the authority and on private contractors. When asked to characterise the transaction costs involved in the CCT process, Mr B maintained:

> "I think it could be incurred whether inhouse or in the private sector. There are significant transaction costs depending on the circumstances, such as the content of the contract, length of the contract and length of time given to tender .... I am sure there are hundreds of other tricks which we could try to deter the private sector."

His comment implies that Local Authority B recognised the possibilities for the use of transaction costs in the interest of the authority in the CCT process. However, he added that:

> "Although the transaction costs associated with the market-orientated public service provision are considerable, and the costs are able to be manipulated by the local authority, [Local Authority B] has had quite a good name as a fair employer. When it comes to CCT, they [private contractors] see us as being impartial and the best contractor gets the job – we go through a fair process."

This indicates that although Local Authority B has known how it could benefit from the CCT process via the use of the politics of transaction costs, it did not seek to do this. One possible reason for this is that it was a hung council with no overall control. Member involvement was generally lower than in any other type of authority, at least partly because there was no very clear overall political approach to competition (Leach and Stewart, 1992; Walsh and Davis, 1993). The other reason is that the councillors and officials of Local Authority B have become very interested in saving money in providing services. Following their experience of the contract for ground maintenance in 1990 which saved them money (25%), they came to think that so long as a contract can save money it does not matter whether the provider is inhouse or an external contractor.

It can be inferred that Local Authority B's motivation towards using the politics of transaction costs during the CCT process was not strong, and that in a sense Local Authority B did not care about the matter.

Conversely, the private contractors' motivation was seen as being very strong, in that many private contractors tendered for the contracts and most of them were keen to use loss-leaders and to take advantage of their status as incumbents. Mr B asserts that private companies which tendered for the contracts in Local Authority B were also able to influence the CCT process via a variety of strategies.

It appears that both the local authority and the private contractors in Local Authority B recognised that transaction costs in the CCT process were high. However, the difference between the two parties is that while the local authority was not motivated to manipulate them, the private contractors were enthusiastic about the use of the politics of transaction costs. This was partly because the private contractors already knew that Local Authority B would not try to manipulate transaction costs to prevent the private sector entering into service provisions, and partly because they already knew many cases where transaction costs could be manipulated by external contractors.

Strategies: Local Authority B was essentially not interested in the unfair CCT process and it employed no prominent strategies to manipulate the transaction costs. Instead, in a sense it sought to decrease the transaction costs on the part of private contractors, including extending the contract period or splitting the contract up, as in the case of ground maintenance.

As regards strategies by the other party, the private sector, loss-leaders were prominent. It is generally assumed that this is a long-term rational strategy. The reason all the contractors came to Local Authority B is that they wanted to establish a base in the area. In reality, there are a great many leisure management facilities. Contractors have appointed an area manager and even now are very competitive in some of the tenders in adjacent local authorities. They have employed a 'base and spread' strategy in the area.

Asset specificity and incumbency are also noteworthy phenomena in Local Authority B. In 1990, when the contract for ground maintenance was tendered, Local Authority B lacked the tools, equipment and facilities to provide the service. Asset specificity was the main factor by which the private company won the contract, because the then DSO was not prepared to compete with the external contractors. Since then the private contractor has made the most of its status as the existing holder of the contract for ground maintenance. As a result, the private contractor has won a series of contracts for ground maintenance.

When asked to elaborate on the private contractors' strategies for winning the award, Mr B noted that the existing holder of the contract had a good knowledge of the bid needed to win follow-up works, as well as easy access to the client for lobbying purposes.

Interplay of contexts, motivations and strategies

As with Local Authority A, in Local Authority B the DSO output is understood to be a result of an interplay of context, motivations and strategies surrounding the CCT process. However, what is remarkable in Local Authority B is that while the local authority was neutral to competition in a certain respect and did not play a major role in deciding who was given the award, the private contractor influenced the CCT process considerably by making the most of its status as the existing holder of the contract. This implies that the politics of transaction costs instigated by the private sector were significant in the process. This became possible with the local organisational culture being neutral to competition and keen on saving money instead of retaining the inhouse provision.

Local Authority B's attitudes towards transaction costs was that although they were high, they could be offset by the savings made by the introduction of CCT. The main reason for this is that over time the neutral stance of the local organisational culture towards CCT has persisted.

The perception councillors and officials in Local Authority B had of CCT, that of a neutral stance, proved to be a major influence on the attractiveness of contracts to the private sector. It is assumed that the councillors and officials were not seriously concerned about the politics of transaction costs. Contexts, motivations and strategies surrounding the CCT process in Local Authority B were advantageous to the private sector.

The strategy used by the private contractor to win the contract has progressively become characterised by a neutral stance on the part of local organisational culture, a legal framework in favour of the private contractor, and a strong motivation on the part of the private company to use transaction costs. The atmosphere in which the private sector played a major role in influencing DSO output and contributed to saving money on service provision in turn enabled the organisational culture (which favoured inhouse services and cooperation with the workforce) to be transformed into a new culture (which, for example, promoted competitive tendering).

Interpretation via the politics of transaction cost framework

One feature of CCT in Local Authority B is that during the process the matter of incumbency arose and prevented the authority from obtaining the lowest price for a contracted service. The private contractor who was awarded the contract for ground maintenance in 1990 won the subsequent contracts for ground maintenance, taking advantage of the strong position of the incumbent in winning rebids.

Asset specificity played a major role in the private contractor winning the ground maintenance contract in 1990.

Asset specificity which cannot be used for other purposes leads to a situation of bilateral monopoly (Walsh, 1995, p 35). Once the investment in special equipment, knowledge or skills has been made it is difficult for the buyer to go to alternative providers, and the person who has made the investment gains quasi-monopoly advantages. In Local Authority B, the contract for ground maintenance is a case in point. The market may not be contestable because of the existing supplier's control of the necessary resources.

The seller may also face a limited market because the buyer is the only purchaser of the specialised products involved. Williamson (1985) argues that many government activities will tend to be characterised by bilateral monopoly because of the highly professionalised nature of many public services. However, in this case, the factor of asset specificity was combined with that of incumbency, resulting in quasi-monopoly advantages on the part of the private contractor.

Asset specificity is an important issue in relation to the politics of transaction costs because where it is prominent, each party (the principal and agent) may become dependent on the other (Walsh, 1995). Principals rely on agents to produce goods and services for them, and agents rely on principals to continue to use them to produce certain goods and services. What is more significant here is that, in Local Authority B, incumbency which resulted from asset specificity enabled the provider to win follow-on contracts, preventing the authority from obtaining the lowest price for contracted services, and the other private contractors from entering the market.

Another characteristic of the CCT process in Local Authority B is rampant opportunism on the part of private contractors, who have used the strategy of loss-leaders. In theory, when the actions of agents are unobservable, they are subject to moral hazard. The need to limit opportunism implies the need for suitable *ex ante* mechanisms (monitoring schemes and incentive-payment contracts) as well as *ex post* ones (auditing and penalties, or other similar safeguards) (Dixit, 1996, pp 55-6).

Local Authority C

Background

Local Authority C has been Conservative-controlled and has had no inhouse provision of 1988 Act services. Local Authority C is a thriving, developing community; agriculture and market gardening continue to be the area's traditional industries and there is a wealth of attractive rural scenery.

Immediately after the Second World War, the district could be described as containing rural communities based around a single market town. However, the district has experienced a tremendous growth in population, and in industrial development. Its overall economic activity rate was particularly high, while it registered an unemployment rate much less than the national median value. Local Authority C also appears to have prospered during the 1980s, being one of the fastest-improving local economies in England, with substantial population growth and a high rate of employment creation. The district has experienced growing prosperity through its concentration on key industrial growth areas benefiting from changes in the British economy in the 1980s.

Politically, Local Authority C has remained predominantly Conservative and middle class. Conservative local councils and MPs have consistently been returned for the past 15 years. The 1990s have seen some incursions into local politics by Liberal Democrats, although overall control remains with the Conservatives. As a consequence of this socioeconomic background, the level of local trade union action has been muted. While there is evidence of opposition to CCT in the late 1980s, there appears to have been no organised trade union movement during the 1990s.

Review of CCT in Local Authority C

Local Authority C became one of the leading exponents of outside tendering for services in the 1980s and 1990s. In its region, it was seen as a model for other like-minded authorities to follow. Since 1990, when Local Authority C was reformed to establish a council Separate Standing Committee to examine contracts, it became a flagship for other local authorities. Unlike those in Local Authority A, councillors and officials in Local Authority C were enthusiastic about competitive tendering and privatisation.

Privatisation in Local Authority C has been a prominent feature of service provision, with all services having been put out to tender since the introduction of CCT. The success of private contractors in this district is linked to the pro-privatisation outlook of the councillors and management. The councillors, for example, have been intent on tendering the services and expecting a high degree of competition from the private sector. As a result, not all the services which were put out to tender since the introduction of CCT were won by the inhouse teams. It seems that a series of measures for decreasing transaction costs on the part of the private sector encouraged tenders from private contractors.

The first instance of contracting out in Local Authority C was the tendering of refuse collection in 1990. At that time the DSO in Local Authority C won the contract initially, but the DSO was not able to make the team of workers successful commercially, so the local authority had to disband the workforce as a business would, then put the contract out to tender again. Finally the contract went to a private contractor. Five private contractors were invited to tender for the service, for a contract which clearly favoured the private sector. The private contractor which had previously been given the award tendered the lowest bid. At this time, unsurprisingly, there appears to have been no protest by the

DSO workforce to the closure of the inhouse service. Lack of the facilities, equipment and workforce necessary for the provision of the service was a characteristic of Local Authority C.

Street cleaning and recyclable collection services were tendered in 1991 and 1993 respectively, with both services won by private contractors. The street cleaning contract received seven private sector competitors, while the recyclable collection contract received six tenders from the major private companies. In the case of the street cleaning contract, a private contractor won because it tendered the lowest bid. In the case of the recyclable collection, the firm which tendered the lowest bid had it rejected by the awards panel for being a loss-leader. The councillors in charge of the contract were uncertain as to the ability of the contractor to run the services for the price quoted and gave the award to the firm who tendered the second lowest bid.

What was noticeable in the process of contracting for the two services was that there was no inhouse workforce opposition to the decisions, and that the district did not try to impose any type of transaction costs on the private candidates. The tender document specifies that the successful contractor can take leases from the council for parts of the premises at no cost and the contractor can hire a sufficient number of the council's existing fleet of vehicles to perform the contract in accordance with the amended conditions of contract. The document also specifies that defects to the required vehicles will be repaired by the council prior to handover or else an appropriate deduction will be given to the contractor. All this implies that the district has endeavoured to lessen any type of burden on private candidates.

In 1994, the contract for the cleaning of buildings was tendered, and the same company that was awarded the contract for street cleaning in 1991 won the contract. When asked to give the reason for this the authority's chief officer, referred to as Mr C, stated that the company was in a much stronger position than any other candidate, in that it had an informational advantage over the other candidates.

In 1994, leisure management and grounds maintenance were tendered, and all contracts were won by the private sector. There were more than six private contractors for both services and the awards went to the lowest bidders.

Analysing contexts, motivations and strategies

Contexts: In Local Authority C, councillors and senior management were keen to see work carried out in the private sector. The culture of efficiency savings through competitive tendering developed in the late 1980s in the authority and has strengthened to the extent that the wisdom of tendering is an accepted part of day-to-day practice.

In Local Authority C, both councillors and officials were keen to encourage competitive tendering. While the majority of the Conservatives were from the old-fashioned paternalistic wing of the Conservative Party, a few individuals were considered hardline Thatcherites. The councillors and officials conceded that competitive tendering had highlighted past inefficiencies in the previous internal service and felt that it had been an important provider of savings.

This district, as a Conservative-controlled local authority, was happy to go along with what central government wanted. Especially after the privatisation of refuse collection services in 1990 had resulted in remarkable savings, officials from Local Authority C radically changed the management philosophy in order to make financial savings.

A significant point to be made about the development of contracting out and the extension of the tendering principle in the authority is that there appears to have been no trade union opposition to the process. The workforce affected by CCT has accepted this line of argument and whatever changes that have occurred as a result. With regard to trade union participation in the decision-making process, unions were not consulted, being eventually confronted with a *fait accompli* in the form of the new service specification for which the DSO would be tendering. Often, no attempt was made to persuade the workforce of the need for change before the specifications were issued.

Industrial relations have been characterised by apathy: the CCT process has not resulted in any industrial action by the workforce and the trade unions' activities have not altered managerial decisions. The authority's workforce has accepted the actions of the decision makers without question. Mr C mentioned that the workforce was cooperative and easy to handle.

Motivations: The district viewed transaction costs as a barrier to the entrance of the private sector and implemented measures to lessen these to attract as many private candidates as possible. Mr C maintained that although the local authority had not got fundamental discretion in the CCT process, it nevertheless had some discretion. He also stated:

> "What the process has revealed is that central government doesn't know how we do our work. The people who draft the regulations, for example, have been revealed as not knowing enough about how local government works to define them accurately. Specifically, there might have been hundreds of tricks to deter the private sector from entering into public service provision. However, we favoured maximum contracting out. We made some efforts to lessen some kinds of imposition on the private contractors."

This statement accords with the measures which have diminished the burdens on the private candidates who tendered for contracts in Local Authority C such as allowing the successful contractor to take leases from the council for parts of the premises and depots at no cost. Unlike other local authorities, which normally set out 10% of the contract size as a performance bond, Local Authority C set out 7%, leading the private sector to tender for the contracts more easily.

When asked to describe the transaction costs involved in the CCT process of Local Authority C, Mr C noted that "the transaction cost is high; however, the local authority did not try to manipulate it for its benefit". In general, the stance was to accept the rationalisation of service provision and efficiency savings through CCT. On this evidence, Local Authority C was not strongly motivated to manipulate transaction costs.

Mr C mentioned four main factors affecting the decision as to who should provide services in Local Authority C:

- service quality;
- the bidding price;
- a lack of requisite tools, equipment or personnel to provide a certain service;
- a high level of confidence in contractors.

Of these factors, he cited asset-specificity-related concerns and the bidding price as the two most important issues in the decision making.

When asked about the relative importance of various factors in contracting out, Mr C believed that the cost of inhouse provision vis-à-vis that of private provision is an important issue in relation to contracting, but that asset-specificity-related factors, and the desire to be cost-efficient, are both 'very important'. This explains why the contract for street cleaning in 1991 went to a private contractor and why the same contractor was awarded the contract for the cleaning of buildings. These comments indicate that Local Authority C did not pay attention to the use of transaction costs in deciding who should win the contract, but rather focused on technical and quality-related criteria.

Whatever the nature of the local organisational culture, one of the most important prerequisites for contracting out is the presence of private firms willing to tender for the contracts in the CCT process. In Local Authority C, street cleaning in 1991 and cleaning of buildings and ground maintenance in 1994 received more than six private contractors on every occasion the service was tendered. However, because Local Authority C had no intention of deterring private contractors from the tendering process, the private sector was in a rather better situation, where it could influence the CCT process using a variety of strategies.

It can be inferred from Mr C's comments that private contractors were strongly motivated to use the politics of transaction costs. Mr C maintained that the pro-privatisation approach of the authority's councillors and officials has allowed the private sector more success. He also noted that throughout the entire history of CCT the bidding strategies of private contractors have targeted Local Authority C because of its good reputation for being pro-privatisation, and the size, nature and other conditions of the contracts it has tendered.

Strategies: Given that the objectives of councillors and officials in the management of Local Authority C were financial savings and the rationalisation of service provision, it is assumed that the strategy for the politics of transaction costs employed by the authority was the alleviation of diverse transaction costs – information, negotiation and monitoring related costs – on the part of the private candidates for the contracts.

By contrast, the private sector used a number of strategies in relation to the politics of transaction costs. One of these, as was shown by the contract for street cleaning, is incumbency. The then incumbent firm for the contract of refuse collection, which was tendered in 1990, had an informational advantage over non-incumbent contractors when the contract for street cleaning was tendered in 1991, because the firm wanted to extend the business scope to street cleaning. This information may be available to the non-incumbent, but only at a cost. Stigler (1966) found that although most economic information is available to all, it may take time and effort to uncover such information in the marketplace.

Another strategy is use of the loss-leader. When asked about certain strategies used by the private sector to win contracts in Local Authority C, Mr C noted that loss-leaders had been employed. For instance, in 1993 when the contract for recyclable collection was tendered and it initially went to the private contractor which tendered the lowest bid, it was rejected by the authority for being a loss-leader.

Interplay of contexts, motivations and strategies

In Local Authority C, the Conservatives historically had a clear majority on the council, dominating the chairmanship and all important posts. The few hardline Thatcherites among them, encouraged by the experience of other contracting authorities, persuaded the authority to undertake a series of efficiency reviews in the early 1980s. By 1982, office cleaning and cattle-market cleaning had been privatised. This pro-privatisation culture made it possible that even before the introduction of the 1988 Act, the authority experienced the smooth privatisation of NHS services and the voluntary competitive tendering of local government services because most of the councillors and officers in Local Authority C were sympathetic with the Conservatives.

This pro-privatisation culture which developed throughout the 1980s and the early 1990s has strengthened, to the extent that the authority, unlike many others, let all relevant DSOs close down, exercising greater discretion both at the contract specification stage and later. The culture has developed around the need to promote savings and develop new ideas about the structure of services for the improvement of efficiency. In the service sector, this philosophy appears to be a driving force throughout the organisation from the councillors and senior officials to the lower workforce. Accordingly, the motivation of the private sector to win the contracts superseded the local authority's motivation towards the politics of transaction costs.

As a result, the market in Local Authority C was dominated by the strategies employed by the private sector to win and keep the contract, with the local authority being indifferent or neutral to diverse strategies exercised by the private sector. The legal framework was also an important factor in that the private sector had no legal requirement to follow in relation to incumbency.

Interpretation via the politics of transaction cost framework

Since the local organisational culture was pro-contracting out and there was no serious industrial relations problem, Local Authority C did not employ any noticeable strategy regarding the politics of transaction costs. Rather, it was this strategy as practised by the private sector which was prevalent and which dominated the market.

One thing characterising the CCT process in Local Authority C from the point of view of the politics of transaction costs was the opportunism employed by the private sector. The perception that Local Authority C was favourable to CCT led many private companies to tender for the contracts it put out. As a consequence, private contractors behaved opportunistically.

Although the pro-privatisation stance of Local Authority C encouraged many private contractors to tender for contracts, the existing holder of the contract won the follow-on contracts. Seeing a chance to hold a local monopoly, the incumbent provider built up detailed information about customer preferences and costs, and so was likely to be difficult to dislodge.

Local Authority D

Background

Local Authority D has been Conservative-dominated, but unlike other such authorities, it has also had high DSO output. Local Authority D is a medium-sized district located in a predominantly rural area containing spectacular countryside, part of which is a national park. The district's four towns are all attractive market towns and there are about 100 smaller villages, many of which have been designated as conservation areas.

The low population density and low rate of population change of Local Authority D reflect its rural characteristics. Its unemployment rate is lower than that of the county to which it belongs and the national median figure. In relation to industry structure, a feature of Local Authority D is that the number of residents in the agriculture industry is relatively high, while that in other industries is comparatively low.

Like most of its neighbouring areas, Local Authority D has a long history of control by the Conservative Party. At the time of the district's controversial tendering exercise in 1988, the Conservatives had a clear majority on the council, controlling the chairmanship and all the council committees.

Review of CCT in Local Authority D

The degree of DSO output in Local Authority D has been relatively high despite the fact that the local authority has been dominated by the Conservatives.

The first instance of contracting out came with the privatisation of refuse collection and its award to a private contractor in 1989. At that time, there were 30 contractors in the region expressing a desire to carry out the refuse collection. According to the authority's chief officer, referred to as Mr D, there are two reasons why many private contractors were tempted to tender in this district:

- the contract for refuse collection was the biggest contract involving manual labour;

- private contractors were able to pick out the Conservative councils and submit tenders to them, knowing that they would be treated more fairly than by Labour councils.

Eventually, three tenders, including the inhouse provider and two private contractors, were received. However, one of the two private contractors, a small family firm, tendered for the contract with a bid about five times higher than the other two bids. This was the first local authority contract that this firm had tendered for. In view of the contractor's excessively high bid, it was felt that this firm should be rejected, without further evaluation.

The other private contractor, a relatively large company, tendered a slightly lower bid than the inhouse provider. As the contractor's tender was the lowest and its supporting information was adequate, Local Authority D had no option but to accept this tender. However, while the officers harboured a great deal of scepticism about whether the contractor's proposed resources and staffing levels would be capable of meeting the specification standards, the contractor stated that additional resources and staffing would be employed if necessary to achieve the specification. Hence there was no reason to believe that the specification could not be achieved. Eventually, the contractor was awarded the contract for refuse collection.

The inhouse workforce was then redundant. There were 40 employees engaged on the work when it was carried out inhouse and the work was eventually carried out by 27 private sector employees.

In early 1990, the contract for toilet cleaning was tendered, and it went to the same private company that had been awarded the contract for refuse collection in 1989. However, both of the privately controlled services provided by this contractor proved unsatisfactory to the council in terms of service quality. These very clear dissatisfactions with privatisation deterred the ruling Conservatives from pushing ahead with similar exercises in other fields. Councillors and officials were aware that the existing task should be re-examined. At a meeting of a committee in late 1990, members agreed to ask officers to prepare a report on the efficiency of a variety of services, including refuse collection and toilet cleaning. Information was to be provided in a way that would allow direct comparisons with other authorities and with private sector firms.

This experience marked a significant change in the style of service provision, resulting in a radical change in management philosophy. In particular, greater emphasis was placed on quality of service and the creation of savings in service provision.

In late 1990, cleaning of buildings was tendered and the tender went to the inhouse team. Five private contractors were invited to tender for the service, the contract for which clearly favoured the retention of the service inhouse. The inhouse tender included projected savings from the authority's rationalisation scheme. Unsurprisingly, the inhouse tender was the cheapest by a considerable margin.

In 1991, grounds maintenance was won by the DSO with no competition. No other private contractor submitted a price despite the fact that there were companies on the select list. The reason there was no private contractor bidding for the contract was that the private companies had no further capacity available to deal with Local Authority D's stringent requirements (eg high level of service quality). The authority made the private candidates very much aware that it would be extremely rigorous in its control of a contract. When asked about the characteristics of the contract for ground maintenance in 1991, Mr D noted:

> **"We did not break any rules. However, we could impose, through supervision of a contract, some fear, as far as the private contractor is concerned, in how rigorously they pursue the conditions of the contract. I know that academically we would say there is a specification there and it's right or wrong, but that isn't quite true. There is a quite grey area. It's my firm belief that the local authority made the private**

> **contractors very much aware that it will be most rigorous in
> the control of a contract."**

In 1992, the contract of leisure management was tendered, and the contract
went to the DSO. At this time the district had difficulties finding private
contractors involved in leisure management to submit a tender. Street
cleaning, cleaning of buildings and housing repairs services were tendered
in 1994. Of these three services, the contract for street cleaning was won
by a private contractor while contracts for the other two services were
won inhouse.

The contract for street cleaning elicited seven bids from private
companies, which were attracted because of the contract's size. Two of
these bids undercut the inhouse tender and eventually the award was
given to the lowest tender despite some misgivings that it looked like a
loss-leader. The contracts for both cleaning of buildings and housing
repair went to the inhouse provider despite the fact that there were
private contractors who undercut the inhouse bids of each contract. The
reason why the inhouse team was finally given the contract was that the
lowest private contractor's bid was seen as a loss-leader, and the committee
found it difficult to see how the specification could be achieved by the
company with its proposed resources and staffing.

As regards the contract for housing repair, the private company which
tendered the lowest bid was seen as having made a number of mistakes in
its submission. Concerning this Mr D stated:

> **"The private contractors submitted a lower price than the
> DSO. I was able to go to the committee and say that the
> contractor had made a number of mistakes in his submission
> and that if this was the standard of work he was submitting
> we couldn't accept it. We'd need to do a lot of work to alter
> the documentation but to be sensible in controlling the
> contract."**

In CCT terms, these two arguments were quite loose and difficult to
sustain. In this connection, Mr D said that:

> **"Had the Conservatives strongly persuaded [it], the authority
> would have taken those two private contractors who tendered
> a lower price than the DSO and who had not put in enough**

resources, on the basis that they would not have liked a challenge from the Secretary of State of the Conservative central government."

However, the Conservative councillors left it to Mr D to decide on the quality of the work that was being offered. What was most crucial for the councillors was not whether the provider should be inhouse or from the private sector, but the quality of service.

It is understood that throughout the CCT process in Local Authority D, tendering was deliberately biased in favour of the inhouse teams.

Analysing contexts, motivations and strategies

Contexts: As in other authorities, in Local Authority D there has been no serious disagreement between the councillors and officials on CCT issues. According to Mr D most of the councillors were Conservative and likely to agree with each other, and all had tremendous faith in the chief officers reporting to them and so were reluctant to go against what they said.

When asked what local councillors and officials in Local Authority D thought of CCT in general, Mr D maintained:

> **"They believe that CCT has been an excellent tool for the authority to document the work it requires to be done and which is done. We think that the competition brought about by the private sector has improved the inhouse manual workforce and its responses to problems. Overall, we've been very pleased with the outcome. We've been disappointed by the fact that not every authority has entered into the spirit of the legislation."**

The general stance of the councillors and officials of Local Authority D was a 'neutral' one of opting for internal and external provision according to what represented the best value for money. Mr D quoted a local councillor as saying that "we would like you to win this work through the DSO, but only win if you can do so very fairly".

What is noticeable in Local Authority D is that the local organisational culture changed following the experience of unsatisfactory financial savings and unexpectedly low quality of service provision through the privatisation of refuse collection and toilet cleaning services in 1989 and

1990 respectively. After the experience, a shift in management philosophy took place with the express intention of creating further savings and a better quality of service regardless of the type of providers. While in the early stages, the authority was almost neutral towards CCT, following the experiences of unsatisfactory service provision in 1989 and 1990, it changed its local organisational culture to an emphasis on friendliness towards the inhouse, hoping that this could result in quality service provision. More specifically, disbelief in service provision by the private sector mounted. A local authority minute emphasised that what was important was not whether the provider was inhouse or private sector, but whether the service provided was good quality.

As regards industrial relations in Local Authority D, trade union power was not strong. In 1989, when the refuse collection service went to a private contractor, the workforce realised that they would be made redundant if work was not won inhouse. In general, Local Authority D councillors and officials had no difficulty in persuading the workforce that the decision makers had to go along these lines. Regarding the workforce Mr D stated:

> **"We are fortunate in the calibre of workers employed on the manual side. We are a farming community and the people within the community are very hard-working people because of that. They realised that if work was not won inhouse they would be taken on by the private sector. The employees don't want to know trade unions and they don't fight battles in the way that perhaps larger authorities would."**

As regards participation in the decision-making process, the trade unions in Local Authority D were either consulted on limited issues (such as health and safety) or informed by management of the already worked-out service specifications. Such involvement was thus 'reactive' – the workforce responding to the exhortations of management to accept already developed plans (often involving new conditions and work practices and some voluntary redundancies).

Characterising local unions' resistance to CCT, Mr D claimed it was 'weak'. In the past there was no widespread opposition to the council's action in relation to CCT, and the trade unions were persuaded to accept CCT as a reality. This was against a background of non-trade-union activity.

Motivations: Local authority D's motivations to engage in the politics of transaction costs were strong. When asked about transaction costs, Mr D said:

> **"It is high. There is considerable work for either the private sector or the DSO to do in tendering for a job. If it's going to be tendered for, I don't think that could be avoided. It is possible to make it difficult for private contractors by the extent of the documentation that they've had to complete in order to submit a tender."**

As regards the relationship between transaction costs and the opportunities for private companies in the CCT process, Mr D emphasised that in the early stages such costs certainly existed, especially in terms of early retirement costs, redundancy costs, underused depot stations and other costs. He also implied that the local authority could influence the CCT process via a variety of strategies, stating that:

> **"... although nowadays it is more difficult to deter private companies from entering the market since new codes were introduced, in the early stages of CCT policy the authority could and did influence the output of the CCT process."**

Since 1990, Local Authority D had been strongly interested in a better quality of service and financial savings. As a result, in 1994 the inhouse service won the contracts for both housing repairs and cleaning of buildings despite, in both cases, the presence of cheaper competition. In both contracts the private bids were rejected because they were regarded as a loss-leader and generated fears that the companies would not be able to run the service at the tendered price. This suggests there had been a greater willingness to rationalise service provision whether the method employed was privatisation or inhouse provision. It also implies that to actualise the philosophy of quality service and financial savings, transaction costs could be used, shifted or manipulated in the CCT process.

According to Mr D, it was possible for the local authority to use transaction costs as it wished, but as time went on it was becoming more and more difficult to bend the relevant rules. Also, it may be assumed that the local authority's motivation to use transaction costs has diminished over time, partly because the relevant regulations have been modified to deter local authorities from using them in their interests and partly because the authority has been keen to rationalise the way in which services have been provided.

From the fact that the management of local authority D recognised that transaction costs played a major role in the implementation of the CCT process in the early stages, and from the fact that it had been keen to make financial savings and provide a good quality of service to residents, it can be inferred that in the early stages, Local Authority D was strongly motivated to engage in the politics of transaction costs.

Since Local Authority D has historically been Conservative-dominated, many private contractors have chosen this area for their business. In most cases, except for the contracts for ground maintenance in 1991 and leisure management in 1992, more than four private contractors tendered for the contracts. As was stated earlier, the private sector was sometimes regarded as implementing a loss-leader. It is assumed that private contractors were motivated to win contracts in order to establish a base in the area, although the proportion of DSO provision was higher than in any other Conservative-dominated local authority.

Strategies: In the early stages, the local authority relied on inserting onerous terms and conditions into tender documents to make the tender for the contracts unrealistic. It let the private sector know that the level of service would need to be so high that the private company could not meet the stipulated requirements.

When asked in respect of which tendering process the local authority could effectively influence the chances of the private sector, Mr D replied that across the *whole* process the council could have an effect. He continued:

> **"For example, the creation of a select list.... We went through our third phase of building cleaning. And we had a number of contractors expressing a wish to be on the select list – five plus the DSO. I recommended to the committee the exclusion of three of those contractors, on the basis that they had no experience of similar work."**

He also maintained that many private companies sought to establish a base in the area, stating:

> **"One of the contractors had similar contracts elsewhere in**

the country. However, it was not enough experience. He would have been on the select list if I hadn't got three other private contractors. It happened to be a company whose main activity is grounds maintenance and he was applying to be on the select list for building cleaning. The reason I didn't want that contractor on the select list was because I thought that if he managed to win the cleaning contract, he would be in an excellent situation to win the ground maintenance contract when that comes up for renewal. That is a local authority really influencing CCT – perhaps wrongly, but in the interests of honest relations throughout [Local Authority D]."

His comments indicate that the local authority could influence the choice of private contractors on the select list in its interests, and that it was conscious of the possibility that the unwanted private contractor would be in a good position to renew the contract. Such a situation is characteristic of incumbency in the CCT process.

Strategies used by the private contractors may be characterised as involving loss-leaders, taking advantage of the legal framework which allows them to obtain information on the inhouse strategy. This loss-leader could be viewed as an investment in information, or as buying a foothold, learning by doing.

Interplay of contexts, motivations and strategies

A feature of the CCT process in Local Authority D is that the local organisational culture changed following experiences of unsatisfactory service provision by the private sector in 1989 and 1990, changing from a neutral stance towards CCT to being adamant that there was no empirical evidence for the effectiveness of the private sector. Since then there has been a significant change in the style of service provision in Local Authority D. Greater emphasis has been placed on financial savings and quality service provision regardless of the type of provider.

Although this research study eliminates from its analysis (see Chapter Six) the role played by the public in the politics of transaction costs, it is worth mentioning briefly the importance of this role. It was generally felt that the public had become a propellant for the incurring of the politics of transaction costs in the CCT process. Since the public was highly dissatisfied with the quality of service provided by the private sector, public dissatisfaction was threatening to push up transaction costs on the part of private bidders. Eventually, Local Authority D changed its principal attitude towards CCT from a neutral stance to what seemed a somewhat biased attitude against the private sector. This indicates that there was not a level playing field in the CCT process of Local Authority D.

Unlike most Conservative-controlled local authorities, this district had no experience of private competition in certain contracts because private companies saw the service requirements as being very stringent. The neutral stance of local councillors towards CCT, and the fact that the councillors left it to the officials to decide the quality of service, made it possible for the authority to use strategies to favour the inhouse providers.

As in other districts, the authority's organisational culture is very important, and has influenced the motivations and strategies of the main interested parties. In Local Authority D, the changed philosophies regarding service provision, followed by the experiences of unsatisfactory service provided by the private contractor, played a major role in changing the overall atmosphere of CCT policy.

Interpretation via the politics of transaction cost framework

In the early stages, the local authority employed a strategy of imposing onerous terms and conditions on tender documents in the hope that this would contribute to better quality of service. The authority also charged for the tender documents, so contractors had to pay for the privilege of submitting a tender – over and above what it had already cost to prepare their proposal. In some cases the amount of information required of the contractors by Local Authority D was excessive.

What was remarkable about Local Authority D was that, emphasising the importance of service quality, it prepared the tenders and the specifications in such a way as to obstruct private contractors. The reason for this, according to Mr D, was that the local authority did not trust the quality of service provided by the private contractors. This implies that an unsatisfactory experience of contracting in the past affected the negative attitudes of the management towards the private sector. In a sense this result reflects the hypothesis that if principals have had good (bad) experiences with contractors in the past, they will be more (less) likely to consider this type of alternative service delivery again in the future (Korosec, 1994, p 269).

The authority made the private candidates very much aware that it will be most rigorous in its control of a contract. As a result, there was no private contractor bidding for the contracts for ground maintenance in 1991 and leisure management in 1992. This state of affairs reflects the negative perception of past contracting experiences in Local Authority D.

The local authority had an influence, even at the stage of selecting candidates on the list. As Mr D said, it could delete some private contractors from the select list on the basis of the assumption that from a long-term perspective they would be inimical to the authority in some respects. This also indicates that the general attitude of the management towards private contractors was negative and that management had the ability to influence the CCT process.

Summary

Contexts

Contexts appear to be a particularly important element in the CCT process. Contexts, in the form of the legal framework, local organisational culture and industrial relations, played a major role in the CCT process.

Legal framework

The main purpose in analysing the legal framework for CCT was to examine whether it gives the major parties involved room for discretionary actions in relation to the use of transaction costs. The Acts and Regulations involved lay down a number of specific requirements about the number of tenders being invited, the time periods between various stages in the tendering process and so on.

Central government intervention can have various direct and indirect effects on the local authority and the private sector during the CCT process. However, much is left to discretion within the two sets of legal framework. For example, the private sector is left with a general proviso that an authority should not act in a manner which restricts, distorts or prevents fair competition or is intended or likely to do so.

Central government has continued to regulate the discretion and power of local authorities in the CCT process. There has been more scrutiny of contract development and processes, and the Department of the Environment has set up an enforcement section to monitor performance. For example, in 1993, the Secretary of State issued 20 notices for alleged anticompetitive behaviour, and gave 12 directions, normally requiring retender. Likewise, central government continued to try to limit the discretion of local authorities and to expand the scope of the activity of private contractors in the CCT process. In brief, although central government and the EU have continued to establish the legal framework concerned with CCT, it appears that there has been some room for discretionary activities on the part of the main interested parties.

Local organisational culture

Regarding the local organisational culture, the main tasks were to examine whether the councillors and officials disagreed on CCT policy and what their general attitudes towards CCT policy were.

On the whole, there was no significant disagreement between the councillors and officials on the principle of CCT and the related issues. In the four cases studied, no conflict was found between councillors and officials. This reflects the fact, that in the UK, member and officer structures are mutually reinforcing, with strong alliances between committee chairs and chief officers (Davis, 1996, p 10). Mr C's explanation that officials did not desire conflict with councillors exemplified this trend.

One of the major differences between the four districts was the approach of the councillors and officials to CCT. Four very distinct organisational cultures emerged, which have played a significant role in determining the basic approaches to CCT.

In Local Authority A, both councillors and officials were keen to retain inhouse service provision, probably because the authority had been dominated by Labour for a long time.

In Local Authority B, the local organisational culture was, in the early stages, not in favour of competition, and was rather supportive towards inhouse service provision. However, over time its position regarding CCT changed from negative to neutral. One factor which influenced this change in culture was a positive experience of financial savings made via service provision by the private sector.

In Local Authority C, both councillors and officials were very keen to encourage competitive tendering. Historically, Local Authority C has been dominated by Conservatives, some of whom were from the old-fashioned paternalistic wing of the party, and a few of whom were considered hardline Thatcherites. As a result, the local organisational culture of Local Authority C was pro-privatisation.

Local Authority D reveals a somewhat different picture of local organisational culture from that revealed by other local authorities. Like Local Authority C, Local Authority D was controlled by the Conservatives, leading it to support CCT at an early stage. However, since it experienced unsatisfactory service provision by the private sector, the emphasis shifted to quality of service and financial savings through the rationalisation scheme, irrespective of whether the services were provided inhouse or by private sector.

Industrial relations

The main focus here was to identify whether trade unions were able to participate in the decision-making process regarding CCT, whether there was industrial action in relation to retention of inhouse service provision, and, finally, what the management's view on the influence of trade unions was.

In Local Authority A trade unions were able to participate in the decision-making process; however, they were not eligible to vote. In Local Authority B, trade unions were also consulted when service specifications were prepared. In Local Authority C, they were almost excluded from the decision-making process, and in Local Authority D they were involved in the process to a limited extent. Local Authority A showed the strongest involvement in the decision-making process, followed by local authorities B, D then C.

There was no radical industrial action over decisions regarding CCT by the trade unions in the four authorities. Although in Local Authority A trade unions were relatively powerful, they were not in a position to influence the CCT process.

All the local authorities had staff who were members of NALGO, NUPE and GMBATU.[9] A joint shop steward committee met with the management team to negotiate about difficulties which could not be resolved within the relevant department works committee. In the four cases studied, trade unions continued to be represented on a variety of working parties, subcommittees, and so on, and had the opportunity to ensure that the views of their members were being heard. However, as was discussed earlier, their role was purely nominal and advisory.

On the whole, the power of trade unions in making decisions in the CCT process was not significant. Although the relatively great power of trade unions in Local Authority A contrasted with the power of the unions in the other three local authorities, it was apparent that even in Local Authority A, such power was not decisive in the retaining of inhouse service provision. In Local Authority A, for example, even though trade union members wanted to participate in committee meetings and attempted to lobby councillors, the influence of the trade unions was not seen as significant.

The other three local authorities had much less militant and strong trade unions. The trade unions had no great power in their decision making regarding CCT. This was partly because one of the Thatcher Government's main policies was to diminish the power of trade unions and partly because the trade unions realised that they could not counter the strong will of central government to implement CCT.

The attitudes of the councillors and officials towards the trade unions varied. In Local Authority A, the trade unions were very strong and had considerable experience of industrial action in the public sector. In the other local authorities they were not strong, and so were viewed as rather cooperative.

Motivations

Motivations of central government

The rhetoric and motivations of central government have been strong, and so, too, have been the constraints it has imposed. For central government there has been the unrelenting task of developing strategies which incorporate the macro and micro aspects of implementation. Even from the limited data set in this study it is apparent that top–down pressures caused by the changing legal framework have meant that central government has been strongly motivated to use the politics of transaction costs to fulfil its objective. This view was echoed in a statement of the then Secretary of State for the Environment, Nicholas Ridley, who was quoted in 1991 as saying:

> **The root cause of rotten local services lies in the grip which local government unions have over those services in many parts of the country. Our competitive tendering provisions will smash that grip once and for all. (Foster, 1993, p 51)**

Motivations of the local authority

To examine the dispositions of the local authority to use, manipulate and transfer transaction costs in the CCT process, the chief officers participating in the case studies were asked about the perception of their local authority regarding transaction costs, and its attitudes towards the relationship between transaction costs and opportunities for private contractors. The propensities of local authorities to use the politics of transaction costs varied depending on their own circumstances.

Criticism of the transaction costs involved in the CCT process has been strongest in Local Authority A, with the argument being advanced that resources have been transferred from service provision *per se* to administration. Mr A emphasised that about two thirds of the initial costs will be incurred every time a contract is let. He also stated that, in his experience, considerable costs, managerial effort and time were required for implementation. He mentioned that the chances of private contractors winning the contract can be affected by the various types of transaction costs. In Local Authority B, the general attitude of management towards transaction costs was that these were high and that the opportunities of the private sector could be influenced by a number of means.

In Local Authority C, as opposed to Local Authority A, the attitude was that transaction costs were basically not high, and to some extent might decrease as the new systems became established and public service managers and politicians learned to operate them more effectively. In this regard, Mr C noted that some of these costs were one-off and that much of this preparatory work would not be repeated for future contracts.

In Local Authority D, councillors and officers thought transaction costs were high, and both parties expended a great deal of time and money in preparing their bids. These costs could not be avoided either by the local authority or by the private sector. It is clear that the relationship between transaction costs and opportunities for the private sector was more significant in the early stages of CCT than in the later stages. However, although Local Authority D recognised that the relationship has been weaker since central government has established a tougher and more sophisticated legal framework, it has still been significant. This indicates that Local Authority D has still been powerfully motivated regarding the politics of transaction costs in the CCT process.

Motivations of private contractors

As regards the motivations of private contractors to use transaction costs, local authorities A and D were similar in this respect. Recognising that opportunities for private contractors in those areas were not good, the main private contractors avoided them. The motivations of private contractors in these two regions were not strong, judging from the results of the three criteria applied in the analysis.

By contrast, in cases B and C, most services attracted private competition on every occasion on which the service was tendered. In most cases, the number of private contractors tendering for contracts was more than five, sometimes reaching seven. This indicates that in two regions, private contractors operated actively to win contracts. The motivation of private contractors in local authorities B and C was relatively strong.

Strategies

Strategies of central government

Central government has introduced a compliance mechanism by which it can spell out sanctions for anticompetitive behaviour. For this purpose, the legal framework for CCT has been supplemented and modified. It has effectively created a legal framework for the operation of DSO. For example, DSOs were required to keep separate accounts for each of the services awarded. Annual accounts and reports had to be published, and each DSO was required to achieve a rate of return on capital, specified by the Secretary of State, in each of the accounting divisions of its operations.

Strategies of the local authority

As was discussed earlier, although central government made some efforts to minimise the scope of the discretion and power of the local authority in relation to the implementation of CCT, the local authority nevertheless retained some discretion – a discretion which some councillors wished to use in ways which reflected their values.

The case study analysis shows that a variety of strategies were employed by the local authority to influence the CCT process. In most cases, local authorities tended to use contract compliance as a means of achieving their policy objectives, through the medium of clauses inserted into contracts, with which prospective or actual contractors had to comply. The strategies of transferring transaction costs to the other party and information asymmetry were also discovered in the individual local authority analysis.

Strategies of private contractors

Private contractors also used a variety of strategies to influence the CCT implementation process. Unlike in local authorities A and D, where the motivations of private contractors to use transaction costs were relatively weak, in local authorities C and B they employed diverse strategies such as opportunism, incumbency, information asymmetry and asset specificity. In the early stages, asset specificity and incumbency were frequently adopted by private contractors, whereas in the later stages information asymmetry and opportunism using loss-leaders were employed.

Discussion

The four case studies examined in this chapter have demonstrated the importance of the politics of transaction cost perspective for understanding why local authorities should follow very different competitive tendering paths. In particular, the study shows that the contexts, motivations and strategies surrounding the CCT process are not static but evolve in a highly dynamic fashion.

Some of the themes of the politics of transaction costs have already been elaborated on and illustrated. What general lessons can be learned from this approach? How does it affect our understanding of the CCT process? What principles should guide economists and political scientists when they analyse or recommend alternative policies? These questions, already fundamental, become even more important in view of the fact that the politics of economic policy is everywhere complex and dynamic, and transaction costs of various types are looming larger in all policy contexts (Dixit, 1996).

Unfortunately, the same analysis also points to the difficulty of giving any general answer to such a question. First, politics intervenes even at the level of spotting and using the degrees of freedom. Normative intervention involves quite subtle informative and manipulative tactics. Second, the nature and severity of transaction costs differ from one authority to another and across time. Any general assertions concerning CCT policy must be few, broad and tentative.

However, many of these balancing considerations are well understood, whereas recognition of the role of transaction costs in the CCT process is relatively new. It is worth pointing out and stressing the implications of the politics of transaction cost approach to understanding the CCT process, so some tentative speculations and suggestions will be offered.

This study is based on the assumption that transaction costs can be altered by administrative, legislative and executive actions, and it is crucial to identify in each case who is altering whose transaction costs, in what manner and under what conditions. With these points in mind, the main points arising from the local authority analysis will be discussed below, using the politics of transaction cost approach. Three main themes that appeared frequently in the four case studies will be summarised as a means of answering the questions raised above.

First, the CCT process is a complex game of strategy with many players. DSO output is a result of the dynamic interaction between the main interested parties. Many apparently inefficient outputs can be understood as the consequence of constraints imposed by various transaction costs, or creditable attempts to cope with them.

The full set of constraints on the CCT process should be recognised: the historically determined rules, the information asymmetries, opportunism, the compliance mechanism, incumbency, and the transfer of transaction costs to the other party. DSO output is the result of the game in which the politics of transaction costs dominate.

The second frequent theme of the case studies is that CCT in Britain is a highly politicised phenomenon. The government's political philosophy is embedded in the CCT process. Very few policies have been enacted in a neutral, pragmatic fashion; most have involved considerable deviations from 'normal' practice (Goodwin, 1994). In some cases, the authority has gone to considerable lengths to placate the unions and put together a viable and acceptable inhouse tender. In other cases, the rules governing the tendering process or the specification itself have been adjusted to improve the competitive position of the inhouse team. In Local Authority A, for example, the decision to ask contractors to quote for work done on their own premises ensured higher bid prices (transaction costs) from contractors than if they had been allowed to quote for work done on the authority premises using existing equipment.

The perception of the government's tendering initiative as an ideological crusade has had a significant impact on the behaviour of the three main interest groups involved in the CCT process: contractors, trade unions and management. The contract service industries felt that they were being 'used' by the government to achieve its ideological aims (Goodwin, 1994; McShane, 1995). This dissatisfaction with the government's failure to take into account their needs and capabilities manifested itself in a number of significant ways. Contractors showed little or no interest in certain local areas and became highly selective about their participation in others, leaving the local authorities with newer and less experienced firms to choose from, and facing the precipitation of loss-leader behaviour on a widespread scale.

The government's political approach to the exercise had an equally significant effect on the behaviour of local councillors and officials. As time has gone on, the legal framework established by central government proved to be biased towards private bidders, leading to an increase in transaction costs on the part of the local authority and a decrease on the part of private bidders. Walsh (1992, p 70) also indicates that it is proposed that the provisions of the 1988 Act be tightened to give the private sector more opportunities for winning tenders. This implies that central government intentionally and politically intervened[10] in the CCT process through the use of the compliance mechanism, creating a non-level playing field that worked in private bidders' favour.[11] Consequently, over time the private sector has come to have more power in the CCT process.

Although the majority of Conservative councillors recognised a certain level of inefficiency in services, few believed that a rigorous and uniform approach to the problem was an appropriate remedy (Walsh, 1991). Their perception of the CCT initiative as being a direct attack on workers fostered a protective attitude towards the workforce. Many officials and councillors who would normally have dismissed union opposition as an inevitable consequence of efficiency improvements took a conciliatory and sympathetic stance during the tendering exercises. This protective attitude manifested itself in many ways.

The events which have occurred in the CCT process in the four local authorities flatly contradict government claims that tendering has been carried out in a commercial fashion. The government's ideological approach and highly political methods of implementation have resulted in a collection of tendering exercises governed not by the rules of the tendering process but by the dynamic interaction of government intervention, political preferences, personalities and trade unions.

Similarly, some of those who have awarded contracts inhouse have done so for political or other reasons, not because direct labour proved the more cost-effective option. Only in a minority of cases have the service needs of the authority or the true economics of the situation been the primary factor in determining the output of the tendering decisions. Not only does this behaviour totally undermine the foundation on which the tendering initiative has been based, it also suggests that local authorities may yet be selecting methods of service provision that are not consistent with their technical needs.

The third main theme to emerge is the fact that the local organisational culture played a major role in determining the output of CCT policy, DSO output. If organisational culture refers to ideologies, then long-held values can either act as barriers or as catalysts to the privatisation of local services. With CCT, the government's reforms have attempted to change the local organisational culture of management. Whereas in the past 'inefficiency practices' in local services were accepted, this has been challenged by CCT. The response of different local authorities to CCT has been influenced by the prevailing or dominant local organisational culture within management. There is no single culture, but a variety of different cultures vying for supremacy. Differences in local organisational culture condition the response to top-down initiatives such as CCT (Goodwin, 1994).

The different local organisational cultures regarding the development of competitive tendering in local authorities can be classified according to the framework put forward by Walsh and Davis (1993, pp 25-7). This was constructed to examine local councillors' attitudes to competition. Walsh and Davis observed four response categories to competitive tendering. Using their classification, the local organisational cultures of the four districts can be divided into the following four groups:

- A hostility to the principles of direct labour and a desire to accept the New Right version of local administration where possible (Local Authority C).

- A neutral stance of opting for internal or external provision according to what represents the best value for money. (This applied in Local Authority B later on.)

- A stance of preferring the DSO to win, but accepting the value of contractors when they could provide a better price and better quality. (This applied in Local Authority D later on.)

- An approach of making every effort to help the DSO win. (This applied all the time in Local Authority A.)

These basic local organisational cultures did not change fundamentally in subsequent years, but there have been some shifts of emphasis (Walsh and Davis, 1993, p 26). The nature of local organisational cultures appears to be a particularly important element of the context and it was this that CCT was designed to change. However, such cultures are diverse, as mentioned above, and, as Local Authority D so clearly demonstrates, can be highly contested and changeable. The CCT process has often represented a struggle for the hearts and minds of individuals. In Local Authority A, for example, a variety of actions by trade unions, councillors and officials helped to nurture an antiprivatisation culture.

However, as regards the attitude of councillors, an indicator used here to analyse the local organisational culture, it appears that this had changed over time, with a significant reduction in the level of member involvement. Competition under the 1988 Local Government Act and the following Acts had gone through the normal political cycle of interest when it was first introduced, followed by a process of institutionalisation. However, basic attitudes towards CCT had not changed fundamentally in the subsequent years. Instead, there had been some shifts of emphasis.

As Walsh and Davis (1993, pp 24 and 26) observed, member involvement was highest in the early stages, when authorities were considering how they should deal with the issue, and clear policy had not developed. However, as time went on other factors, including private interest, also significantly affected the output of the CCT process. This trend coincides with the results of the path analysis given in Chapter Four.

The extent to which political party composition affected DSO output had changed to some degree. Member involvement in the continuing management of competition was limited, and member involvement overall therefore declined. Basically, it was still a matter of basic political polarisation, with Labour against and the Conservatives in favour, but that opposition was less clear because, speaking more generally, the shift in priorities has been away from that of winning under competition towards a focus on the customer and on the services. The preservation of the DSO was the initial priority, but that has lessened in significance as the local authority has placed more and more emphasis on the interest of customers (Walsh and Davis, 1993). These results coincide with those of the path analysis for the two years.

If transaction costs function in the CCT process in the way identified in the case studies, it is necessary to come up with the mechanisms to cope with them. This study has not dealt centrally with the development of mechanisms to cope with the politics of transaction costs. Rather, it has examined the four cases through the politics of transaction cost lens and identified the roles the politics of transaction costs played in the

CCT process, with special regard to the DSO output. For these reasons the mechanisms that have been developed for coping with the politics of transaction costs have only briefly been examined.

The transaction cost approach recognises that all parties to an economic transaction can benefit if they can develop ways to economise on transaction costs, just as they can reap mutual gains by economising on the resource costs of production, by specialising according to comparative advantage (Dixit, 1996, p 61). It is expected that ordinary citizens can also benefit if transaction costs can be reduced, because economic inefficiency and irrationality can be minimised in the economic policy process.

Each of the parties to a contract exhibits some divergence of interests from that of the others, some informational advantage, and some freedom of action. The institutions or processes must evolve to address problems such as opportunism and informational asymmetry, either with feasible external enforcement mechanisms or with credible internal ones. The success or failure of economic ventures and transactions can depend on the ability of the participants to devise such institutions and enforcement mechanisms.

Some constraints on policy can be removed or relaxed in the course of time. Some exist to cover contingencies that are no longer relevant or are mere historical accidents; these can in principle be removed when an opportunity for a reform of rules arises. Some information asymmetries can be reduced by developing better monitoring techonologies or different institutions, organisations or cultures. Calculations of the economic benefit that can in principle be achieved by removing or reducing constraints have value as guides to long-term action (Dixit, 1996, p 147).

Rules and institutions should evolve for the purpose of economising on transaction costs (Dixit, 1996, p 61). In this enterprise, transparency is desirable when it reduces information asymmetries and removes some transaction costs, but there may be some merit to opacity if it conceals relatively efficient ways of coping with transaction costs, when exposing these to public scrutiny and criticism would merely lead to the use of substitutes that are worse and more deeply hidden.

Conclusions

The case studies have attempted to spell out the political dimensions of the transaction costs involved in the CCT policy process by analysing the three dimensions of transaction costs that can characterise the contractual arrangements. They have exposed a variety of transaction costs involved in the four different implementation efforts, uncovering the importance of the politics of transaction cost framework for understanding how DSO output has been produced.

Taken as a whole, the case study analysis has indicated that the CCT policy process at the local government level is characterised by a complex series of games of strategy involving central government, the local authority and private contractors. Accordingly, much, even if not all, of the DSO output of each local authority is understood as being the result of a political game[12] in which the transaction costs incurred were shifted, used or manipulated by the interested partes to their political and economic ends. The contexts were not static but evolved in a highly dynamic fashion, being affected by the strategies employed by the interested parties and their motivations towards the politics of transaction costs.

From the beginning, the legal framework for CCT set by central government has not been perfect as regards its interpretation. Consequently, the interested parties, the local authority in particular, have had some degree of discretion to use, shift or manipulate transaction costs to their advantage in the CCT process. This is made clear by Hill (1997b, pp 186-7), who maintained that all work, however closely controlled and supervised, involves some degree of discretion. Hill points out that whenever work is delegated, the person who delegates loses some measure of control, and in complex organisational situations, gaps readily emerge between intentions and outcomes.

At the same time, the legal framework has influenced the occurrence of transaction costs in the direction of granting a favour to the private sector, thus creating a bias towards the private sector. As Leone (1986) states, government regulation creates winners and losers. Hence, conflicts can arise regarding the precise form regulation is to assume. The contributions of any form of regulation towards making markets more efficient might be called into question, owing to an interested emphasis on the costliness of regulatory intervention. From the point of view of the politics of transaction cost framework, this means that transaction costs in the CCT process have been decreased for private bidders and increased for local authorities.

The local organisational cultures have been a particularly important factor that characterises the local context, and they have played an important role in shaping the actions of individuals. One of their characteristics is that in the early stages of CCT, the political variable primarily shaped the organisational cultures, while over time, service quality and economic considerations influenced the change in organisational cultures. The public's satisfaction or dissatisfaction with service provision also impacted on changes in the organisational cultures, eventually influencing transaction costs. Industrial relations in the local authority was also an important factor in influencing the CCT policy process, although in most cases, it was not crucial.

It is difficult to clarify the motivations of the interested parties towards the politics of transaction costs, partly because this study did not interview the private bidders and partly because motivations *per se* are difficult to investigate. As a result of the analysis made using the proxy variable, it may be inferred that the motivations of the interested parties also played an important role in deterring or encouraging them from engaging in the politics of transaction costs.

The case studies exposed a variety of transaction cost strategies, employed by the parties to influence the implementation process either positively or negatively. These included the exploitation, manipulation and transfer of transaction costs. What is chiefly noticeable is that in the early stages of CCT, local authorities could take the initiative in the implementation process, employing such strategies as information asymmetry, incumbency and so on, whereas over time, the private bidders led the process via the use of opportunistic strategies which mainly include the strategy of loss-leading to establish a base and to then eventually extend their business area, or they went through a process of being accepted on to a select list and then not submitting a bid. These strategies on the part of the private bidders possibly owed primarily to the legal framework for CCT, which was biased towards them and their business strategies deriving from their experience.

It is hoped that the results of this case study analysis will be of service to students of policy implementation in various disciplines, practitioners of contracting out and competitive tendering policy making and evaluation, whose work is influenced by what happens during the policy implementation process, and competitive tendering policy makers who are interested in a more explicit description of their implementation problems and alternatives.

Notes

[1] The Act attempts to prevent authorities from taking into account any of a number of 'non-commercial matters' in the course of tendering procedures. It specifically prohibits councils from introducing particular considerations in drawing up contracts, inviting tenders or making or terminating contracts (Carnaghan and Bracewell-Mines, 1993, pp 44-5).

[2] DoE Circular 10/93.

[3] The Transfer of Undertakings (Protection of Employment) is European law in relation to contracts of employment. One matter which had caused uncertainty, casting a shadow over the policy of competitive tendering and the contracting out of services, is whether the 1981 Transfer of Undertakings (Protection of Employment) Regulations would apply to the transfer of an activity from a council to a private company or other body in the context of competitive tendering. Where these regulations apply, the new employer takes over responsibility for the employees who transfer on the same terms and conditions, with consequences for the ability of the new employer to reduce labour costs. Judgments in a number of UK industrial tribunal cases and in the European Court of Justice have generated wide debate. Although the circumstances under which TUPE applies are still contested, TUPE is likely to deter many private contractors from getting involved in council service provision (Bailey, 1997, pp 194-5; Byrne, 1994, pp 471-2; Walsh and Davis, 1993, p 3; Walsh et al, 1997, p 104).

[4] The directives had three basic elements: the Community-wide advertising of contracts; establishing objective criteria for the award of contracts; banning adoption of technical standards which are only used nationally and, hence, have the effect of discriminating against contractors based in other European Community states (Clarke and Pitelis, 1994, p 161).

[5] The Association of Metropolitan Authorities (AMA) has pointed out that since the threshold of 200,000 ECU, above which the EC Directive applies, refers to the total value of a contract, not its annual value, a six-year contract worth about £22,000 a year would be subject to the procedures. Thus, "a contract for the cleaning of a secondary school in Sheffield may have to be advertised all over the EC" (AMA, 1991, p 3).

[6] Local Government (Direct Service Organisations) (Competition) Regulations, 1993 and guidance under those regulations (Walsh and Davis, 1993, p 2).

[7] The following descriptions of the case studies are based on interview results, tender evaluation documents, unpublished inside materials, minutes and reports. The footnotes are designed to ensure the anonymity of each local authority. See Goodwin, 1994, pp 132-95; Walsh et al, 1997, pp 105-13.

[8] Loss of contracts could force the inhouse to shed staff and even to shut down completely. This could result in the local authority having to incur considerable redundancy costs. Thus the 1988 Act permits an authority, in assessing the overall costs of accepting a contractor's bid, and therefore deciding whether to let a contract externally as opposed to awarding it to an inhouse provider, to take account of the potential redundancy costs. This must be on the basis of spreading the cost of redundancy over the length of the contract, and these costs should be fairly stated and not deliberately inflated. However, this provision can only be used once, and if the redundancy cost argument is used to enable a contract to be awarded to an inhouse in the first round of tendering, it cannot be used again when that particular defined activity comes up for tender again (Prowle and Hines, 1989, p 17).

[9] NALGO: National and Local Government Officers'Association; NUPE: National Union of Public Employees; GMBATU: General Municipal, Boilermakers and Allied Trade Union (formerly GMWU: General and Municipal Workers' Union).

[10] For details concerning justifications for state regulation see Francis, 1993, pp 10-18.

[11] Williamson's explanation of the role of power (1997, p 12) indicates that central government can play an important role in the contractual arrangements. He states:

> **Because B is bigger than A, B enjoys a power advantage in the exchange relation between them. Or because A is dependent on B, B has a power advantage over A. Or if A and B were initially on a parity, but a disturbance has occurred that works in B's favour, then parity is upset and B now has more power.**

[12] In other words, it is a cat-and-mouse game.

EIGHT

Conclusions

Theoretical and empirical understanding of the main factors affecting public service contracting, and the role institutions, culture and legal frameworks play in it, is still incomplete. This book has attempted to contribute to a deeper understanding of the main determinants of CCT output and the roles played by the main interested parties in the CCT process, and thus to enable more balanced and better-founded policy decisions to be taken in relation to the restructuring of the public sector via the contracting system.

Unlike the work of various academic, social and professional commentators who have argued about the utility of competitive tendering, this research has not attempted either to promote CCT or to deter local authorities from competitive tendering and contracting out. It has attempted to take a step back from the often heated controversy concerning privatisation, to investigate the determinants of the output of CCT policy and to examine how these determinants are related to DSO output. It is hoped that such an approach will help to fill a void in positive social research in that it draws on the concept of the politics of transaction costs, which has rarely been utilised in the analysis of privatisation policy. The research has also attempted to address how transaction costs can be manipulated, shifted and exploited by the interested parties in the CCT process and to show that unless transaction costs are dealt with properly the CCT process will be distorted and eventually result in undesirable output.

The main conclusions of the study will now be summarised, focusing on the lessons to be learned from both the path analysis and the case studies of CCT. The first section of the chapter summarises the main findings from the path analysis, the case study analysis and the triangulation analysis, which is the analysis made from the two combined perspectives. The second assesses the utility of the two analyses. The third section examines what contributions this study has made to an understanding of the output of CCT policy. It explores what implications for theory result from these findings; in particular, it examines the value of the politics of transaction cost approach for understanding the CCT process.

Research results

Path analysis results

Two sets of data, that for 1991 and that for 1994, were employed in the path models. Model 1, for 1991, and Model 2, for 1994, used the same independent and dependent variables.

The results of the two path models indicated the following. In Model 1, contract size, proportion of Labour councillors, proportion of Conservative councillors, population size, degree of urbanisation and geographical location were significant variables which affected DSO output. Of these variables, contract size, proportion of Labour councillors and proportion of Conservative councillors affected DSO output directly and positively, whereas population size affected it directly and negatively. Degree of urbanisation and geographical location influenced DSO output indirectly through the mediating political variable. Of these variables, the political variable, proportion of Labour councillors, was the strongest, followed by proportion of Conservative councillors, population size and contract size.

In Model 2, proportion of Labour councillors, proportion of Conservative councillors, population size, degree of urbanisation and geographical location were significant, with geographical location (*dum3*) being the strongest. The explanatory power of the path model for 1994 was slightly lower than that for 1991. However, what is remarkable is that the strongest variable affecting DSO output changed from being the political variable in 1991 to being the strategic variable, geographic location, in 1994. As to the reasons for this, the case study portion of this research was expected to provide additional evidence.

Case study results

For the case study analysis, key contracting officials from the four local authorities, and one lawyer, were interviewed. Criteria including political party composition and degree of DSO output were considered in selecting the local authority districts.

The case studies brought into focus the dynamic interactions between the contexts, motivations and strategies behind the CCT process of each local authority. At the early stages of CCT implementation, the involvement of councillors was significant, whereas as time went on, instead of councillors' involvement, private contractors influenced the CCT process via diverse strategies.

In explaining these findings, the research undertook a review of three dimensions: contexts (legal framework, local organisational culture and industrial relations), motivations and strategies. While no single factor appeared to explain the dynamics behind the CCT process, some factors were more likely to be important at various times than others. A hierarchy of influences appeared to exist. The first level of this hierarchy included two prerequisites for CCT: a local organisational culture prepared to put services up for competitive tender at the early stage, and interest from the private sector (at the later stage). These results coincide with the results of the path analysis, which showed that in 1991 the most important factor affecting DSO output was political party composition, whereas in 1994 it was the strategic variable, geographic location.

What is noticeable in this analysis is the role of the private sector in the CCT process, a role which has been given very little attention in previous research. This study showed that the impact of private sector bidding strategies had a fundamental impact on DSO output. For example, the motivations and strategies of the private sector have been instrumental in fashioning the pattern of DSO output since private companies have been dissuaded from bidding by some local authorities with an antiprivatisation culture, whereas they have been attracted to other local authorities which have pro-privatisation cultures.

Another explanation is that the private sector sought to establish a base in a certain area using loss-leaders, or other such strategies to extend its business to the adjacent areas. In this process, the legal framework for CCT, which has been disposed towards the private sector, the private contractors' accumulated experience of the bidding process and their opportunism, the reduction of local councillors' involvement in the CCT process and the public's increasing interest in service quality and financial savings all played an important role, eventually leading to regional variances in DSO output.

Local organisational culture was particularly important for the local variation of the DSO proportion in the early years of CCT, when many 'hostile' districts refused to comply with the policy. There appears to be what Goodwin (1994, p 187) calls a 'leaders' and 'laggard' pattern in the local variation of DSO output associated with the attitudes of councillors and officials towards CCT. The 'leaders' are authorities that worked on positive lines soon after the tendering policy was introduced. This appears to be the case in Local Authority C, where precedents for the role of private companies had been established so that CCT could advance quickly. 'Laggards' are districts that were slow to accept CCT and which have remained opposed to CCT. In Local Authority A, for example, the continued antiprivatisation culture identified appears to have influenced the continued maintenance of the inhouse provision and to have perpetuated the local variation of DSO output.

One of the conclusions that could be drawn from the case studies is that the CCT process is a complex game of contexts, motivations and strategies with many players. While all local authorities in Britain were forced to introduce CCT, some local authorities which were perceived to maintain an antiprivatisation culture, or which offered relatively poorer deals, were avoided by private contractors because the markets were seen as unprofitable.

While the environmental variables, political and strategic variables in particular, have helped to explain the general pattern of DSO output over time, the ways in which they have affected DSO output have been far less easy to predict because of the complex nature of the CCT process and the contradictory nature of the factors involved. How the variables have exhibited such wildly different levels of DSO output could not be explained adequately by the path analysis. In the light of these findings, an analytical framework was developed for the case studies, based on the politics of transaction cost approach, to investigate more fully how the dynamically interacting CCT process could produce different DSO outputs in local authorities.

Triangulation[1] results

Together, the path analysis and the case studies begin to illustrate the factors which affected DSO output and the ways in which they did so. Regarding the path analysis, in the 1991 model proportion of Labour and Conservative councillors, contract size and population size were significant factors which directly affected DSO output, while in the 1994 model proportion of Labour and Conservative councillors and geographical location were the significant factors. In the case studies, contexts, motivations and strategies associated with the politics of transaction costs were each found to have played a major role in the CCT policy implementation process. In this analysis the DSO output of each local authority is understood as a function of the three dimensions, context, motivation and strategy, associated with the politics of transaction costs of the main participants in the CCT process.

While it has been difficult to describe the complex nature of the interaction between context, motivation and strategy, it has not been difficult to observe in the case studies some of the ways in which the three dimensions have acted, both as a constraint in certain situations and as a propellant in others. The DSO output has not been the result of a simple process. Rather, the CCT process, in any particular location, evolves over time through a series of actions and interactions which may have the effect of enhancing the process of privatisation or of developing barriers, in the form of transaction costs, to this change.

One of the most important findings of this research is that the parties to a contract try to influence the policy process in their own favour, and various transaction costs play important roles in this process. The triangulation analysis results have indicated that the CCT policy implementation process is characterised by a complex series of diverse linkages between context, motivation and strategy associated with the politics of transaction costs.

Utility of the path analysis and of the politics of transaction cost approach

Utility of the path analysis

The chief rationale behind this research was the fact that output study of CCT is a neglected topic. This research has sought to address this issue through the analysis of manual services subject to the 1988 Act. The aim has been to further understanding of locally different privatisation.

Path analysis was used in an attempt to discover which variables were significant in DSO output. The path analysis employed in this study extends and broadens the prior limited, descriptive and explanatory research concerning the output of privatisation policy by examining the causal relationships among key indicators affecting the output of CCT policy, DSO output. Path analysis based on a direct and indirect causal effect model, including independent variables and a dependent variable, was conducted.

Via path analysis of the dataset, the research has shown that locally uneven DSO output is more complex than previous research had perceived. The analysis had an advantage over previous research in that it was able to examine from a causal relationship point of view which factors influence DSO output. It was also able to reveal how DSO output developed over time. The path analysis was able to arrive at new findings about the uneven nature of privatisation.

Utility of the politics of transaction cost approach

The politics of transaction cost framework used in this study has aimed to contribute to the understanding of uneven privatisation in a number of ways.

First, it was noted in Chapter Two that previous theoretical enquiries into privatisation and competitive tendering failed to articulate the relationship between policy output and the policy implementation process. One of the major difficulties with these works was their derivation from older theoretical frameworks which could not cope with the empirical complexities of the CCT process. In Stubbs and Barnett (1992), for example, the geographically uneven nature of privatised ancillary contracts in New Zealand is interpreted through the use of public choice theory, managerialism and Marxian theory. As the researchers point out, the Marxian perspective was too crude, because it did not take into account the important role of elected bodies and managerial influences, while public choice theory and managerialism could not explain how local decision making was constrained by the operation of the wider political economy (Goodwin, 1994). Stubbs and Barnett (1992) conclude that it is necessary to invoke all three theories to explain the spatial, temporal and sectoral dimension to contracting out.

In this study, to examine the ways in which the statistically significant factors discovered via path analysis affected the policy output, DSO output, the focus has been on the politics of transaction costs involved in the CCT policy implementation process. Far from being institutionally neutral and isolated from power relationships, the implementation of

CCT policy can be understood in terms of the politics of transaction costs that shape the probabilities of success or failure.

The framework developed in this study has made it possible to spell out the political dimension of economic transaction costs in the CCT policy implementation process by allowing analysis of the complex types of linkage and inter-relationships that characterise the CCT process. As a result, a number of constraints in the CCT process have been exposed. Also, the study has attempted explicitly to examine and illustrate the various types of transaction costs that can plague the implementation process. Although past research has recognised the importance of politics in privatisation policies, evidence suggests that much of the political dynamic behind privatisation decisions at the local level has not been understood.

The neo-classical view of economic policy relies heavily on the notion of rational, maximising behaviour by all parties, is predicated on the absence of information problems, and is preoccupied with movements towards equilibrium states. In contrast, this study emphasises the uneven capacity of the main parties to acquire and filter information from a competitive environment, which is constantly changing its rules and assumptions. To this extent it shares the concerns of institutional economists that competition is not merely a matter of price-mediated transactions in markets (Pettigrew and Whipp, 1991, p 274). Rather, it is supported by a range of political, economic and social institutions which operate according to each of the three conditions identified by this study. This is the second way in which the politics of transaction cost approach contributed to an understanding of uneven privatisation.

The third way is through its emphasis on context, motivation and strategy and the way in which these interact. Most importantly, it has emphasised the dynamic nature of contexts in influencing uneven privatisation. The dynamic view of competitive tendering means that the CCT process is characterised by uncertainty and possibility. While the uneven DSO output in England suggests that some contexts are more receptive to privatisation than others, the idiosyncratic combination of the three dimensions can lead to local variations in DSO output, even where the location and the political and socioeconomic environments are similar. Accordingly, this approach allows understanding of local variations in privatisation because of the characteristics it underlines, the contested nature of the tendering process and the uncertainty of output (Dixit, 1996; Goodwin, 1994; Pettigrew and Whipp, 1991).

Contributions and implications of the study

Study's contributions to the field

Studies of competitive tendering and contracting out have advanced from debating whether to contract out to investigating what actually takes place during implementation. However, what remains largely unexplored is the question of what the main factors are and how they affect the policy output of privatisation. This study has synthesised previous work on policy output studies and literature in transaction cost theory. It can not only describe local government's contractual policies but also provide a prescription for the implementation of centrally imposed policy in particular. It is hoped that the study will advance understanding of the theoretical issues surrounding the privatisation of local government services.

The literature on transaction cost theory, which served as a foundation of the analytical framework developed for the case studies, has provided a primarily abstract conception of the policy dimensions – context, motivation and strategy – suggested by this study. With the exception of a few which focus on competition policies, few studies on contracting out have systematically analysed and observed the transaction costs involved in the policy process. Few studies have explicitly claimed and identified any intertwining relationships and interplay between the policy dimensions in relation to transaction costs.

Equally importantly, through the use of path analysis this study has empirically identified the main factors that underlie the policy output of CCT, DSO output. The identification of such underlying factors has aimed to further understanding of the major ingredients of CCT policy. The path analysis results that link the major factors of policy output to the policy implementation process should also help to direct researchers' and public policy makers' attention towards how DSO output has been provided.

Finally, few, if any, studies of the privatisation of local government services have attempted systematically to link policy output to the policy implementation process. One reason for the lack of such research may be that an appropriate method that captures the multiple inputs and outputs of the CCT process was not readily available. This study, through the application of the politics of transaction cost framework, has attempted to offer an approach which does capture the inter-relationships between policy output, DSO output and CCT policy implementation.

Theoretical implications

This research might serve as a starting point for attempts to combine the policy output and its implementation process through use of the concept of the politics of transaction costs. This will allow other researchers to build on the concepts and theories designed in this model, and possibly create a more comprehensive model of privatisation policy.

This study has implications for both normative and positive theory. While much of the present debate and literature on both contracting out and competitive tendering has in general revolved around normative bases, it is hoped that this research may represent an important step in focusing on how and why CCT policy imposed from above results in different policy outputs at the local level. It is expected that the realisation that centrally imposed CCT policy has been implemented differently at the local level because the politics of transaction costs has functioned differently will help the theorist to develop more informed theories concerning both the implementation and the applications of CCT.

Practical implications

To implement successfully a centrally imposed CCT policy, policy makers, in establishing contractual policies and interacting with local authorities and private contractors, should focus their attention on the three dimensions of the politics of transaction costs identified in this study. They should also consider the sub-components of these dimensions in particular, recognising that the politics of transaction costs incurred by the main interested parties can pervert the whole process of competitive tendering in various ways, with unintended and unexpected outcomes both for the parties concerned and for service recepients. What makes the situation more complicated is that as the public service contracting system gets on the right track, the ways in which the interested parties manipulate, exploit and transfer transaction costs to their own advantage in the competitive tendering process become more sophisticated and refined. This highlights the importance of the dynamics of public service contracting and in particular how the interested parties in it adapt to new circumstances, especially when the introduction of contracts into public service delivery is not accepted as natural.

Transaction costs should be minimised in the CCT process. To minimise these costs, the main information policy should be capable of deterring local governments and private contractors from manipulating, exploiting and transferring transaction costs and in so doing possibly causing serious and unresolvable problems for the CCT process. Public managers in central government should pay more attention to, and spend more resources on, designing and implementing effective incentives and disincentives. Specifically, public agencies must maintain the capability to sanction effectively local governments and private contractors in whatever way necessary. They must also show a determination to take penalising action when predetermined conditions occur.

At the same time, central government should also alleviate problems such as the non-level playing field, either through changes to the legal framework or through introducing credible internal or external enforcement mechanisms. Unless there is a fair competition rule and a level playing field for the interested parties in the competitive tendering process, the process is likely to become a cat-and-mouse game, resulting in endless efforts to use, shift or manipulate transaction costs to the party's own end. Local governments, when renewing service contracts with present contractors, must take their service performance into consideration in determining forthcoming contracting levels and contractual relationships.

The data contained in this study is both quantitative and qualitative. It provides the reader both with statistics regarding privatisation and with 'behind the scenes' explanations of why and how local authorities exhibit different levels of privatisation. The advantage of this triangulation approach is that it reveals both the quantitative and qualitative aspects of the CCT process, allowing the reader to become much better informed than if he or she had relied exclusively on either methodology alone.

As Painter (1992) notes, given that differing local organisational cultures existed at the local level and their resistance or acceptance to CCT proved to be an important element in differing DSO outputs, important questions need to be raised concerning the ability of government to create a new managerialism among local councillors and officials. The meaning and impact of local organisational culture is an important issue that needs to be addressed by policy scientists.

Concluding comments

It is well known that initiatives pursued in one country cannot always be transferred successfully to other countries owing to differing cultural, constitutional and demographic circumstances. Nevertheless, if practitioners are able to draw on the experiences of other countries by refining and adapting an established system to new circumstances, they should be able to avoid the financial costs and practical pitfalls associated with 'reinventing the wheel'.

This study has attempted to provide an objective survey of CCT drawing on a range of statistical data and case study analysis. Such a survey is necessarily prone to limitations, both methodological and intrepretative. Both the path analysis and the case studies are complex, and interpreting the research results is often fraught with difficulty. The study is essentially exploratory in nature, and should be viewed as only an initial attempt to understand the complex dynamics of public service contracting in the UK. Nevertheless, it represents an advance on previous work in the field since, in adopting a neutral and objective standpoint towards CCT, it eschews the partisan approach on which most previous research on the subject in Britain has been based. To this end it has, unlike previous studies, identified the actual determinants affecting public service contracting, with the aim of offering policy makers useful suggestions for redesigning and restructuring the current public service system.

Public service contracting is set to become even more important in the future as policy makers in both developing and industrialised countries strive to create ever greater efficiency in the provision of public services. It is hoped that this study will be of both practical and theoretical value to policy makers and others in enabling them to understand and draw on British experiences of CCT.

Note

[1] Since research programmes involve multiple studies, they provide a ready context for combining different types of study in order to obtain the particular strengths each offers. Denzin's concept of *data triangulation* is perhaps the most muddled in that it encompasses focused sampling, the use of case studies and replications of the same study in different settings, and – most importantly – introduces the idea that research should

be carried out at both the micro level (to cover interpersonal interactions in small group settings) and the macro level (to cover structuralist explanations) (Hakim, 1987, p 144).

Bibliography

Abbott, B., Blackburn, R.A. and Curran, J. (1996) 'Local authority privatisation and markets for small business', *Local Government Studies*, vol 22, no 3, pp 72-89.

Adam Smith Institute (1990) *The tender traps*, London: Adam Smith Institute.

Adonis, A. (1991) 'Most tenders from councils won by their own workers', *Financial Times*, 13 May.

Aiken, M., Newton, K., Friedland, R. and Martinotti, G. (1987) 'Urban systems theory and urban policy: a four-nation comparison', *British Journal of Political Science*, vol 17, pp 341-58.

Akerlof, G.A. (1970) 'The market for "lemons": quality uncertainty and the market mechanism', *Quarterly Journal of Economics*, vol 84, pp 488-500.

Alexander, A. (1982) *The politics of local government in the United Kingdom*, Harlow: Longman.

Alvesson, M. (1993) 'Transaction costs, clans and corporate culture', *Journal of Management Studies*, vol 30, May, pp 427-52.

AMA (Association of Metropolitan Authorities) (1991) *AMA response to the proposal for a council directive relating to services*, London: AMA.

Arrow, K.J. (1962) 'Economic welfare and the allocation of resources for invention', in National Bureau of Economic Research (ed) *The rate and direction of inventive activity: Economic and social factors*, Princeton, NJ: Princeton University Press. [Reprinted in Lamberton, 1971.]

Arrow, K.J. (1969) 'The organisation of economic activity: issues pertinent to the choice of market versus nonmarket allocation', in US Joint Economic Committee (ed) *The analysis and evaluation of public expenditure: The PPB system*, Volume 1, Washington, DC: US Government Printing Office.

Asher, K. (1987) *The politics of privatisation: Contracting out public services*, Basingstoke: Macmillan.

Ashford, D.E., Berne, R. and Schramm, R. (1976) 'The expenditure-financing decision in British local government', *Policy & Politics*, vol 5, no 1, pp 5-24.

Atkins, J. (ed) (1996) *The council's handbook 1996*, London: CDC Publishing Limited.

Audit Commission (1989) *Preparing for compulsory competition*, London: HMSO.

Audit Commission (1993) *Realising the benefits of competition: The client role for contracted services*, London: HMSO.

Austin-Smith, D. and William H.R. (1987) 'Asymmetric information and the coherence of legislation', *American Political Science Review*, vol 81, no 3, pp 897-918.

Bach, S. (1990) 'Competitive tendering and contracting out: prospects for the future', in H. Cook (ed) *The NHS private health sector interface*, Harlow: Longman.

Bailey, S.H. (1997) *Cross on principles of local government law*, London: Sweet & Maxwell.

Baldwin, R. (1997) 'Rules, discretion and legitimacy', in M. Hill (ed) *The policy process: A reader*, London: Prentice Hall.

Ball, D. (1984) 'Striking hospital cleaners commission work report', *Health and Social Services Journal*, 20 September.

Bamberg, G. and Spremann, K. (1987) *Agency theory, information and incentives*, NewYork, NY: Springer Verlag.

Banks, J.S. (1991) *Signalling games in political science*, Reading: Harwood Academic Publishers.

Bardach, E. (1977) *The implementation game*, Cambridge, MA: MIT Press.

Barker, L. (1993) *Competing for quality*, Harlow: Longman.

Barnekov, T., Boyle R. and Rich, D. (1989) *Privatism and urban policy in Britain and the United States*, Oxford: Oxford University Press.

Barnett, R.R., Levaggi, R. and Smith, P. (1990) 'The impact of party politics on patterns of service provision in English local authorities', *Policy & Politics*, vol 18, no 3, pp 217-29.

Barringston, T.J. (1991) 'Local government in Ireland', in R. Batley and G. Stoker (eds) *Local government in Europe: Trends and developments*, London: Macmillan.

Beck, P.A. and Sorauf, F.J. (1992) *Party politics in America*, New York, NY: Harper Collins.

Beresford, P. (1987) *Good council guide: Wandsworth 1978-1987*, London: Centre for Policy Studies.

Boaden, N. (1971) *Urban policy making: Influences on county boroughs in England and Wales*, London: Cambridge University Press.

Bosanquet, N. (1983) *After the New Right*, London: Heinemann.

Bouttes, J.-P. and Hamamdjian, P. (1997) 'Contractual relationships within the firm', in C. Menard (ed) *Transaction cost economics: Recent developments*, Cheltenham: Edward Elgar.

Boyne, G.A. (1987) 'Median voters, political systems and public policies: an empirical test', *Public Choice*, no 53, pp 201-19.

Boyne, G.A. (1992) 'Regional influences on local policies: the case of the Welsh effect', *Regional Studies*, vol 26, pp 569-80.

Boyne, G.A. (1995) 'Population size and economies of scale in local government', *Policy & Politics*, vol 23, no 3, pp 213-22.

Boyne, G.A. (1996a) 'Assessing party effects on local policies: a quarter century of progress or eternal recurrence?', *Political Studies*, vol 44, pp 232-52.

Boyne, G.A. (1996b) 'Competition and local government: a public choice perspective', *Urban Studies*, vol 33, pp 703-21.

Braunig, D. (1992) 'Management of local authorities in Germany and The Netherlands', *Local Government Policy Making*, vol 19, no 3, pp 29-41.

Bryson, J. (1984) 'The policy process and organisational form', *Policy Studies Journal*, vol 12, pp 127-41.

Buchanan, J.M. (1973) 'The Coase theorem and the theory of the State', *Natural Resources Journal*, vol 13, no 4, pp 579-94.

Buchanan, J.M. (1975) 'A contractarian paradigm for applying economic theory', *American Economic Review*, vol 65, no 2, pp 225-30.

Buchanan, J.M. (1987) 'The constitution of economic policy', *American Economic Review*, vol 77, no 3, pp 243-50.

Buchanan, J.M. (1988) 'Contractarian political economy and constitutional interpretation', *American Economic Review*, vol 78, no 2, pp 135-9.

Buchanan, J.M. and Tullock, G. (1962) *The calculus of consent*, Ann Arbor, MI: University of Michigan Press.

Bulpitt, J.G. (1967) *Party politics in English local government*, London: Longman.

Butler, E. (ed) (1988) *Privatisation in practice*, London: Adam Smith Institute.

Byrne, T. (1994) *Local government in Britain*, Harmondsworth: Penguin Books.

Calista, D.J. (1987) 'Transaction cost analysis as a theory of public sector implementation', *Policy Studies Journal*, vol 15, pp 461-80.

Cameron, D.K. (1978) 'The expansion of the political economy: a comparative analysis', *American Political Science Review*, vol 72, no 4, pp 1,243-61.

Carnaghan, R. and Bracewell-Milnes, B. (1993) *Testing the market*, London: Institute of Economic Affairs.

Caudrey, A. (1984) 'Firms' bid to cut cleaner's pay sparks off 24-hour walkout', *Health and Social Services Journal*, 4 March.

Central Statistics Office (1995) *Regional trends*, London: HMSO.

Chakravorty, S. (1996) 'Urban inequality revisited: the determinants of income distribution in US metropolitan areas', *Urban Affairs Review*, vol 31, no 6, pp 759-77.

Chandler, J.A. (1988) *Public policy making for local government*, Beckenham: Croom Helm.

Chandler, T.D. and Feuille, P. (1991) 'Municipal unions and privatisation', *Public Administration Review*, vol 51, no 1, pp 15-22.

Cheshire, P. and Carbonaro, G. (1996) 'Urban economic growth in Europe: testing theory and policy prescriptions', *Urban Studies*, vol 33, no 7, pp 1,111-28.

Chi, K.S., Devlin, K.M. and Masterman, W. (1989) 'Use of the private sector in delivery of human services', in J.W. Allen, K.S. Chi, K.M. Devlin, M. Fall, H.P. Hatry and W. Masterman, *The private sector in state service delivery: Examples of innovative practices*, Washington, DC: Urban Institute.

CIPFA (1991; 1994) *Direct service organisations statistics*, London: CIPFA.

CIPFA (1991; 1994) *Finance and general statistics*, London: CIPFA.

CIPFA (1991; 1994) *Local government comparative statistics 1991, 1994*, London: CIPFA.

CIPFA (1995) *Councillors' guide to local government finance*, London: Chartered Institute of Public Finance and Accountancy.

Clarke, T. and Pitelis, C. (ed) (1994) *The political economy of privatisation*, London: Routledge.

Clements, S. (ed) (1991; 1994; 1996; 1997) *The municipal yearbook*, London: Municipal Journal Limited.

Coase, R.H. (1937) 'The nature of the firm', *Economica*, vol 4, pp 386-405.

Coase, R.H. (1960) 'The problem of social cost', *Journal of Law and Economics*, vol 3, pp 1-44.

Cochrane, A. (1991) 'The changing state of local government: restructuring for the 1990s', *Public Administration*, no 69, pp 281-302.

Cohen, W.S. (1983) 'The competition in contracting Act', *Public Contract Law Journal*, vol 14, no 1, pp 178-90.

Coleman, J. (1990) *Foundations of social theory*, Cambridge, MA: Harvard University Press.

Commons, J.R. (1934) *Institutional economics*, Madison, WI: University of Wisconsin Press.

Cooper, P.J. (1980) 'Government contracts in public administration: the role and environment of the contracting officer', *Public Administration Review*, vol 40, no 5, pp 459-68.

Coulson, A. (1997) 'Transaction cost economics and its implications for local governance', *Local Government Studies*, vol 23, no 1, pp 107-13.

Council of Europe (1993) *The role of competitive tendering in the efficient provision of local services*, Research Report No 49, Local and Regional Authorities in Europe, Strasbourg: Council of Europe Press.

CQBB (1991) *Competing for quality – Buying better public services*, London: HMSO.

Crano, W.D. and M.B. Brewer (1986) *Principles and methods of social research*, Boston, MA: Allyn & Bacon.

Creswell, J.W. (1994) *Research design: Qualitative and quantitative approaches*, London: Sage Publications.

Cross, M. and Mallen, D. (1987) *Local government and politics*, London: Longman.

Cubbin, J., Domberger, S. and Meadowcroft, S. (1987) 'Competitive tendering and refuse collection: identifying the sources of efficiency gains', *Fiscal Studies*, vol 8, no 2, pp 49-57.

Dahl, R. (ed) (1976) *Modern political analysis*, Baltimore, NJ: Prentice Hall.

Daintith, T.C. (1982) 'Legal analysis of economic policy', *Journal of Law and Society*, vol 9, no 2, p 2.

Danziger, J.M. (1976) 'Twenty six outputs in search of a taxonomy', *Policy & Politics*, vol 5, pp 201-12.

Danziger, J.M. (1978) *Making budgets*, London: Sage Publications.

Davis, H. (1996) 'The fragmentation of community government', in H. Davis (ed) *Enabling or disabling local government*, Buckingham: Open University Press.

Davis, H. (ed) (1986) *The future role and organisation of local government*, Birmingham: Institute of Local Government Studies.

Davis, H., Leach, S. and Associates (1996) *Enabling or disabling local government*, Buckingham: Open University Press.

Davis, L.E. and North, D.C. (1971) *Institutional change and American economic growth*, Cambridge: Cambridge University Press.

Davis-Coleman, C. (ed) (1995; 1996) *The contracts handbook*, issues 12, 13 and 14, London: CDC Publishing Limited.

Dawson, R.E. and Robinson, J.A. (1963) 'Inter-party competition, economic variables and welfare policies in the American States', *Journal of Politics*, vol 25, pp 265-89.

Dearlove, J. (1973) *The politics of policy in local government*, Cambridge: Cambridge University Press.

Dearlove, J. (1979) *The reorganisation of British local government: Old orthodoxies and a political perspective*, Cambridge: Cambridge University Press.

DeHoog, R.H. (1983) *Government manipulation of constitutional-level transaction costs: An economic theory and its application to off-budget expenditure through the federal financing bank*, Doctoral dissertation, University of Washington.

DeHoog, R.H. (1984a) *Contracting out for human services*, Albany, NY: State University of New York Press.

DeHoog, R.H. (1984b) 'Theoretical perspectives on contracting out for services: implementation problems and possibilities of privatising public services', in G.C. Edwards (ed) *Public policy implementation*, Greenwich, CT: JAI Press.

DeHoog, R.H. (1985) 'Human services contracting: environmental behavioural and organisational conditions', *Administration and Society*, vol 6, no 4, pp 427-54.

Demsetz, H. (1964) 'The exchange and enforcement of property rights', *Journal of Law and Economics*, vol 7, pp 11-26.

Denes, T.A. (1996) *The success of contracting out services in a quasi-open market*, Doctoral dissertation, University of Pennsylvania.

Denhardt, R. and Hammond, B.R. (1992) *Public administration in action: Readings profiles and cases*, Pacific Grove, CA: Brooks/Cole Publishing Company.

Department of the Environment (1985) *Competition in the provision of local authority services*, London: DoE.

Department of Health (1989) *Working for patients*, London: HMSO.

Dexter, L.A. (1970) *Elite and specialising interviewing*, Evanston, IL: North-Western University Press.

Dietrich, M. (1994) *Transaction cost economics and beyond*, London: Routledge.

Digings, L. (1991) *Competitive tendering and the European Communities*, London: AMA.

Dixit, A. (1996) *The making of economic policy*, Cambridge, MA: MIT Press.

Domberger, S., Meadowcroft, S. and Thompson, D. (1987) 'The impact of competitive tendering on the costs of hospital domestic services', *Fiscal Studies*, vol 8, no 4, pp 39-54.

Donahue, J.D. (1989) *The privatisation decision*, New York, NY: Basic Books.

Dunleavy, P. (1980) *Urban political analysis*, London: Macmillan.

Dunn, W.N. (1994) *Public policy analysis*, Englewood Cliffs, NJ: Prentice Hall.

Dye, T.R. (1976) *Policy analysis*, Tuscaloosa, AL: University of Alabama Press.

Easton, D. (1965) *A systems analysis of political life*, New York, NY: John Wiley & Sons.

Elcock, H. (1994) *Local government*, London: Routledge.

Engelbrecht-Wiggans, R., Milgrom, P.R. and Weber, R.J. (1983) 'Competitive bidding and proprietary information', *Journal of Mathematical Economics*, vol 11, pp 161-9.

Etzioni, A. (1964) *Modern organisations*, Englewood Cliffs, NJ: Prentice Hall.

Etzioni, A. (1976) *Social problems*, Englewood Cliffs, NJ: Prentice Hall.

Fenwick, J. (1995) *Managing local government*, London: Chapman & Hall.

Ferris, J.M. (1986) 'The decision to contract out: an empirical analysis', *Urban Affairs Quarterly*, vol 22, no 2, pp 289-311.

Ferris, J.M. and E. Graddy (1986) 'Contracting out: for what? With whom?', *Public Administration Review*, vol 46, no 4, pp 332-55.

Ferris, J.M. and Graddy, E. (1991) 'Production costs, transaction costs, and local government contractor choice', *Economic Inquiry*, vol 29, July, pp 541-54.

Ferris, J.M. and Graddy, E. (1994) 'Organisational choices for public service supply', *The Journal of Law, Economics and Organisation*, vol 10, no 1, pp 126-41.

Fisher, S. (1977) 'Long-term contracting, sticky prices, and monetary policy: comment', *Journal of Monetary Economics*, no 3, pp 317-23.

Forsyth, M. (1980) *Reservicing Britain*, London: Adam Smith Institute.

Forsyth, M. (1982) *Reservicing Health*, London: Adam Smith Institute.

Foster, C.D., Jackman, R. and Perlman, M. (1980) *Local government in a unitary state*, London: Allen & Unwin.

Foster, D. (1991) *Privatisation policy in local government: The response of public sector trade unions*, Doctoral dissertation, University of Bath.

Foster, D. (1993) 'Industrial relations in local government: the impact of privatisation', *The Political Quarterly*, vol 64, no 1, pp 49-59.

Francis, J. (1993) *The politics of regulation*, Oxford: Blackwell.

Frankfort-Nachmias, C. and Nachmias, D. (1996) *Research methods in the social sciences*, London: Martin's Press Inc.

Frater, M. (1988) 'The challenge of competition', *Municipal Journal*, 11 March.

Fried, R.C. (1975) 'Comparative urban policy and performance', in F.J. Greenstein and N.W. Polsyby (eds) *The handbook of political science*, Reading, MA: Addison-Wesley.

Fry, B.R. and Winters, R.F. (1970) 'The politics of redistribution', *American Political Science Review*, no 64, pp 508-22.

Gamble, A. (1988) *The free economy and the strong state*, London: Macmillan.

Gaver, K.M. and Zimmerman, J.L. (1977) 'An analysis of competitive bidding on Bart contracts', *National Contract Management Journal*, Summer, pp 80-95.

Girvin, B. (ed) (1988) *European Consortium for Political Research: The transformation of contemporary Conservatism*, London: Sage Publications.

Globerman, S. and Vining, A.R. (1996) 'A framework for evaluating the government contracting-out decision with an application to information technology', *Public Administration Review*, vol 56, no 6, pp 577-86.

Goodman, P.S. and Dean, J.W. (1982) 'Creating long-term organisation change', in P.S. Goodman (ed) *Change in organisations*, San Fransisco, CA: Jossey Bass.

Goodwin, N. (1994) *Privatisation and the NHS: The geography of contracting out*, Doctoral dissertation, University of Southampton.

Goodwin, N. and Pinch, S. (1995) 'Explaining geographical variations in the contracting out of NHS hospital ancillary services: a contextual approach', *Environment and Planning*, vol 27, pp 125-39.

Gorden, R.L. (1969) *Interviewing – strategy, techniques, and tactics*, Homewood, IL: Dorsey Press.

Goss, S. (1989) *Local labour and local government*, Edinburgh: Edinburgh University Press.

Green, D. (1990) *It can all be done better*, Okehampton: Devon District Council Technical Association.

Green, L.P. (1959) *Provincial metropolis*, London: Allen & Unwin.

Griffith, B., Illiffe, S. and Raynerl, G. (1987) *Banking on sickness: Commercial medicine in Britain and the USA*, London: Lawrence & Wishart.

Grossman, G.M. and Helpman, E. (1994) 'Protection for sale', *American Economic Review*, vol 84, no 4, pp 833-50.

Grossman, S. and Hart, O. (1986) 'The costs and benefits of ownership: a theory of lateral and vertical integration', *Journal of Political Economy*, vol 94, no 4, pp 691-719.

Guba, E.G. and Lincoln, Y. (1988) 'Do inquiry paradigms imply inquiry methodologies?', in D.M. Fetterman (ed) *Qualitative approaches to evaluation in education*, New York, NY: Praeger.

Gunn, L.A. (1978) 'Why is implementation so difficult?', *Management Services in Government*, vol 33, no 4, pp 169-74.

Hakim, C. (1982) *Secondary analysis in social research*, Boston, MA: George Allen & Unwin.

Hakim, C. (1987) *Research design*, London: Unwin Hyman.

Ham, C. and Hill, M. (1993) *The policy process in the modern capitalist states*, London: Harvester Wheatsheaf.

Hammersley, M. (1995) *The politics of social research*, London: Sage Publications.

Hampton, W. (1987) *Local government and urban politics*, London: Longman.

Hampton, W. (1991) *Local government and urban politics*, London: Longman.

Hanke, S. (ed) (1987) *Prospects for privatisation*, San Francisco, CA: ICS Press.

Hansen, T. (1981) 'Transforming needs into expenditure decisions', in K. Newton (ed) *Urban political economy*, London: Francis Pinter.

Hanushek, E.A. and Jackson, J.E. (1977) *Statistical methods for social scientists*, New York, NY: Academic Press.

Hartley, K. and Huby, M. (1985) 'Contracting-out on health and local authorities: prospects, progress and pitfalls', *Public Money*, vol 5, no 2, pp 23-6.

Haworth, C.T., Long, J.E. and Rasmussen, D.W. (1978) 'Income distribution, city size and urban growth', *Urban Studies*, vol 19, pp 1-7.

Headey, B. (1978) *Housing policy in the developed economy*, London: Croom Helm.

Heckathorn, D.D. and Maser, S.M. (1987) 'Bargaining and the sources of transaction costs: the case of government regulation', *Journal of Law, Economics and Organisation*, vol 3, no 1, pp 69-98.

Hendricks, K. and Porter, R.H. (1988) 'An empirical study of an auction with asymmetric information', *American Economic Review*, vol 78, no 5, pp 865-83.

Hepworth, N.P. (1990) *The finance of local government*, London: Unwin Hyman.

Hewitt, C. (1977) 'The effect of political democracy and social democracy on equality in industrial societies', *American Sociological Review*, vol 42, pp 450-64.

Hilke, J.C. (1992) *Competition in government financed services*, New York, NY: Quorum Books.

Hill, M. (1993c) *The welfare state in Britain*, Cheltenham: Edward Elgar.

Hill, M. (1994) *Understanding social policy*, Oxford: Blackwell.

Hill, M. (1996) *Social policy*, London: Prentice Hall.

Hill, M. (1997a) *The policy process in the modern state*, London: Prentice Hall.

Hill, M. (ed) (1993a) *The policy process: A reader*, London: Harvester Wheatsheaf.

Hill, M. (ed) (1993b) *New agendas in the study of the policy process*, London: Harvester Wheatsheaf.

Hill, M. (ed) (1997b) *The policy process: A reader*, London: Prentice Hall.

Hill, M. and Bramley, G. (1990) *Analysing social policy*, Oxford: Blackwell.

Hirsch, B.T. (1982) 'Income distribution, city size and urban growth: a final re-examination', *Urban Studies*, vol 19, pp 71-4.

Hirsch, W.Z. (1995) 'Factors important in local governments' privatisation decisions', *Urban Affairs Review*, vol 31, no 2, pp 226-43.

Hogwood, B.W. and Gunn, L.A. (1984) *Policy analysis for the real world*, Oxford: Oxford University Press.

Hood, C.C. (1976) *The limits of administration*, London: John Wiley & Sons.

HPSS (1991) *Health and personal social services statistics for England*, London: HMSO.

Hunt, R.G. (1984) 'Cross-purposes in the federal contract procurement systems: military R & D and beyond', *Public Administration Review*, vol 44, no 3, pp 247-56.

Huws, U. and De Groot, L. (1985) 'A very ordinary picket', *New Socialist*, January, pp 8-10.

Hyde, A. (1984a) 'Barking contracts row brings staff out on strike', *Health and Social Services Journal*, 5 April.

Hyde, A. (1984b) 'OCS must clean up its practices warns HA', *Health and Social Services Journal*, 5 April.

Hyman, H.H. (1975) *Interviewing in social research*, Chicago, IL: University of Chicago Press.

ICMA (1984) *Rethinking local services: Examining alternative delivery approaches*, Washington, DC: International City Management Association.

ICMA (1989) *Service delivery in the 90s: Alternative approaches for local governments*, Washington, DC: ICMA.

Itani, M. (1989) 'The privatisation of local authority services in Japan', *Planning and Administration*, vol 16, no 2, pp 51-8.

Jackson, R.M.J. (1965) *The machinery of local government*, London: Macmillan.

Jennings, M. (1987) 'Contracting out – key issues for councils', *Local Government Chronicle*, 25/31 December.

John, P. (1990) *Competitive tendering*, London: Policy Studies Institute.

John, P. (1994) 'Central–local relations in the 1980s and 1990s: towards a policy learning approach', *Local Government Studies*, vol 20, no 3, pp 412-36.

Johnson, G.W. and Douglas, J.W. (1991) 'Privatisation: provision or production of services? Two case studies', *State and Local Government Review*, vol 23, no 2, pp 82-9.

Joint NHS Privatisation Research Unit (1990) *The NHS privatisation experience: Competitive tendering for NHS services*, JNHSPRU.

Kane, M. (1996) 'The nature of competition in British local government', *Public Policy and Administration*, vol 11, no 3, pp 51-66.

Kanter, R.M. (1985) *The change masters: Corporate entrepreneurs at work*, London: Allen & Unwin.

Kerley, R. (1994) *Managing in local government*, London: Macmillan.

Kerlinger, F.N. and Pedhazur, E.J. (1973) *Multiple regression in behavioural research*, New York, NY: Holt, Rinehart & Winston.

Kettl, D.P. (1988) *Government by proxy: Mismanaging federal programs*, Washington, DC: Congressional Quarterly Press, Inc.

Key, A. (1987) 'Contracting out in the NHS', in A. Harrison and J. Gretton (eds) *Health care UK*, Policy Journals.

Key, V.O. (1956) *American state politics*, New York, NY: Knopf.

Klein, P.G. and Shelanski, H.A. (1995) 'Empirical research in transaction cost economics: a review and assessment', *Journal of Law, Economics and Organisations*, vol 11, no 2, pp 335-61.

Kleinman, M., Eastall, R. and Roberts, E. (1990) 'What determines local authorities' capital expenditure on housing? An evaluation of various models', *Urban Studies*, vol 27, no 3, pp 401-19.

Kolderie, T. (1986) 'The two different concepts of privatisation', *Public Administration Review*, vol 46, no 4, pp 285-300.

Korosec, R.P.L. (1994) *Privatisation of local governments: Contracting out as a service delivery option*, Doctoral dissertation, State University of New York at Binghamton.

Kramer, R.M. and Grossman, B. (1987) 'Contracting for social services: process management and resource dependencies', *Social Service Review*, vol 61, no 1, pp 32-55.

Kydland, F.S. and Prescott, E.C. (1977) 'Rules rather than discretion: the inconsistency of optimal plans', *Journal of Political Economy*, vol 85, no 3, pp 473-92.

Labour Research Department (1983) *Privatisation: Who loses? Who Wins?*, London: Labour Research Department.

Le Grand, J. and Barltett, W. (eds) (1993) *Quasi-markets and social policy*, London: Macmillan.

Leach, S. and Stewart, J. (1992) *The politics of hung authorities*, London: Macmillan.

Leedham, W. (1986) *The privatisation of NHS ancillary services*, Workers Educational Press.

Leone, R. (1986) *Who profits: Winners, losers and government regulation*, New York, NY: Basic Books.

Levy, D.T. (1985) 'The transaction cost approach to vertical integration: an empirical examination', *Review of Economics and Statistics*, vol 67, pp 438-55.

Levy, F.S., Meltsner, A.J. and Wildavsky, A. (1974) *Urban outcomes*, Berkeley, CA: University of California Press.

Lewis-Beck, M.S. (1977) 'The relative importance of socio-economic and political variables for public policy', *American Political Science Review*, vol 71, no 2, pp 559-84.

Lewis-Beck, M.S. (1994) *Research practice*, London: Sage Publications.

LGA (Local Government Association) (1998) *Modernising local government: Improving local services through best value*, London: LGA.

LGMB (Local Government Management Board) (1991) *Local government: A councillor's guide*, London: LGMB.

LGTB (1987) *Competition and contracting out*, London: Local Government Training Board.

Lineberry, R.L. 1989) *Government in America*, Glenview, IL: Scott, Foreman & Company.

Lineberry, R.L. and Sharkansky, I. (1978) *Urban politics and public policy*, New York, NY: Harper & Row.

Lipsky, M. (1980) *Street-level bureaucracy: Dilemmas of the individual in public services*, Russel Sage Foundation.

Local Government Chronicle Elections Centre (1994) *Local elections in Britain: A statistical digest*, Plymouth: Local Government Chronicle Centre, University of Plymouth.

Lockard, D. (1963) *The politics of State and local government*, New York, NY: Macmillan.

Lowi, T.J. (1979) *The end of liberalism*, New York, NY: W.W. Norton & Company.

LRD (1984) *Defending the health services*, Labour Research Department.

MacInnes, J. (1987) *Thatcherism at work: Industrial relations and economic change*, Milton Keynes: Open University Press.

McAfee, R.P. and McMillan, J. (1988) *Incentives in government contracting*, Toronto: University of Toronto Press.

McGinnis, H. (1994) 'Determining the impact of economic factors on local government growth policy: using time-series analysis and transfer function models', *Urban Studies*, vol 31, pp 233-46.

McGuire, R.A., Ohsfeldt, R.L. and Van Cott, T.N. (1987) 'The determinants of the choice between public and private production of a publicly funded service', *Public Choice*, no 54, pp 211-30.

McGuirk, T. (1992) *The competitive edge*, Croydon: Institute of Public Finance.

McMaster, R. (1992) *Competitive tendering and service quality: A brief examination utilising an amended transaction cost framework*, Discussion Paper, Aberdeen: Department of Economics, University of Aberdeen.

McShane, F.M. (1995) *Compulsory competitive tendering for local authority services: A legal analysis of the Local Government Acts 1988 and 1992*, Doctoral dissertation, University of Glasgow.

Marsh, D. (1990) 'Privatisation under Mrs Thatcher: a review of the literature', *Public Administration*, vol 69, pp 459-80.

Marston, M.W. (1990) *The use of contract compliance as a legal technique in attaining policy objectives*, Doctoral dissertation, Sheffield University.

Menard, C. (ed) (1997) *Transaction cost economics: Recent developments*, Cheltenham: Edward Elgar.

Miller, T.A. (1988) *Contracting out the operations and management of local hospitals: An analysis of the determinants of local government choice*, Doctoral dissertation, University of Southern California.

Milne, R.G. (1987) 'Competitive tendering in the NHS: an economic analysis of the early implementation of HC (83) 18', *Public Administration*, vol 65, Summer, pp 145-60.

Milne, R.G. (1993) 'Contractors' experience of compulsory competitive tendering: a case study of contract cleaners in the NHS', *Public Administration*, vol 71, Autumn, pp 301-21.

Minogue, M. and O'Grady, J. (1985) 'Contracting out local authority services in Britain', *Planning and Administration*, Spring, pp 82-90.

Moe, T. (1984) 'The new economics of organisation', *American Journal of Political Science*, vol 28, no 4, pp 739-77.

Moe, T. (1990) 'Political institutions: the neglected side of the story', *Journal of Law, Economics and Organisations*, no 6, pp 289-311.

Mohan, J. (1986) 'The geography of NHS privatisation', *Public Service Action*, no 21, p 8.

Morgan, D.R., Hirlinger, M.W. and England, R.E. (1988) 'The decision to contract out city services: a further explanation', *Western Political Quarterly*, vol 41, no 2, pp 363-90.

Mueller, D. (1979) *Public Choice (1)*, Cambridge: Cambridge University Press.

Nagel, S.S. (ed) (1994) *Encyclopaedia of policy studies*, New York, NY: Marcel Dekker, Inc.

Nakamura, R.T. and Smallwood, F. (1980) *The politics of policy implementation*, New York: St Martin's Press.

NAPA (1989) *Privatisation: The challenge to public management*, National Academy of Public Administration.

National Audit Office (1987) *Competitive tendering for support services in the NHS*, London: HMSO.

Newton, K. (1976) *Second city politics*, Oxford: Clarendon Press.

Newton, K. (ed) (1981) *Urban political economy*, London: Francis Pinter.

Newton, K. and Sharpe, L.J. (1977) 'Local output research: some reflections and proposals', *Policy & Politics*, vol 5, no 1, pp 61-82.

NHS Unlimited (1984) *Contracting out ancillary services: The health authority views*, NHS Unlimited.

Niskanen, W.A. (1971) *Bureaucracy and representative government*, Chicago, IL: Aldine-Athertons.

Nordlinger, E.A. (1981) *On the autonomy of the democratic state*, Cambridge, MA: Harvard University Press.

North, D.C. (1990a) *Institutions, institutional change, and economic performance*, New York, NY: Cambridge University Press.

North, D.C. (1990b) 'A transaction cost theory of politics', *Journal of Theoretical Politics*, vol 2, no 4, pp 355-67.

North, D.C. (1997) 'Transaction costs through time', in C. Menard (ed) *Transaction cost economics: Recent developments*, Cheltenham: Edward Elgar.

Oliver, F.R. and Stanyer, J. (1969) 'Some aspects of the financial behaviour of county boroughs', *Public Administration*, no 47, pp 18-31.

Ostrom, V. and Ostrom, E. (1977) 'Public goods – public choices', in E.S. Savas (ed) *Alternatives for delivering public services*, Boulder, CO: Westview Press, Inc.

Paddon, M. (1994) 'EC public procurement directives and the competition from European contractors for local authority contracts in the UK', in T. Clarke and C. Pitelis (eds) *The political economy of privatisation*, London: Routledge.

Page, E., Goldsmith, M. and Kousgtaard, P. (1990) 'Time, parties and budgetary change: fiscal decisions in English cities, 1974-88', *British Journal of Political Science*, vol 20, pp 43-61.

Painter, J. (1990) *Seconds out, round two: The first round of compulsory competitive tendering*, Manchester: Centre for Local Economic Strategies.

Painter, J. (1991) 'The geography of trade union responses to local government privatisation', *Transactions IBG*, vol 16, no 4, pp 214-26.

Painter, J. (1992) 'The culture of competition', *Public Policy and Administration*, vol 7, no 1, pp 58-68.

Painter, J. (1995) *Politics, geography and 'political geography': A critical perspective*, London: Arnold.

Parker, D. and Hartley, K. (1990) 'Competitive tendering: issues and evidence', *Public Money and Management*, Autumn, pp 9-16.

Parsons, W. (1995) *Public policy: An introduction to the theory and practice of policy analysis*, Aldershot: Edward Elgar.

Pearce, D.W. (1981) *Dictionary of modern economics*, London: Macmillan.

Pedhazur, E.J. and Schmelkin, L.P. (1991) *Measurement, design, and analysis*, New Jersey, NJ: Lawrence Erlbaum Associates.

Perrow, C. (ed) (1986) *Complex organisations: A critical essay*, New York, NY: Random House.

Peters, B. (1974) 'Income redistribution: a longitudinal analysis of France, Sweden and the United Kingdom', *Political Studies*, vol 22, no 3, pp 311-23.

Pettigrew, A. and Whipp, R. (1991) *Managing change for competitive success*, Oxford: Blackwell.

Pettigrew, A., Ferlie, E. and McKee, L. (1992) *Shaping strategic change*, London: Sage Publications.

Pettigrew, A.M. (ed) (1988) *The management of strategic change*, Oxford: Blackwell.

Pfeffer, J. and Salancik, G.R. (1978) *The external control of organisations: A resource dependence perspective*, New York, NY: Harper & Row.

Pinch, S.P. (1989) 'The restructuring thesis and the study of public services', *Environment and Planning*, vol 21, pp 124-43.

Pinch, S.P. and Witt, S. (1988) 'The restructuring of health services in Southampton', Paper presented to the IBG, Loughborough, 8 January.

Pirie, M. (1985) *Privatisation*, London: Adam Smith Institute.

Pirie, M. (1988) *Privatisation: Theory, practice and choice*, London: Adam Smith Institute.

Plunkett, W.R. and Attner, R.F. (1994) *Introduction to management*, California: Wadsworth Publishing Company.

Posner, R.A. (1972) *Economic analysis of law* (2nd edn), Boston, MA: Little Brown.

Pressman, J.I. and Wildavsky, A. (1973) *Implementation*, Berkeley, CA: University of California Press.

Prowle, M. and Hines, G. (1989) *Local government competition: Meeting the challenge*, London: Certified Accountants Education Trust.

Putnam, R. (1993) *Making democracy work*, Princeton, NJ: Princeton University Press.

Pyper, R. (1990) 'Compulsory competitive tendering', *Social Studies Review*, May, pp 187-205.

Rainnie, A.L. (1994) *Fighting the tender trap: UNISON and competitive tendering*, Research Report Hertfordshire County Branch, UNISON.

Rehfuss, J.A. (1989) *Contracting out in government*, San Francisco, CA: Jossey-Bass.

Rehfuss, J.A. (1990) 'Contracting out and accountability in state and local governments – the importance of contract monitoring', *State and Local Government Review*, vol 22, no 1, pp 254-65.

Rein, M. and Rabinovitz, F.F. (1978) 'Implementation: a theoretical perspective', in W.D. Burnam and M.W. Weinberg (eds) *American politics and public policy*, Cambridge, MA: MIT Press.

Reve, T. (1990) 'The firm as a nexus of internal and external contracts', in M. Aoki and B. Gustafssonan (eds) *The firm as a nexus of treaties*, London: Sage Publications.

Rhodes, R.A.W. (1979) 'Research into central–local relations in Britain: a framework for analysis', Unpublished paper, Colchester: Department of Government, University of Essex.

Rhodes, R.A.W. (1981) *Control and power in central–local government relationships*, Aldershot: Gower.

Rhodes, R.A.W. (1986) '"Power dependence" theories of central–local relations: a critical assessment', in M. Goldsmith (ed) *New research in central–local relations*, Aldershot: Gower.

RIPA (1984) *Contracting out in the public sector*, London: RIPA.

Rose, R. and Page, E. (1982) *Fiscal stress in cities*, London: Cambridge University Press.

Rothkoph, M.H. (1983) 'Bidding theory: the phenomena to be modelled', in R. Engelbrecht-Wiggans, M. Shubik, and R.M. Stark (eds) *Auctions, bidding, and contracting: Uses and theory*, New York, NY: New York University Press.

RSHG (1987) *Facing the figures: What is really happening to the NHS*, Radical Statistical Health Group.

Sabatier, P.A. (1986) 'Top-down and bottom-up approaches to implementation research: a critical analysis and suggested synthesis', *Journal of Public Policy*, no 6, pp 21-48.

Savas, E.S. (1977) *Alternatives for delivering public services: Toward improved performance*, Boulder, CO: Westview Press, Inc.

Savas, E.S. (1982) *Privatising the public sector: How to shrink government*, Chatham, NJ: Chatham House Publishers, Inc.

Savas, E.S. (1987) *Privatisation: The key to better government*, Chatham, NJ: Chatham House Publishers, Inc.

Savas, E.S. (1992) 'Privatisation and productivity', in M. Holzer (ed) *Public Productivity Handbook*, New York, NY: Marcel Dekker.

Schafritz, J.M. and Hyde, A.C. (1978) *Classics of public administration*, Chicago, IL: Dorsey Press.

Schelling, T.C. (1960) *The strategy of conflict*, Cambridge, MA: Harvard University Press.

Schoford, J.A. (1978) 'Determinants of urban service expenditure', *Local Government Studies*, April, pp 65-80.

Self, P. (1993) *Government by the market*, London: Macmillan.

Shann, E.D. (1990) 'Tender debate deserves a fair hearing', Business Review Weekly (Australia), *Industrial Relations Journal*, vol 19, no 2, p 42.

Sharkansky, I. (1980) 'Government contracting', *State Government*, vol 53, no 1, pp 22-7.

Sharp, E.B. (1990) *Urban politics and administration: From service delivery to economic development*, New York, NY: Longman.

Sharpe, L.J. (ed) (1981) *The local fiscal crisis in Western Europe: Myths and realities*, London: Sage Publications.

Sharpe, L.J. and Newton, K. (1984) *Does politics matter?: The determinants of public policy*, Oxford: Clarendon Press.

Shaw, K. and Fenwick, J. (1995) 'Compulsory competition for local government services in the UK: a case of market rhetoric and camouflaged centralism', *Public Policy and Administration*, vol 10, no 1, pp 63-75.

Shaw, K., Fenwick, J. and Foreman, A. (1994) 'Compulsory competitive tendering for local government services: the experiences of local authorities in the North of England 1988-1992', *Public Administration*, vol 72, Summer, pp 201-17.

Shaw, K., McCarthy, A. and Fenwick, J. (1992) *Compulsory competitive tendering in local government: An annotated bibliography*, Winteringham: Earlsgate Press.

Sheaff, M. (1988) 'NHS ancillary services and competitive tendering', *Industrial Relations Journal*, vol 19, no 2, pp 93-105.

Sherman, J. (1984a) 'London ancillary workers strike against privatisation', *Health and Social Services Journal*, 1 March.

Sherman, J. (1984b) 'Hammersmith cleaning contract may have to go outside NHS', *Health and Social Services Journal*, 26 July.

Sherman, J. (1985) 'Waiting for the big bite', *Health and Social Services Journal*, 13 August.

Silverman, D. (1993) *Interpreting qualitative data: Methods for analysing talk, text and interaction*, London: Sage Publications.

Simon, H.A. (1972) 'Theories of bounded rationality', in C. McGuire and R. Radner (eds) *Decision and organisation*, Amsterdam: North Holland.

Simon, H.A. (1978) 'Rationality as process and as product of thought', *American Economic Review*, vol 68, pp 1-16.

Simon, H.A. (1987) 'The proverbs of administration', in M. Shafritz and A.C. Hyde (eds) *Classics of public administration*, Chicago, IL: Dorsey Press.

Smith, T.B. (1973) 'The policy implementation process', *Policy Sciences*, no 4, pp 197-209.

Snape, S. (1994) *Contracting out by Dutch municipalities, marketisation in Europe*, MIE Research Papers, Newcastle: University of Northumbria.

Spencer, K. (1984) 'Assessing alternative forms of service provision', *Local Government Studies*, March/April, pp 14-20.

Starr, P. (1991) *The case for scepticism*, in W.T. Gormley (ed) *Privatisation and its alternatives*, Madison, WI: University of Wisconsin Press.

Stewart, J. (1996) 'An obituary: Kieron Walsh', *Public Administration*, vol 74, Spring, pp 149-55.

Stigler, G.J. (1966) *The theory of price*, New York, NY: Macmillan.

Stiglitz, J.E. (1994) *Whither socialism?*, Cambridge, MA: MIT Press.

Stoker, G. (1988) *Privatising local government*, London: Macmillan.

Stoker, G. (1991) *The politics of local government*, London: Macmillan.

Stubbs, J.G. (1990) *Towards a theory of geographically uneven development of privatisation: The case of New Zealand hospital ancillary services*, Doctoral dissertation, Canterbury: University of Kent.

Stubbs, J.G. and Barnett, J.R. (1992) 'The geographically uneven development of privatisation towards a theoretical approach', *Environment and Planning*, vol 24, pp 1,117-35.

Sullivan, H.J. (1987) 'Privatisation of public services: a growing threat to constitutional rights', *Public Administration Review*, vol 47, no 6, pp 461-67.

Sword, J. (1992) *The advent of compulsory competitive tendering of local government services in Scotland*, MBA dissertation, Dundee: University of Dundee.

Talbot, P. (1986) 'Are local authorities ready for competitive tendering?', *Public Finance and Accountancy*, 5 December.

Tiebout, C. (1956) 'A pure theory of local expenditure', *Journal of Political Economy*, vol 64, pp 24-42.

Tory Reform Group (1984) *High noon in the National Health Service*, TRG.

Townsend, A. (1987) *Middlesbrough locality study*, Working Paper No 4 Rationalisation and Change in the South Teeside Health Service, Durham: Department of Geography. University of Durham.

Tullock, G. (1965) *The politics of bureaucracy*, Washington DC: Public Affairs Press.

Twight, C. (1983) *Government manipulation of constitutional-level transaction costs: An economic theory and its application to off-budget expenditure through the Federal Financing Bank*, Doctoral dissertation, Washington, DC: University of Washington.

Twight, C. (1988) 'Government manipulation of constitutional-level transaction cost: a general theory of transaction-cost augmentation and the growth of government', *Public Choice*, no 56, pp 131-52.

Twight, C. (1990) 'Regulation of asbestos: the microanalytics of government failure', *Policy Studies Review*, no 10, pp 9-39.

Twight, C. (1992) 'Constitutional renegotiation: impediments to consensual revision', *Constitutional Political Economy*, no 3, pp 89-112.

Twight, C. (1994) 'Political transaction-cost manipulation', *Journal of Theoretical Politics*, vol 6, no 2, pp 189-216.

UNISON (1997) *Best value: A strategic approach*, UNISON.

Van Dyke, W.A. (1990) *An analysis of the impact of the Competition in Contracting Act (CICA) of 1984 on technical and professional services contractors serving the US Navy*, Doctoral dissertation, George Washington University.

Van Meter, D. and Van Horn, C.E. (1975) 'The policy implementation process: a conceptual framework', *Administration and Society*, vol 6, no 4, pp 445-88.

Vickers, J. and Yarrow, G. (1988) *Privatisation: An economic analysis*, Cambridge, MA: MIT Press.

von Hayek, F.A. (1986) *The road to serfdom*, London: Routledge.

Vroom, V.H. and Deci, E. (1992) *Management and motivation*, London: Penguin.

Walker, J. and Moore, R. (1983) *Privatisation of local government services*, Workers' Educational Association.

Walsh, K. (1989) 'Competition and services in local government', in J. Stewart and G. Stoker (ed) *The future of local government*, London: Macmillan.

Walsh, K. (1991) *Competitive tendering for local authority services*, London: HMSO.

Walsh, K. (1992) 'The extension of competitive tendering', in K. Walsh (ed) *The Heseltine review of local government*, Birmingham: Institute of Local Government Studies.

Walsh, K. (1995) *Public services and market mechanisms*, London: Macmillan.

Walsh, K. and Davis, H. (1993) *Competition and service: The impact of the Local Government Act*, London: HMSO.

Walsh, K., Deakin, N., Smith, P., Spurgeon, P. and Thomas, N. (1997) *Contracting for change: Contracts in health, social care, and other local government services*, Oxford: Oxford University Press.

Weaver, R.K. (1988) *Automatic government: The politics of indexation*, Washington, DC: The Brookings Institution.

Weisbrod, B.A. and Schlesinger, M. (1986) 'Public, private, nonprofit ownership and the responses to asymmetric information: the case of nursing homes', in S. Rose-Ackerman (ed) *The economics of nonprofit institutions: Studies in structure and policy*, Oxford: Oxford University Press.

West, E.G. and Winer, S.L. (1980) 'Optimal fiscal illusion and the size of government', *Public Choice*, no 35, pp 607-22.

Wildavsky, A. (1973) 'If planning is everything, maybe it is nothing', *Policy Sciences*, no 4, pp 127-54.

Williamson, O. (1971) 'The vertical integration of production: market failure considerations', *American Economic Review*, no 61, pp 112-27.

Williamson, O. (1975) *Market and hierarchies: Analysis and antitrust implications*, New York, NY: Free Press.

Williamson, O. (1976) 'Franchise building for natural monopolies – in general and with respect to CATV', *Bell Journal of Economics*, no 7, pp 73-131.

Williamson, O. (1979) 'Transaction-cost economics: the governance of contractual relations', *Journal of Law and Economics*, no 22, pp 233-61.

Williamson, O. (1985) *The economic institution of capitalism*, New York, NY: Free Press.

Williamson, O. (1989) 'Transaction cost economics', in R. Schmalensee and R. Willig (eds) *Handbook of industrial organisation* (vol 1), New York, NY: Elsevier.

Williamson, O. (1991) 'Comparative economic organisation: the analysis of discrete structural alternatives', *Administrative Science Quarterly*, no 36, pp 269-96.

Williamson, O. (1997) 'Hierarchies, markets and power in the economy: an economic perspective', in C. Menard (ed) *Transaction cost economics: Recent developments*, Cheltenham: Edward Elgar.

Wilson, D. and Game, C. (1994) *Local government in the United Kingdom*, London: Macmillan.

Wilson, J.Q. (1989) *Bureaucracy: What government agencies do and why they do it*, New York, NY: Basic Books.

Wolf, C. Jr (1988) *Markets or governments: Choosing between imperfect alternatives*, Cambridge, MA: MIT Press.

Yager, E.M. Jr. (1993) *The politics of municipal contracting decisions: A resource dependency approach*, Doctoral dissertation, Santa Barbara, CA: University of California at Santa Barbara.

Interview questionnaire

1 Personal background information

- How many years have you worked in this local authority?

- What is your position?

- What were the major tasks that you were responsible for in your position from 1991 to 1994, as it related to CCT for services?

2 Attitudes towards CCT

- Could you please briefly describe the CCT in your local authority in general.

- What do you think of CCT in general?

- Has your local authority ever used private contractors for local service provision at any time since 1988? (*yes or no*)

  (*If no*) Would you please give details of why your local authority has had no private contractors to provide local service.

- Since 1988 it has been government policy to put some manual services (refuse collection, street cleaning, building cleaning, schools and welfare catering, other catering, vehicle maintenance, grounds maintenance and the management of sports and leisure facilities) out to competitive tender. From your local authority's point of view, in what ways do you think this policy has been a success and in what ways has it been disappointing?

- In brief, it might be possible to divide the attitudes of local authorities towards CCT into two main types, agreement with and avoidance of CCT. How would you rate your authority's general position? Why?

- Have your local authority's views on CCT changed since 1988? If so, how and why?

- On average, how would you characterise CCT during the period of its introduction since the 1988 Local Government Act, particularly in terms of merits and demerits?

- If you were given a free hand what would you change in the CCT process?

3 CCT and local politics

- Who was officially responsible for making decisions during the CCT process?

- Who (or what agency) was primarily influencing the process of evaluating and eventually deciding upon the contract award?

- In your opinion, was there a general consensus of opinion between the council members and the officials within your local authority during the process of tendering or were there stages at which the members and the officials disagreed (eg over the policy in general or over specific issues)? Please give details.

- In your opinion, what were your authority's primary reasons for seriously considering trying to get work for the DSO or a private company?

- During the CCT process were there any stages at which representatives from the workforce, or their trade union, were able to participate in the process? (*If yes*) At what stages were these parties able to express their views?

- To what extent did trade unions lobby management during the CCT process (eg was there any threat of industrial action)?

4 The presence of transaction costs and related issues

- In my opinion, the proportion of tenders won by DSOs varied considerably, according to the political composition of local authorities. Why do you think it has been so? How has it been possible?

- Compared to other local authorities, particularly Conservative-controlled ones (or Labour-controlled ones), the DSO output in your local authority has been relatively higher (or lower). What is the main reason for that? How has it been possible?

- If some local authorities, for example Labour-controlled ones (or Conservative-controlled ones), opposed (or supported) CCT, how did they affect CCT, particularly in deciding who should be awarded the contract? Did they have some effective measures to affect the chances of the private sector?

- Some people say that so-called transaction costs on the client side, such as the costs of setting service standards, preparing contracts, inviting and evaluating tenders, and monitoring the work of contractors, are high when CCT is implemented. What do you think of that?

- How would you evaluate the transaction costs, such as the costs of tendering for and carrying out the work of contracts?

- What would you say about the relationship between transaction costs and the chances of private companies in the CCT process?

- How likely was it that the local authority had influenced the CCT process in its own interest?

- In which tendering process could the local authority have effectively influenced the chances of a private company?

- What measures do you think could be considered to affect the chances of a private company or DSO?

Sources of information used in case studies

Interviews with the four chief officers and one lawyer

The municipal yearbook 1991, 1994, 1996

Local government comparative statistics 1991, 1994

Direct Service Organisations Statistics 1991, 1994

Minutes of the competitive tendering subcommittee

Tender documents relating to tendering of services

Internal memoranda concerning progress, savings of CCT and so on

Reports to councillors

Index

[NOTE: Page numbers followed by *fig* indicate information to be found in a figure; page numbers followed by *n* indicate information to be found in a note; page numbers followed by *tab* indicate information to be found in a table.]

Barnett, R.R. 55, 58, 62, 134*n*
Barringston, T.J. 35
'base and spread' strategy 115, 119, 128-9, 231-2, 248-9, 269
see also incumbency
Bay Area Rapid Transit (BART) contractors 72
Beck, P.A. 78
Beresford, P. 39
Best Value framework 2, 10, 30-1, 33
12 Principles of Best Value 30, 31
key objectives 30
timetable for 31, 32*tab*
Boaden, N. 54, 64
Bosanquet, N. 17
'bounded rationality' concept 143, 147-8, 149, 164
Bouttes, J.-P. 66, 168-9
Bow Group 25
Boyne, G.A. 61, 62, 63, 65, 73, 91*n*, 120, 134*n*
Bracewell-Milnes, B. 2, 5, 6, 9, 17, 18
competitive tendering 21, 22, 23, 24, 26, 29, 37, 213
compulsory competitive tendering 33
Labour and CCT 63-4, 106, 124
legal framework 28, 67, 204, 210, 265*n*
private sector 72, 130, 209
Bramley, G. 55
Braunig, D. 34
Bryson, J. 141-2
Buchanan, J.M. 138, 139, 182
Bulpitt, J.G. 62
Butler, E. 21
Byrne, T. 9, 70, 78, 79, 93*n*, 265*n*

C

Calista, D.J. 144
Cameron, D.K. 62
Carbonaro, G. 76
Carnaghan, R. 2, 5, 6, 9, 17, 18
competitive tendering 21, 22, 23, 24, 26, 29, 37, 213
compulsory competitive tendering 33
Labour and CCT 63-4, 106, 124
legal framework 28, 67, 204, 210, 265*n*
private sector 72, 130, 209
case studies 8, 10-11, 13-14, 203-66
analysis 203-66, 267, 268-70
analytical framework 185-201
legal framework 204-16
Local Authority A 217-26, 252, 253-4, 255-6, 258, 260, 261, 270
Local Authority B 226-34, 252, 253, 255, 256, 260
Local Authority C 234-41, 252, 253, 255, 256, 260, 270
Local Authority D 241-51, 252-3, 255-6, 260, 261
methodology 194-200
case selection 198-200
interviewing 195, 196-8, 199, 200
Caudrey, A. 44
causal relationships *see* path analysis
CCT *see* compulsory competitive tendering
central government
case study representation 199-200
discretionary power 166-7, 251-2